Closet Reading

500 years of humour on the loo

Phil Norman

GIBSON SQUARE

To my parents, Peter and Judith, for all their help

This edition published for the first time in 2010 by

Gibson Square

UK Tel: +44 (0)20 7096 1100
      Fax: +44 (0)20 7993 2214

US Tel: +1 646 216 9813
      Fax: +1 646 216 9488

Eire Tel: +353 (0)1 657 1057

info@gibsonsquare.com
www.gibsonsquare.com

ISBN 9781906142483

Printed by Clays, Bungay.

Contents

ACKNOWLEDGEMENTS

Thanks to the following people for giving their time for interviews, interrogations and general impertinent requests: Russell Ash, Gyles Brandreth, Terence Blacker, Anthony Cohen, Katy Hepburn, Graeme Garden, Mark Lucas, Mark Leigh, Mike Lepine, David McCandless and Richard Herring, and especially to John Lloyd and Geoffrey Strachan, for help and patience above and beyond the call of duty. Thanks for valuable help with research and textual nit-picking to Tim Worthington, Graham Kibble-White, Johnny Trunk, Steve Berry, Louis Barfe, Jem Roberts and Peter Gordon. Parts of this book are taken from articles by the author in Kettering: the Magazine of Elderly British Comedy. *Special thanks to Martin Rynja for taking a punt on such a ridiculous idea, and Scott Pack for kicking it into some sort of shape. Extra special thanks to the second-hand booksellers and book-hoarders of Britain and beyond, without whom this book would be a leaflet full of bracketed question marks. Finally, thanks to my wife Suzanne, for everything.*

Introduction

Here I sit, alone and sixty,
Bald and fat, and full of sin;
Cold the seat and loud the cistern
As I read the Harpic tin.

Alan Bennett, *Place-Names of China*.

Many call them 'gift books'. Others plump for 'novelty books'. For a third of the year they become 'Christmas books'. Bookshops, more often than not, label them 'humour books'. At least, they do in public: round the back of the shop, they huddle over their cocoa and make disparaging noises about 'non-books'.

But perhaps the most cutting nickname has to do with the part of the house to where these flimsy, whimsical publishing afterthoughts are often relegated: judged unfit to stand proud between the *Encyclopaedia Britannica* and the *Complete Sherlock Holmes*, they find themselves instead keeping company with the sort of reading matter that limits itself to stern warnings about not getting bleach in your eyes.

For want of a worse word, we're talking about toilet books.

Whatever you call them, you can't mistake them. We all know their type. Cosy collections of showbiz anecdotes and outlandish random facts. Brightly coloured paperbacks full of jokes about cats. An opportunistic gag about the latest fad in the news, padded out to book length with a few cartoons. The hit TV show of the year unceremoniously stuffed between hard covers. A hundred pages of showboating sarcasm with a very rude word slapped on the front. Not the sort of thing to trouble Booker judges, cultural historians, or anyone but the proprietors of overflowing charity shops come the New Year clearout.

They trouble the bestseller lists, though. More often than your average literary pundit would care to admit. Your bookshelves may be entirely free of literary classics, but it's a racing certainty there'll be a *Schott's Miscellany*, or a yellowing *Kenneth Williams's Acid Drops*, a dog-eared *Wicked Willie*, maybe even *Frank Bough's Breakfast Book* lurking in a long-undusted corner. No, nothing to be ashamed of at all. Yes, of course it was a present. Of course.

Snobbery rules the publishing roost. Woe betide the book that refuses to play the prestige game. But every year, dozens of titles opt out of the quality rat-race and set up shop in that most inhospitable of ghettoes, the bookshop 'humour table' – twenty yards from the door, over on your right, tastefully concealed behind the fat pile of Updikes.

But should we so readily brush them aside? All human life is here, after a fashion. From the theatre to sport, music to cookery, science to politics: for every non-fiction category, there's a small but dedicated wing of wry, unassuming works whose take on the subject can prove every bit as sociologically enlightening as their more considered counterparts. Much as we might like the idea of future civilisations judging ours by the stature of Bertrand Russell's *History of Western Philosophy*, who's to say their archaeologists won't unearth Paul Manning's *How to be a Wally* instead?

So if we're going to allow these books some sort of posterity, let's do it right. They do, after all, have a history as long and varied as the novel. Granted, it's a rather more messy history, and one that has as much to do with newspapers, magazines, advertising, the stage, radio and the telly as it does with literature. If we have some grasp of that, maybe we'll see where these odd little tomes fit into the fabric of what we like to call culture.

So here, for the first and probably last time, is the full story of publishing's worst kept secret. It's a tale of audacious publicity stunts, fraught battles with WH Smith over swearword allowances, and mad rushes to turn great aunt Edith's scrapbooks into six-figure publishing phenomena. We'll witness wet dreams about Barry Manilow, the secret origins of Jimmy Hill's beard and Enoch Powell's recipe for Crème Brulée. It's a timely story that demands to be read.

Or you could wait for a bit and pick it up on Amazon next March for 50p.

What is a toilet book?

Although we all *sort of* know what we mean by a 'toilet book', mapping the boundaries of the genre is a task the great universities of the west have strangely elected to pass on, so we'll have to bodge a definition together ourselves. The literal description's no good, as any tome, from *Finnegans Wake* to the Screwfix catalogue, can gain 'toilet book' status with a quick trip to the business side of an 'engaged' sign. We need a solid working guide before we dive into the paperback ocean, so let's get rigorous for a moment.

FORM: In a word, bitty. The toilet book is first and foremost a smorgasbord of tempting prose morsels rather than a meaty, well-broiled narrative slog, the better to be dipped into as and when the mood takes the reader. Thus, for example, a showbiz memoir, with its surefooted trudge from birth to Palladium to divorce to dotage, isn't a true toilet book, but if our loveable old trouper organises his or her life experience into a loose collection of bite-size anecdotes, in it goes.

CONTENT: Light. Most of the titles here come under that broad and uninspiring banner of 'humour', but out and out comedy needn't be the order of the day. Trivia, whimsy and other deeply unfashionable nouns will crop up just as often. If they conjure up the image of a fusty dinner party for obsessive-compulsive Edwardian civil servants, don't worry – the reality is infinitely more varied and far less tweedy. That said, it wouldn't be a bad idea to pack a stout pair of slippers for the journey.

STATUS: The lowest of the low. With reviews rare and awards non-existent, the toilet book is a true literary pariah. Their authors tend to be all too aware of this, and lard their introductions with pre-emptive apologies and blushing self-deprecation. If they then go on to produce a book that's every bit as good as the best of its legitimate cousins, they don't expect to be praised for it, although the royalty cheques may offer some consolation.

So, with minds wedged dangerously open, ready to take the rough with the smooth, and vowing not to judge a Michael Parkinson book by its cover photo of Michael Parkinson, let's do what the average toilet book reader never does, and begin at the beginning.

RENAISSANCE FILTH

When did the toilet book begin?

Depending on how far you're prepared to stretch the point, you could do worse than start with Giovanni Boccaccio's *Decameron* (1353), a satire of the corrupt society of medieval Florence in 100 tiny chunks. It may be a bona fide literary classic, but it has much in common with the modern toilet book: the average tale can be polished off in under ten minutes; many of the stories are 'borrowed' from other sources; it brims with in-jokes and satirical snipes at well-known figures of the day; and majors in practical jokery, witticisms and bawdiness. Lashings of bawdiness.

Most copies tend to fall open at part three, tale number ten, in which an innocent fourteen-year-old girl visits a pious hermit, who soon decides his vow of chastity wasn't such a hot idea after all, and introduces the girl to an exciting new holy act: 'putting the Devil in Hell'. This begins with a swift removal of clothing, upon which the hermit's lust 'was more than ever inflamed at the sight of her beauty, and the resurrection of the flesh came to pass.' The girl innocently enquires 'what is it thou hast that thrusts itself out in front, and that I have not?' This, it transpires, is 'the Devil'. The location of 'Hell' isn't too hard to deduce, and before long the pair are re-enacting the Fall of Lucifer on every available surface. Eventually the girl's appetite for this most invigorating of ecclesiastical metaphors outstrips the hermit's Satan-summoning powers ('at times he could satisfy her, but so seldom that it was like feeding an elephant with peas') and she hops off to inherit a pile of cash, shack up with a local playboy, and carry on her Good Work in plusher surroundings.

Around 1462 a French *Decameron* homage appeared, *Les Cent Nouvelles Nouvelles* (translated into English as *One Hundred Merrie and Delightsome Stories Right Pleasaunte to Relate in All Goodly Companie by Way of Joyance and Jollity*). These stories are on average less than half the length of Boccaccio's (even the ones pinched directly from him), lighter in mood and bawdier still in content. Wives are swapped, knights run rampant, chamberpots are emptied over heads, women compare their husbands' penises unfavourably to donkeys', clerks pretend to have no testicles in order to wangle dates with their master's wives, a gentleman surreptitiously sleeping with a chambermaid is found out via a loud fart, and plenty of eel pasties are consumed. It's *Confessions of a Renaissance Man* all the way, punctuated by the odd comical parp on a crumhorn.

Apes, geese and toilet seats

Eventually the fashionable mini-tale crossed the channel with the publishing by John Rastell, brother-in-law to Sir Thomas More, of the first major English language joke book, *A Hundred Merry Tales* (c. 1525). It contained such slapstick capers as the tale of a young man caught on the job by his partner's dad, who ends up running madly through the streets with a toilet seat round his neck, to much horse-frightening consternation.

Elsewhere, we're served up a glutinous broth of laboured gags. A country bumpkin mistakes a lute player for someone strangling a goose. A foolish Welsh messenger delivers an important document to an ape by mistake. Here's a typical story, with the random spelling of the day retained to enhance the hilarity:

A yonge gentylman of the age of xx [twenty] yere,

somwhat dysposed to myrth and gaye, on a tyme talked wyth a gentylwoman whyche was ryght wyse and also mery. Thys gentylwoman as she talked with hym happenyd to loke vpon hys berde which was but yonge and somewhat growen vpon the louer lyppe, and but lyttell growen benethe as all other yonge mennys berdes comynly use to grow and sayd to hym thus: 'Syr. ye haue a berde aboue and none beneth,' and he herynge her say so, sayde in sporte, 'Maystres, ye haue a berde beneth and none aboue. 'Mary,' quod she, 'then set the one agaynst the tother,' which answere made the gentylman so abasshed that he had not one worde to answere.

Contemporary attitudes to this drollery were mixed. In Shakespeare's *Much Ado about Nothing* (1600), Benedick ridicules Beatrice's wits, claiming she cribs gags from *A Hundred Merry Tales* —as heinous a crime as stealing jokes from Cannon and Ball. But Shakespeare owned a copy of the book himself, and wasn't above pinching the odd gag for his plays. Tale LXXV, in which St Peter clears Heaven of Welshmen by standing at the gates and shouting 'roasted cheese!' is referenced in *The Merry Wives of Windsor*. A ripe bit of farce in which a husband plans to hide under his wife's bed and leap out to accost her lover, only to bottle it, cowering under the randy pair pretending to be a sheep, turns up in *Love's Labours Lost*. Basic and bawdy they may have been, but these jokes had legs.

Unholy japes

Short, punchy tales like these were often used by Catholic priests in sermons to drive home a moral point. Called *exempla*, they took classical tales and trimmed them down to the bare bones – the idea being to keep the congregation interested and alert, in the same way a good joke should. Geoffrey Chaucer's

The Miller's Prologue and Tale satirized their use by trendy clerics to liven up a tedious sermon. There were rules for delivery of these stories, again much like the Rules of Comedy: make the stories believable, make sure they're appropriate for your audience (or congregation), eliminate all extraneous faff and get to the point.

Not everyone followed these rules. William Painter collected sixty well-known tales for his *Palace of Pleasure* (1566), often relying on the familiarity of the old chestnuts and taking the action as read, instead putting emphasis on fruity language and rambling digressions, like a 16th-century Frankie Howerd. Collections like the *Mensa Philosophica* (1479) lumped *exempla* in with less morally upstanding bits of literary fluff, either elevating the latter or degrading the former, depending on which side of the debate you took.

Despite this constant exchange of gags between the two disciplines, comedy and religion remained mutually mistrustful. Nowhere was this more apparent than at the English royal court, where bishops rubbed shoulders with the court fool. The fool was first felt as a regular presence in the court of Edward II, who for some reason liked his fools to be called Robert. An exception, Roland le Pettour, was called to a Royal Command Performance for the king on Christmas Day his speciality act, 'a leap, a whistle and a fart', and was rewarded with 30 acres of prime Ipswich real estate for his trouble.

Church and comedy collided spectacularly at Christmas when the December *festum fatuorum,* or Feast of Fools took place. This was a raucous upending of the traditional Mass, in which an Archbishop of Dolts was appointed from the lower ranks of society to lead an alternative ceremony, which included satires on leading churchmen, vulgar songs and dances, and even the odd bucket of water flung by the congregation. This blasphemous end-of-term festival was curtailed in the 14th century, but the link between comedy and Christmas would prove indelible, and increasingly lucrative.

Star turns

Some court fools achieved fame not only in the palace, but across the nation and even internationally. Will Somer was the servant of a Northamptonshire gentleman who was caught sending shirts to a disgraced priest. Somer pleaded for clemency for his master and got it, impressing Henry VIII with his wit and loyalty. Consequently he was appropriated by the King as court fool, and achieved such fame that, long after his death, a jest book, *A Pleasant History of the Life and Death of Will Summers* [sic] (1676), appeared, in which many corny old tales from older sources were recycled, with Somer's name slapped on them as a readily recognisable brand. Celebrity merchandising had arrived.

If the anecdotes were rarely genuine, sometimes the person was also mythical. John Scoggin may have been court fool to Edward IV, but more likely was a mythical composite of various individuals. Nevertheless, *The Jestes of Skogyn* (c. 1600), written by Andrew Borde, physician to Henry VIII was plundered by many comics, and even Shakespeare himself was said to have cribbed from a copy.

Fabricated fools were hardly necessary, though, when the real article was so strange and varied. Thomas Brandon, a contemporary and often bitter rival of Somer, found infamy as a conjuror. One routine involved causing the death of a nearby pigeon by repeatedly stabbing a picture of it with a dagger. The scholar Reginald Scot, in his *Discoverie of Witchcraft* (1584), a fascinating catalogue of debunking and trickery with such entries as To Drawe a Cord Through Your Nose, Mouth or Hand so Sensible as is Woonderful to See, spent many hours trying to fathom Brandon's pigeon gag but couldn't work it out, despite conducting his own meticulous experiments on 'crows and pies'.

The traditional image of the fool was not always accurate. They weren't all male, or genuine 'simpletons' – some were learned jokers such as John Pace, 'the bitter fool' who used his

Eton and Cambridge education to regale Elizabeth I with wordy, satirical humour, which she seemed to tolerate more than enjoy.

Much more to the taste of Queen Bess, and indeed the nation, were the low physical comedy and face-pulling antics of Richard Tarlton, England's first true star comedian. Whereas Pace would lay a finger alongside his nose and mutter something knowing about the King of Spain, Tarlton would cover himself in bacon and get the Queen's lapdog to chase him manically about the palace, much to Liz's delight. He also did a mean drunk act, could act, sing, fence and tumble with the best of them, and could improvise comic verse on subjects suggested by his audience – a versatile amalgam of John Sessions and Freddie Starr. Inevitably, the apocryphal jest books in his name began rolling off the presses within two years of his death, including *Tarlton's Newes out of Purgatorie; Onely such a Jest as his Jigge, Fit for Gentlemen to Laugh at an Houre, &c.* (1590). Other fools failed to reap such acclaim. Sir Walter Raleigh was reportedly so enraged by the noisome gadzookery of Elizabethan fool Charles Chester he sealed his mouth up with wax.

By the time of Elizabeth's reign, the traditional fool was giving way to a new breed of theatrical idiot. Theatre, even before Shakespeare, underwent something of a revolution, particularly in comedy. Actor-writer-fools emerged, such as Robert Armin, who wrote the first histories of fooling, *Foole Upon Foole* (1600) and *A Nest of Ninnies* (1608), and actor and Globe Theatre shareholder Will Kemp, who once left the Queen's court and Morris-danced to Norwich (as one does), a famous stunt immortalised in *Kemp's Nine Daies Wonder* (1600). He also toured Europe, where he was welcomed as a comic genius even though he spoke no foreign language, an Elizabethan Norman Wisdom.

People do the funniest things

Court fools were not the only celebrities to have posthumous books of their alleged jests published. Richard Johnson's *The*

Pleasant Conceits of Old Hobson the Merry Londoner. Full of Humorous Discourses, and Witty Meriments Whereat the Quickest Wits May Laugh, and the Wiser Sort Take Pleasure (1607) detailed the eccentric sayings and doings of William Hobson, a renowned character who worked as a haberdasher during the 16th century. Some of these tales may well have been genuine Hobson capers, but many were clearly not, such as this one, which is a straight rip-off of a particularly corny *exemplum* attributed at various times to several priests:

In Christmas Holy-dayes when Maister Hobson's wife had many pyes in the oven, one of his servants had stole one of them out, and at the tauerne had merrily eat it. It fortuned, the same day, that some of his friends dined with him, and one of the best pyes were missing, the stealer of, after dinner, he found out in this manner. He called all his servants in friendly sort together into the hall, and caused each of them to drinke one to another, both wine, ale, and beare, till they were all drunke; then caused he a table to be furnished with very good cheare, whereat hee likewise pleased them. Being set altogether, he saide, 'Why sit ye not downe fellows?' – 'We bee set already,' quoth they. – 'Nay,' quoth Maister Hobson, 'he that stole the pye is not yet set.' – 'Yes, that I doe!' quoth he that stole it, by which means Maister Hobson knewe what was become of the pye; for the poor fellowe being drunke could not keepe his owne secretts.

It was the way he told them. Some jest-books bracketted their vignettes in a skeletal narrative, such *as Jacke of Dover, his Quest of Inquirie, or his Privy Search for the Veriest Foole in England* (1604). Others chronicled the ineptitude of fictional idiots, such as Andrew Borde's *Merie Tales of the Mad Men of Gotam* (1630)[1] and *The Sack-Full of News* (1673), which lampooned the supposedly inferior intellects of country bumpkins for metropolitan amusement. (In *Sack-Full* oafish Essex men loom large, while Anthony Copley's *Wits, Fittes and Fancies* (1595) has a thing about an idiot farmhand called John-a-Nokes.) And if the tales themselves weren't especially hilarious, a bit of bawdiness could always be dragged in to spice things up. *Sack-Full of News* delights with this choice morsel:

> There was a man and his wife lying in bed together, and the good man laid his buttocks on his wives knees, and so they lay sleeping, and the man dreamed that he was dead, and as he thought was carried into heaven, and being there he dreamed that he did shite through the moon into the world, but he did shite into his wives lap. And when he awaked, he told his wife his dreame, and as she would have turned on the other side, she felt that she was all to be shitten? Cocks body, quoth she, you have dreamed fair, for you have all to be shitten my knees; and so they were both faine to rise to make themselves clean.

As the years wore on they became more populist yet. In 1739 a shilling bought you a copy of *Joe Miller's Jests*, a repository of zingers attributed to the popular comic who flourished around the turn of the 18th century. Among the expected bawdiness nestles the odd relatively sophisticated gag that wouldn't be out of place in a 20th-century stand-up act, or at the very least would make the cut at a *Crackerjack* script meeting:

'An Irish lawyer of the Temple having occasion to go to dinner, left this direction in the keyhole; Gone to the Elephant and Castle, where you will find me, and if you cannot read this, carry it to the stationer's and he will read it for you.'

2

LET'S LOOK SIDEWAYS

The Renaissance may have seen unparalleled expansion in scholarship, but all this newfangled academic study began to take its toll on scholars' spirits, bringing mental exhaustion and homework melancholy to the attention of worried physicians. Their prescription must have seemed a trifle corny even back then: a dose of gaiety. Textbooks were joined by light-hearted treasuries of wit, to help learned minds kick back after a hard day at the lectern. Science, philosophy and art played their part in lifting Europe out of the Dark Ages, but the Renaissance wouldn't have been half the social revolution it was without the advent of the sideways look.

These collections were appropriately dubbed *facetiae*. The most famous practitioner was Poggio Bracciolini, a randy papal secretary who fathered some twenty children and married an 18-year-old at 55. His *Liber Facetiarum* (1451) collects nearly three hundred witty nuggets of Florentine life, ranging from the classically suggestive ('A certain gentleman, being called a pimp, consoled himself saying: "Why should I complain at being called by this name? I live according to the laws of nature, and I do for others what I would have them do for me."') to the plain silly ('Messer Matteo Franco, whose cat mewed when he pulled its ears, threw it out of the window, saying: "Now, I will catch my own mice."').

More scholarly fun was to be had via the riddle. Dutch émigré and printing pioneer Wynkyn de Worde published *The*

Demaundes Joyous in 1511, a collection of conundrums that would do the *Beano* proud:

> *Demaunde:* How many calues tayles behoueth to reche
>   frome the erthe to the skye?
> *Answere:* No more but one if it be longe ynough…
> *Demaunde:* Why doth an oxe or a cowe lye?
> *Answere:* Bycause she can not sytte…
> *Demaunde:* What beast is it that hath her tail between her
>   eyes?
> *Answere:* It is a cat when she licketh her arse…

(Perhaps not that last one.) Riddles were still in demand a century later. Anthony Copley was a poor poet and, as accessory to the failed 1603 Bye Plot, an even worse would-be kidnapper of James I, but a highly serviceable riddler. His opus was the exhaustingly titled *Booke of Merrie Riddles, Together with Proper Questions, and Witty Proverbs, to Make Pleasant Pastime. No Lesse Usefull then Behoovefull, for Any Young Man or Childe, to Knowe Whether he be Quicke-Witted or No.* (These deep-breath book titles may seem risibly overloaded now, but their function was important in those halcyon pre-cover blurb days.)

'Every cocke is proude on his owne dunghill'

Copley augmented his stock of riddles with some 130 proverbs, which have aged rather better than his confusing rubrics. 'Chuse not a woman, nor linnen cloth, by a candle.' 'Marvell is the daughter of ignorance.' 'He that goeth to bed with dogs riseth with fleas.' All this was as old as civilisation, but the Tudor period saw a snowballing fashion for the proverb, the epigram, the pithy observation, a trendiness capitalised upon by John Weever's *Epigrammes in the Oldest Cut, and Newest Fashion* (1599). John Heywood, court dramatist to Henry VIII, followed his *An Hundred Epigrammes, Invented and Made by John Heywood* (1550) with the expanded *Two Hundred Epigrammes* (1555) and later *A Fourth*, *A Fifth* and *A Sixt Hundred of Epygrams* (1560-2): one of the earliest literary franchises.

The epigrammatists were soon consigned to the critical dumper. Scholars dismiss them as second-rate poets, but many of their coinages live on to this day. 'Would ye both eat your cake and have your cake?' and 'A man may well bring a horse to the water, but he cannot make him drink' are two examples that have survived, slightly mangled, down the centuries. Many others, naturally, haven't aged quite so well ('One day men shall catch hares with tabers', 'The still sow eats up all the draffe') though yet more could perhaps do with a revival ('Hungry dogges will eate durty puddinges', 'He who is hanged in May shall eate no flannes in midsummer').

While many of these collections had morally reformist zeal, they nonetheless attracted the derision of more highbrow authors. John Rastell, playwright (and publisher of *A Hundred Merry Tales*, and therefore a right one to talk), bemoaned the waste of wit and paper that went into such 'toys and trifles'. More seriously, royalty began to turn censorious. Henry VIII, initially a vocal supporter of printed books, found enough examples of anti-monarchist satire by 1533 to warrant a suppression of 'fond books, ballads, rimes and other lewd treatises in the English tongue'. Queen Mary cast aspersions on the motives of 'printers and stationers, of an evil zeal for lucre and covetous of vile gain'. The finger of suspicion had fallen on the 'gutter press' and would never be lifted. But the censors' chief concern was with a seemingly innocuous literary form: the ballad.

A handful of songs

For centuries, the ballad was the primary news source for the masses. Not lyrical ballads of the type sung by a strolling minstrel in feathered cap and puffy shirt, but topical ballads printed on a single-sheet 'broadside' in heavy type and stuck up in the town square for ribald dispersal in mass tavern sing-a-longs.

The printed ballad dates back to *A Lytel Geste of Robyne Hood* (1506), and lasted well into the 19th century, until public order acts curtailed mass singing in the pubs, and the tradition gave way to its twin progenies, the newspaper and the music hall turn. Despite its heritage, the topical ballad has never been taken as seriously as its high-flown lyrical cousin, which after all went on to spawn classical poetry, while the broadside bequeathed us *Pop Goes the Weasel* and Richard Stilgoe's sideways look at the week's events.

A tavern packed with learned balladeers must have resembled an especially boisterous, risqué edition of *Nationwide*, as if Frank Bough had been left in charge of all departments. There would be major news (*The Death of the Right Honourable Sir Robert Peel*), rolling news (*Another Fearful Explosion Has Just Happened as We Hear*) and expert analysis (*War: What is All This Row About?*). Then discussion might turn to matters of politics (*Hallo ye Poor Tories What Slumped Once Again*); free trade (*The Fullwood Anti-Corn Law Soirée; Butchers of England Are Growing Quite Cranky*) or even consumer issues (*The Price of Flour Keeps Falling, They Want to Stop our Sunday Beer and Shove a Tax on Matches*).

Weighty topics dealt with, drinkers could move onto some serious frivolity. There were ballads of domestic distress (*To Be Drunk on the Premises; Barbers, I Have Lost my Wig!*). Local characters could be celebrated (*Jack Muggins the Donkey-Balancer*), or ridiculed (*Humphrey Dickins the Queer-Looking Man!*). The world of fashion was put under the microscope (*Great Flopping Bonnets*). And there was always a bout of pure, unadulterated whimsy (*Merrily Fuddle Thy Nose*).

A huge chunk of the repertoire was, inevitably, amorous. There was the straight romantic ballad (*Colin Stole My Heart Away*). There was the lovelorn lament ('I'm a broken-hearted milkman/In grief I am arrayed'). Inns being all-male affairs, there was the inevitable bout of off-colour misogyny (like grimly enthusiastic wife-beating paean *Bang Her Well, Peter*). Most, however, were just plain randy, from the charmingly upfront *Pull Down the Blind* ('Did you ever make love?/If not, have a try') via the less innocent *She Cannot Hold her Legs Together* right down to unwitting anthems of acute desperation like *The Brown Cunts of Old England*.

If the latter suggests that the real thing wasn't as abundant as some balladeers anticipated, the same went for food. Many ballads combined grub and sex in ingenious ways. You had *The Sausage Man; Beef Pork Mutton Will You Buy (Or the Amorous Butcher Boy)* and *The Eel Pie Shop! (That Girl Belongs to Me)*. Below-stairs servants were apt to get lucky in the larder in such songs as *Frying Pan Courtship* and *Cupboard Love (or Butter, Cheese and All)*. Or try this verse from the heart-warming *Rosannah, Don't You Sigh for Me (I'm Going to Northampton)*: 'Now when you see Rosannah/You'll say she is a good 'un/For she has got a tidy mouth/For eating Yorkshire pudding.' Often the composer's mind would drift away from sex entirely, leaving just the food (*The Turnip Song; The Great Meat Pie; You Shouldn't Buy Tripe On a Friday*). As a reliable source of news, the ballad was clearly flawed, but this was journalism genuinely by, about and for the people, and all to a thumping good tune.

The world on a tray

The Civil War caused an epidemic of printers, turning out propagandist pamphlets for both sides. Come the Restoration, with presses lying idle and creditors hovering, printers turned to the lowest common denominator to survive. 'Garlands' of ballads were collected in chapbooks, pocket-sized pamphlets printed with second-hand wooden type recycled from more prestigious jobs, and decorated with whatever chunky woodcuts were lying about the press room (if they happened to match the subject of the text in some vague way, then so much the better).

These scrappy sheaves of salvaged print were mainly sold by the chapman, a travelling hawker bearing all manner of cheap tat in his 'budget' – a large tray strapped round the neck – ranging from mirrors and trinkets through assorted haberdashery to the odd penny chapbook. Innkeepers too kept up a good stock of pamphlets and broadside ballads – as essential to 17th-century alehouse entertainment as Sky Sports today.

If literacy wasn't as rare in the 17th century as is often assumed, paper certainly was, so chapbooks were the first literal 'toilet' books, kept in the outdoor privy to help pass the time during the morning's business, then deployed to help clean up afterwards. As one ballad had it, 'Bum-Fodder or Wast-Paper proper to wipe the nation's rump with'.

All classes of literate Briton read chapbooks, but many were aimed at the simpler variety of countryman, and made no bones about it. Inaugurating a long toilet book tradition of apologetic introductions, *The Shifts of Reynardine, Son of Reynard the Fox* began:

I here offer the present Work... well knowing that a Clown is as well pleased with a Cock's Feather in his Cap, as a young Gentleman with a costly Plume... because such Books as these are more frequently read by persons of mean Understanding, than by Men of sound Judgement; I have good Reason to expect less Censure, or more Praise than I deserve.

Many chapbooks were 'improving' religious tracts or cat-on-mat language primers. Almost as prevalent were the 'pleasant histories'. There were easy-to-read accounts of biblical figures, biographies of noted worthies, and action-packed myths like the perennially popular tale of *Sir Bevis of Southampton* which, with its sidelining of character development in favour of an episodic narrative jumping from a double dragon-slaying to a fight with a 20-foot ogre and back again, reads like a modern Hollywood fantasy blockbuster, and was aimed at pretty much the same adolescent audience.

Also profiled on the cheap were famous witches like Mother Shipton, folk heroes such as Robin Hood and Wat Tyler; and underclass legends like Mother Bunch, licentious alewife and teller of many well-worn jests, who could 'talk as much without book as ony Inholder betwixt Brainford and Bagshot'. (Many chapbook publishers, likewise, had a second income as innkeepers.) At the bottom of the heap, citizens of ill repute were celebrated, including Edward IV's concubine Jane Shore, *The Merry Life and Mad Exploits of Capt. James Hind, the Great Robber of England* and *The Comical Cheats of Swalpo a Notorious Pick Picket, Together with the Merry Pranks of Roger the Clown.*

Then there was whimsy. Jests and riddles figured heavily, with the butt of many bumpkin jokes shifting to Wales (*The Unfortunate Welchman; The Pleasant History of Taffy's Progress to London*). If they weren't laughing at the daft immigrants, chapbook readers were guffawing at pretty much the same smut as ever. Giggling innuendo was not yet seen as immature schoolboy amusement. Fart gags were fit for all.

Porn abounded too. Salacious European dialogues were loosely translated, with a few topical references thrown in: very much aimed at the horny male reader, of course. Samuel Pepys recorded a solitary encounter with a copy of *L'Escholle des Filles* in his diary for February 1668, using a discreet secret code, which is nevertheless fairly easy to crack:

> ... a lewd book, but what doth me no wrong to read for information sake (but it did *hazer* my prick *para* stand all the while, and *una vez* to *decharger*); and after I had done it, I burned it, that it might not be among my books to my shame.

Elsewhere third-rate poets scraped a living with lewd verse epics starring King Bolloxinian and General Buggeranthus, lists of (genuine) London prostitutes were printed, such as *A Catalogue of Jilts, Cracks, Prostitutes, Night-Walkers, Whores, She-Friends, King Women and Others of the Linnen-Lifting Tribe* (1691), and serialised memoir *The Wandering Whore* (1660) whipped up a storm of carefully manufactured publicity over the identity of its anonymous author, of the sort familiar to modern readers of 'Belle de Jour's *Intimate Adventures of a London Call-Girl* (2005). Most prurient of all were mock medical tomes like *Rare Verities: the Cabinet of Venus Unlocked and her Secrets Laid Open* (1658), featuring temptingly titled chapters:

Which is more lustful, a woman or a maid?

Concerning some men that have had wonderful great genitals.

Whether to copulate backwards after the manner of beasts is best.

Concerning pendulous venery, and also many other fantastical venereal postures.

Undistinguished as they were, the wide circulation of these booklets throughout the country gave the masses some semblance of the education they would need to hold their own during the coming social upheavals of the Industrial Revolution. Could Marxism ever have taken off without the solid groundwork laid down by *Funny Dick's Grinning Made Easy*?

3

FOR THE BUSY WAY
YOU LIVE TODAY

Authors of literary classics can take their immortality for granted. Creators of less revered works melt into obscurity as the centuries pass. *The Boke of St Albans* (1486) is a case in point. This combined almanac of hawking, hunting and heraldry is commonly attributed to Dame Juliana Berners (or maybe Barnes), who was the prioress of a local nunnery. (Possibly.) Or maybe she was the daughter of Sir James Berners of Essex. (Doubt it, though.) She may even, since a lady of that era writing a book of all things is a bit much for most scholars, have been a monk named Julian Barnes all along. (Hmm.) Chaucer never had this sort of trouble getting noticed.

The book is mainly a solemn treatise on the noble field sports, brimming with medieval pomp. ('Here endyth the proceis of hawkyng. And now foloys the naamys of all maner of hawkys and to whom they belong.') But the parts that have lasted aren't concerned with how to make those twee little tufty leather hoods for falcons. They are tidbits chucked in, seemingly at random, and possibly for no other reason than to pad out the original manuscript. This filler is varied stuff. A gazetteer of 'Bestis of the chace of the swete fewte and stinking' nudges up to a list of Biblical proverbs, which in turn neighbours a guide to fine wines. The real historical winner, though, is 'The Companys of beestys and fowlys', a list of 164 collective nouns of an increasingly daft nature.

We begin with the expected flocks, covens and herds, then move into more whimsical-poetic territory with an unkindness of ravens, a kindle of kittens, and a business of ferrets; before the animal kingdom is left behind for a series of nudge-nudge comedy collectives ('a multiplying of husbands, a non-patience of wives, a superfluity of nuns'). This, in popular terms, is the book's legacy. The hunting poems are long forgotten, but everyone knows a couple of these silly names. The whimsical afterthought has outlasted the learned manual by centuries. And it was this practice of bunging in all manner of random stuff to create books of variety and amusement which led to a major literary fashion some two centuries after Dame Julian Whoever noted her (or his) last shrewdness of apes: the miscellany.

Looke and learne

The 16th century saw the flourishing of the miscellany. *The Court of Venus* (1538), Tottel's *Songs and Sonnettes* (1557) and *The Paradyse of Daynty Devises* (1576) collected pious sonnets together for the edification of young gentlemen. Fair enough, but what about the growing numbers of fashionable young men whose busy modern lifestyles (that ever-popular, punter-flattering code for chronic laziness) didn't permit endless hours perusing such fusty tomes? Where are they to get their education?

Some said such fops didn't deserve pandering to. Henry Peacham's *The Complete Gentleman* (1622) was a self-styled etiquette bible laying down the law on the 'most necessary and commendable qualities concerning minde or bodie that may be required in a noble gentleman'. Peacham poured scorn on the ungentlemanly masses ('that pestilent ayre of the common breath'). He also railed against the growing fashion for idle foppery, or as he put it 'the common Education; which is, to weare the best cloathes, eate, sleepe, drinke much, and to know nothing.'

He was answered by John Raymond's *Folly in Print* (1667), a book designed not to improve, but to entertain. As Raymond saw it, 'the whole world (imaginably) is but one great market; and all mankind in it, are distinguished into buyers and sellers, who either truck for, or buy commodities; particularly in Books.' Publishing was a trade, and the less highfalutin of writers set about the lucrative task of pushing common denominators down as far as possible.

William Winstanley was a former barber and eager, but ultimately rather clueless, author of a largely plagiarised catalogue of English poets. In the more forgiving world of the miscellany, however, he could run with the best of them. *The New Help to Discourse: or, Wit, Mirth and Jollity Intermixt with More Serious Matters* (1680) began with an earnest justification of his half-cocked endeavours:

> Thou hast here... the marrow of many Voluminous Authors of that bulk and bigness, that many people have not time to read them, and... seeing the tediousness of attaining knowledge, break off their journey at the beginning of the Race. [When] they come into company of knowing persons, they are feign to fit like dumb Images or Statues, for fear by speaking they betray their ignorance.

In other words, what's knowledge for, if not showing off? But these bluffer's guides had a practical application. Poetry is the language of romance, is it not? So, just as you don't need to be able to understand Racine in order to buy a litre of cheap wine at a French supermarket, there must be a similar crafty shortcut one can take through the daunting wasteland of poetry to get one's hands on... oh, you know. Enter the poetry miscellany as universal leg-over phrasebook.

'How must a man behave himselfe among Ladyes?'

The first rule of wooing was the same for men of the Stuart period as it is for the lad of today: don't make a pranny of thyself. Unfortunately for those idle fops too 'busy' to learn the first thing about social interaction, elevating one's wits above 'complete buffoon' was harder than it looked. So a single slim volume, solving a young milksop's personal shortfall in wit and gallantry at a stroke, was a guaranteed bestseller.

The Character of a Town-gallant; Exposing the Extravagant Fopperies of Some Vain Self-conceited Pretenders to Gentility and Good Breeding (1675) is a stinging mock day-in-the-life of one of these idle fops, 'a painted Butter-flye; a Baboon, usurping Humane Shape… made up of Complements, Cringes, Knots, Fancies, Perfumes, and a thousand French Apish tricks. His whole Library consists of *The Academy of Complements, Venus Undress'd, Westminster Drollery,* half a dozen Plays, and a bundle of Bawdy Songs in Manuscript.'

Let's take the first of these, John Gough's *The Academy of Complements* (1639). Gough dices sonnets into handy morsels of flattery for easy application by the fledgling crumpeteer. The reader can choose phrases from the greats praising his sweetheart's hair, forehead, eyes, cheeks, breath, chin, tongue and breasts (Shakespeare's 'ivory globes' of course).

Courtly bluffing reached its zenith with the 'model dialogues', enchanting scripted conversations with a member of the fairer sex to be learned by rote and – surely only with a great deal of luck – replicated on a stroll in the park or during a hansom cab journey. The shame at being caught doing this was so acute that later miscellanies added to their model dialogues lines with which to deflect any accusations of using model dialogues. It was a jungle out there.

The sheer social panic engendered by these manuals reaches paranoid levels by the time we get to John Cotgrave's *Wits*

Interpreter, the English Parnassus (1655). Chatting up birds has now become a science. Obscure diagrams show the apprentice wooer which phrases to drop in at which points in which conversation – providing he can make sense of the thing. The furtive philanderer often had recourse to espionage tactics. 'How to Write Love-letters Secretly that they Cannot be Discovered' proffers a complicated system of cut-out ciphers as used by Cardinal Richelieu. Learn from the best in the deceit business, lads!

Something for the ladies

While young gentlemen were being coached in the mysterious ways of having it away with the womenfolk, the womenfolk were plied with their own miscellanies instructing them in the various ways of sitting there and putting up with it. John Dunton printed *The Ladies Dictionary; Being a General Entertainment for the Fair-sex: a Work Never Attempted Before in English* (1694). Part beauty manual and part etiquette guide, it was, claimed Dunton (one of literature's first hucksters), 'a compleat Dictionary to the Female Sex in all Relations, Companies, Conditions and States of Life; even from CHILDHOOD down to Old-Age, and from the Lady at the Court, to the Cook-maid in the Country'.

Perhaps mindful of the large number of periwigged fops going about the place armed with *The Academy of Complements* in their pocket, Dunton urged caution before marriage ('you'll get better Conditions if the Enemy does not know how weak you are within')[2] and fidelity after (nine pages on 'Adultery and Uncleanness'). Other topics in this wide-ranging A-Z include Amazons (nine pages); Big-belly'd women in need of self-governance; Naked Breasts ('the sight of a fair Neck and pretty swelling Breasts, are no less dangerous for is than that of a Basilisk', but those that 'hang loose, and are of an extraordinary largeness, lose their charms, and have their beauty buried in the grave of uncomliness') and Nuns. The (male) authors veer between condescending advice and fierce prohibition in a manner made all the more comical by their matter-of-fact prose. A lady's education is a serious matter.

Nothing much changed for a century. With Victoria a few years from the throne, *The New Female Instructor; Or, Young Woman's Guide to Domestic Happiness* (1834) expended over 600 tightly printed pages on preserving the female *status quo*. After all, as the introduction proclaimed:

> By the arts of *pleasing* only it is, that WOMEN can attain to any degree of consequence or power: and it is by pleasing only that they can hope to become objects of *love* and *affection*… In their forms lovely, in their manners soft and engaging, they can infuse, by their smiles, air and address, a thousand nameless sweets into society, which, without them, would be insipid, and barren to sentiment and feeling.

Temptation, more than ever, was waiting to drag the respectable young lady into the mire of iniquity. The solution: keep your head down, keep away from men, and above all, don't get any ideas. 'Look into yourselves, learn wisdom, and acquire experience, before you venture into the dangerous vortex of beguiling pleasure.' Your friends may mock your virtuous lifestyle, but don't give in to their bitter words: 'Fear not the being reproached with *prudery*… At any rate, it is better to be thought ridiculous than loose.'

A helpful list of prohibited activities is provided: card games and gambling in general are not on ('Old maids are the only class of females who may be allowed to spend some of their tedious hours in such absurd and unhealthy pastimes'); nor are novels ('to indulge in a practice of reading novels is, in several other particulars, liable to produce mischievous effects'); swearing is 'utterly INEXCUSABLE, and bear-baiting is right out.

With her entertainment options drastically reduced, the lady is free to knuckle down and apply the book's numerous medical recipes. ('Hard breasts: Apply turnips roasted till soft, then mashed and mixed with a little oil of roses; change this twice a day, keeping the breast very warm with a flannel.') It's easy to laugh at these mad, condescending primers now, but this domineeringly unctuous drivel sold like hot posset for decades.

There was the odd voice of dissent. *Mundus Muliebris: or, The Ladies Dressing-room Unlock'd, and her Toilette Spread* (1690) is an odd little book by diarist, gunpowder magnate and tree expert John Evelyn, written with considerable help from his daughter Maria. A satire on the mad ranks of published courtship advice, it featured a demented cosmetic recipe:

> *To Make Pig, or Puppidog, Water for the Face*
> Take a Fat Pig, or a Fat Puppidog, of nine days old, and kill it, order it as to Roast, save the Blood, and fling away nothing but the Guts; then take the Blood, and Pig, or the Puppidog, and break the Legs and Head, with all the Liver and the rest of the Inwards, of either of them, put all into the Still if it will hold it, to that, take two Quarts of old Canary, a pound of unwash'd Butter not salted; a Quart of Snails-Shells, and also two Lemmons, only the outside pared away; Still all these together in a Rose Water Still, either at once or twice; Let it drop slowly into a Glass-Bottle, in which let there be a lump of Loaf Sugar, and a little Leaf-Gold.

17th-century society was a tad more complex than the miscellany's overall picture of the idle, witless young man running lustily after the chaste, turnip-smeared young woman. William Winstanley's *The Muses Cabinet, or, Delights for the Ladies* (1655) promised fun fun fun, in the shape of poems such as The Jealous Husband, On the Entity and Goodness of God, and On One Whose Nick-name was Stiffy. If that wasn't enough, there were 'three useful as well as delightful Recreations in Practical

Mathematics', and all for 'the easy price of Three Shillings only'. The miscellanies had something for everyone, whether they liked it or not.

Coffee mates

During the 17th century a new kind of watering hole appeared on London's streets: the coffee-house. Despite the name, leisurely imbibing of the newly discovered Turkish stimulant was their least important attraction. Clay pipes, newsletters and gossip were the main draws. Gentlemen in the know, or keen to appear to be in the know, paid their penny for a cup of Eastern restorative and congregated in a civilised world of conviviality and banter, where all men (over a certain social standing) were equal, moping and fighting were frowned upon, betting was tolerated up to a five shilling limit, and swearing carried a twelve penny fine.

Pioneering hack-about-town Ned Ward captured the snugly manic essence of these places in *The Weekly Comedy: as it is Dayly acted at most Coffee-Houses in London* (1699). Set in the fictional Bohee's Coffee House, it teems with whimsical types dashing in and out of the sitcom setting as they go about their frenzied business, among them Prim the Beau, Truck the Merchant, the 'Jingling Poet', the 'Frothy Punster', and Scribble the News-Hound, desperately hunting the latest town gossip. In a typical episode, Whim the Inventor concocts a Periwig-making machine for turning out oversize headjoy 'after the Newest French Mode'. Prim inevitably stumps up fifty guineas to be first in line, and turns up at the Coffee-House later that day in the elephantine result, to the loud amusement of the rest of the company, looking 'like the Fundament of a Peacock with its Tail spread; for I can scarce see any part of your Face but your Mouth for Periwig'. These distinctly *Blackadder*-esque goings-on were turned into a popular three-act play a few years later.

A real life coffee-house frequenter was Captain William

Hicks, former butler, landlord, military instructor, dance tutor and all-round 'sharking and indignant fellow' who hung up his shoes when he grew too old to prance and turned to publishing miscellanies for a living. His chief sales trick was to identify his books with specific centres of urban wit. Hence his *Oxford Drollery: Being New Poems, and Songs Made by the Most Eminent and Ingenious Wits of the Said University* (1671), *London Drollery* (1673) and *Coffee-house Jests* (1677), all purporting to feature nuggets of wit and mirth overheard amongst the witty fellows who frequented these places, gathered for the edification of those who did not. Here's an example from the latter volume:

> A cleanly woman of Cambridgeshire made a good store of butter, and whilst she went a little way out of the town about some earnest occasions, a neighbour's dog came in in the meantime, and eat up half the butter. Being come home, her maid told her what the dog had done, and that she had locked him up in the dairy-house. So she took the dog and hang'd him up by the heels till she had squeez'd all the butter out of his throat again, whilst she, pretty, cleanly soul, took and put it to the rest of the butter, and made it up for Cambridge market. But her maid told her she was ashamed to see such a nasty trick done. 'Hold your peace, you fool!" says she; "'tis good enough for schollards. Away with it to market!'

Evidently, there hasn't been a great leap of sophistication since the days of the old jest books. But what is new here is the presentation of these gags as the by-product not of a single comedian, but of a large and matey society. The detached humour of the solitary outsider has become the inclusive, conservative humour of the club.

Away from the tense and complicated art of womanising, the miscellanies were in their element on the subject of kicking back with the boys. *Wits Interpreter*'s 'Labyrinth of Fancies, New

Experiements and Inventions' includes many exciting party
tricks, or 'Petty Conceits': To Heave up a Bottle with a Straw;
How a Pear, or an Apple may be Parted into many Parts without
Breaking the Rind; and, worryingly, How a Man may put his
Finger in, or Wash his Hands in Melting Lead without Danger
of Burning. All this led, inevitably, to the topic of boozing,
which Cotgrave's fun-loving miscellany enshrines as the
'Schoole of Bacchus', a droll academy of heavy drinking whose
graduates can easily be recognized:

> A fat corpulent fellow, is a *Master of Arts*. A lean
> drunkard, a *Bachelour*. He that hath a purple face enshrin'd
> with rubies, a *Bachelour of Law*.

This larking about sent out a defiant message in the
17th century, as to be vocally pro-booze – pro-'fun', even
– was implicitly to be identified as a Royalist, giving such
otherwise frivolous 'lusty drollery, joviall fancies, and *a la
mode* lamponnes' a cocky Restoration swagger after the
grim days of the Protectorate. Tomfoolery was a symbol
of freedom, but the problem remained – how to make it
pay?

4

DUNCES' CORNER

The condition of an Author, is much like that of a Strumpet... and if the reason be requir'd, why we betake our selves to so scandalous a Profession as Whoring or Pamphleteering, the same exclusive answer will serve us both, viz. That the unhappy circumstances of a narrow Fortune, hath forc'd us to do that for our Subsistence, that we are much asham'd of.

Ned Ward, *A Trip to Jamaica* (1698)

Milton Street, London EC2 must be the dullest street in Britain. At the top, there's St Paul's Tavern, a traditional London pub with old-fashioned snugs and wooden ale casks suspended from stout brass chains. Original oak beams support television sets bearing silent Sky Sports News.Polished wood panelling creates a welcomingly Dickensian atmosphere in which to play *Super Prize Bullseye*. The rest of the street flows uneventfully into the Barbican Centre. The only hint of history lies in the cobbled Georgian square of The Brewery, once the capital's largest beer factory, now an Olde Worlde corporate banqueting centre. Here you will be met by a delightful man in bowler hat and handlebar moustache who will, with impeccable politeness, ask you to clear off.

Submerged somewhere underneath all this is Milton Street's original incarnation as Grub Street, 17th-century bohemian hang-out of writers, artists and general layabouts. Long after the name change, Grub Street lived on as journo-slang for that stage of a writer's career when hack work, writing for hire, is the only way to keep solvent. In the 18th century, Grub Street acquired extra significance. The publishing boom that followed the abolition of the Licensing Act in 1695, giving everyone and anyone the right to print anything, brought a rocketing demand for copy. Much of this unregulated material was bad, mad, even dangerous – if not to national security like anarchist pamphlets then dangerous, at least, to noble ideals of art and civilised society. Writers cast their eye over the trade, and what they saw worried them.

Anyone with a bit of spare cash could publish a pamphlet. Facile tracts of Restoration ribaldry were, appropriately enough, multiplying like rabbits. Literature seemed to be heading for the slagheap with gathering speed. Concerned writers of the establishment banded together to form a reactionary clan dedicated to the ridicule of hackery. This was the Augustan age, and literature was to be on its best behaviour at all times. No coarseness, no blasphemy, no rambling, no punning, no ducking, no diving, and no soiled work clothes in the foyer please.

The chief clique of this movement was the Scribblerus Society, a loose group of writers including literary worthies Jonathan Swift and Alexander Pope. The Scribblerians' prime weapon was parody. Swift published *A Tale of a Tub* (1704), a breathless tract written in the style of a wide-eyed, eager, yet gullible consumer of the shiny new publishing age. Driven half mad with a surfeit of information of wildly varying reliability, he digresses from his point, then digresses from that digression, and soon spirals into a frenzy of pointlessly hyperactive chatter, all the while convinced that, in the vanguard of an exciting new dawn for civilisation, he is the equal of any writer in history.

The key players in this literary mob rule were satirised in Pope's mock epic poem, *The Dunciad* (1728). Here Pope laid into Grub Street's 'dunces' (the hacks, bad poets and all-round enemies of clarity and decorum), as they went about their dishonourable craft, and worshipped at the feet of the goddess of commercial scribbling, Dulness. There was an element of protective snobbery in all this. Pope was vocal in his hatred of the 'taste of the Rabble', fearing a 'world turned upside down' by this 'vast involuntary throng'. Grub Street in the eyes of the Scribblerians was a cancer on the cultivated world of English literature.

Hackery's financial rewards were undeniable, however, and the Scribblerians weren't above dabbling in Grub Street's murky waters for a furtive shilling. Jonathan Swift's *Miscellanies* (1722) brought together several light-hearted pamphlets discussing the art of punning, and the possible benefits to the British treasury of a national swearbox, along with *The Benefit of Farting Explain'd*,[3] a mock address to the fairer sex, positing that many female distempers might be the result of rectal gas inadequately vented. (Swift later denied authorship of *Farting*, insisting it was the work of 'one Dobbs, a surgeon', though this may have been an embarrassed fib.)

Bog standards

Trawling through 18th-century literature is like sifting junk mail in an asylum. All human life really is here. The titles alone are enough to make discerning eyeballs revolve heavenwards. Try John Dunton's *Bumography: or, a Touch at the Lady's Tails* (1707), or the more philosophical *A Turd is as good for a Sow, as a Pancake: Or, The Story of a COCK and a BULL.*

Complicating the mare's nest further, many writers operated under pseudonyms to save face, and often gratingly whimsical ones at that. Imagine a few hours in the relentlessly convivial company of 'Ferdinando Funny', 'Sir Toby Tickleside' and 'Tim Gape, Grin-master General'. This desire for anonymity is understandable, and probably hides the work of many well-known men of letters. There are two ways for a writer to stand out in the madhouse: be scrupulously sane (possible, but there's not much money in it), or be louder and madder than everyone else. The latter method helped some authors rise above the delirious throng.

Take Samuel Johnson, for instance. Not Dr Samuel Johnson of Dictionary fame, but Half-Mad Samuel 'Maggoty' Johnson of Cheshire, sometime jester of Gawsworth Hall, accomplished dancer, mean fiddler, poet, clown, stilt-walker and dramatist whose mock opera *Hurlothrumbo, or the Supernatural* enjoyed an eighty-night sell-out run at the Haymarket Theatre, thanks to such nonsense songs as the one describing the side-effects of imbibing a cocktail of brandy and gunpowder: 'Then Lightning from the Nostrils flies/Swift Thunder-bolts from Anus, and the Mouth will break/With Sounds to pierce the Skies, and make the Earth to quake.'

In 1731, James Roberts of London published a series of four sixpenny pamphlets entitled *The Merry-Thought: Or, the Glass-Window and Bog-House Miscellany,* a collection of public graffiti, either inscribed with diamonds into the windows of coffee-houses, or written on the inside walls of public bog-houses using whatever medium came to hand, compiled by one 'Hurlo Thrumbo', a pseudonym for either Johnson or Roberts, most likely a collaboration of the two.

A compendium of comic verse scratched away in idle (above the belt, at least) moments, it tends towards homely craphouse philosophy with such ditties as An Encomium on a Fart ('I sing the Praises of a Fart/That I may do't by Rules of Art… For sure I must not use high Strains/For fear it bluster out in Grains') and, 'in a Bog-House at Hampstead', 'There's Nothing foul that we commit/But what we write, and what we shit'. It's at once a pastiche of learned Augustan miscellanies and a demented celebration of the lowest form of poetry for its own sake, as 'H-T' explains in his preface, which, appropriately enough, is in the middle of the book. ('You will pardon the Editor that he does not put Things better in Order; but he is so engaged in reading the Letters sent him… that he believes the Preface is in the Middle of the Book; but I dare swear you'll find it somewhere or other.')

'Hurlo Thrumbo' boasts, with mock seriousness, his mighty

achievement in preserving works which 'might have been lost, by the Effects of Wine, Punch, and strong Beer, in the Christmas Time… I have myself taken Care to visit most of the Glasiers in Town where I just came Time enough to save some few Scraps of Wit; and have bribed a great Number of Football-Players'. As a record of what people used to write on toilet walls, it's historically useful; as a cheeky swipe at the tutting elite on behalf of the uneditable masses, it's a stylish masterstroke.

Dunton checks in

As much a part of Samuel Johnson's character as his eccentricity was a wide streak of good honest opportunism. It took both qualities to make a great dunce, and no one better exemplified them than John Dunton.

As a publisher, Dunton was a busy man (he claimed to have published over 600 titles) who lived on his wits, a great deal of credit, and a relentless thirst for the spirit of the age: novelty. Nothing was too far-out for Dunton's consideration: secret histories, political tracts, conduct books and anecdote collections rolled off his press. 'Unless a Man can either think or perform something out of the old beaten Road, he'll find nothing but what his forefathers have found before him,' claimed his doorstop compilation *Athenianism: Or, the New Projects of Mr. John Dunton* (1710).

One of his many mad deals resulted in Charles Gildon's *The Post-Boy Rob'd of His Mail: Or, the Pacquet Broke Open* (1692). This was a collection of 500 disparate letters, supposedly stolen in transit and mockingly sampled by a coterie of coffeehouse wits. Tapping into the ever-present paranoia of communications going AWOL, it was a great success, though Dunton was sufficiently embarrassed by it to later pen a furtive dismissal: 'This Project obtained so well, that both Volumes are now out of print. It is true there are many unwary and prophane expressions scattered through these Volumes, so that I am heartily sorry I had any concern in them: but the Author sent the Copy to the press as he wrote it off, and in regard I had no suspicion of him, I did not peruse the Letters till it was past time to alter them.'

Athenianism as Dunton defined it was 'an endless search for novelty', a garden shed hobby version of the Enlightenment's explosion of scientific and philosophical discovery. If that sounds like an absurdly vague brief, it didn't matter to the ever-keen Dunton. Every aspect of life was up for excitable amateur dissection, but it was best to hurry, as there was a lot to get through. *Athenian Sport: Or, Two Thousand Paradoxes Merrily Argued* (1707) is another typically mammoth work, wherein Dunton discusses such 'Pleasant Theses' as, 'A marry'd Woman may be twice a Virgin', 'Content is the greatest Misery', and 'Fruition's nothing, or a Paradox proving there's no Pleasure in Copulation'.

Dunton moved from publishing to writing after the death of his first wife in 1697. He retreated from the raucousness of Grub Street to the country, where he wrote *The Art of Living Incognito* (1700), a rambling discourse on whatever matters came to mind. What came to Dunton's mind most often was Dunton, and much of the book expounds on the (evidently) endlessly fascinating topic of his life, including an essay on his own funeral.

'And this is me.'

But the peak of Dunton's solipsistic obsession came with his 1705 autobiography. At a time when autobiography was the preserve of a handful of bluebloods and the odd poet, a publisher's memoir would have been novel enough, but Dunton went further, producing *The Life and Errors of John Dunton Late Citizen of London; Written by Himself in Solitude. With an Idea of a New Life; Wherein is Shewn How He'd Think, Speak, and Act, Might He Live Over His Days Again: Intermix'd with the New Discoveries the Author has Made in His Travels Abroad, and in His Private Conversation at Home. Together with the Lives and Characters of a*

Thousand Persons Now Living in London, &C. Digested into Seven Stages, with their Respective Ideas. Here things really start to get out of hand.

Dunton offers up densely detailed chapters on his boyhood and apprenticeship, alternating with musings on what might have been had events taken a different turn. This may sound like monstrous self-indulgence, and indeed it was, but Dunton's not so much self-satisfied as self-excited. When he comes to the chapter dealing with his tragically short first marriage, he rockets off for nearly 300 pages of minuscule detail and shambolic soul searching. Then, as if suddenly realising he'll never get the job done at this rate, he apologetically promises to tell the rest of his life story in a second volume (which never arrived), before randomly launching into 'A Panegyrick of Eminent Persons' ('Mr. Accepted Lister, of Thornton in Bradford-dale, is a little man, but one that has a great soul…') and other essays which push the twin envelopes of sense and readability beyond all previous records. It's among this book's many achievements to be one of the few autobiographies that plagiarise substantial chunks of other people's books. Alexander Pope marveled at Dunton's effrontery, if nothing else.

Dunton's unwitting gift to the Augustans came in the form of the mostly fabricated *A Voyage Round the World; or, a Pocket-Library* (1691), another sprawling, digressive work that tries to cram everything possible between its covers. This extract, attempting to describe the scope of the book's ambitions, should give some idea of the attractions of his manic stream-of-consciousness prose to the Scribblerian's satirical eye:

I cannot better or fuller describe it, than telling you in two words, 'tis *every thing*. For as the Lives and Actions of great Princes contain one way or other, the greatest part of the *History of the times and Ages* they live in, so the Reader will find in the Life of *one Traveller,* my individual self, *Don Kainophilus,* alias *Evander,* the whole Description of, I scorn to say one *Country, one Age, or one World;* but of all the Habitable and Uninhabitable Creation:

every *Foot, Pearch and Inch on't; Virtue and Vice, Wit and Folly*, all the Humours, Religions, Customs, Whims and Connundrums of Mankind... Should I tell you, as the *virtuosi* do, that I was shaped at first like a Todpole, and that I remember very well, when my Tail *Rambled off*, and a pair of little Legs sprung out in the Room on't: Nay, shou'd I protest I pulled out my Note-book, and slap-dash'd it down the very minute after it happen'd – let me see – so many Days, Hours, and seconds after Conception, yet this Infidel World wou'd hardly believe me...

Such passages of concentrated brush-daft riches were grist for Lawrence Sterne, whose *Life and Opinions of Tristram Shandy, Gentleman* (1759) bears an uncanny resemblance to Dunton at times. Dunton's *Voyage* was even reprinted in 1762 as *The Life, Travels, and Adventures of Christopher Wagstaff, Gentleman, Grandfather to Tristram Shandy*, for the ironic delectation of the sophisticated consumers of Sterne's parody, in much the same way as today's publishers plunder the innocent books of the past for our amusement. So John Dunton did achieve some measure of the literary immortality he was constantly fretting about, though perhaps not in the way he planned.

Multi-platform madness

As my Monkeys and me and my Dogs am promised to go to L'Haye and Vienna after some Days more, the grand Noblemans and Gentlemans of this Nation England do desire me to perform every Night, and so me shall do with Mrs Midnight at the Haymarket Playhouse this Thursday Night. Ballard Mango, my big Monkey, will talk the *Prologue*.

So proclaimed an Italian animal trainer in a 1752 press adver-tisement for *Mrs Midnight's Oratory*, a raucous and highly popular musical and comedic free-for-all revue hosted by an ageing, cantankerous midwife, played by a fellow of Pembroke College, Cambridge in old-fashioned drag. This demented all-nighter may seem like just another one of many rowdy variety evenings that were flooding Covent Garden's theatres at the time, paving the way for the Victorian music hall and trouncing Shakespeare at the box office. But it's a crucial part of the strange and tragic tale of one of the most remarkable of all dunce writers: poet, scholar and pioneering spirit of British nonsense humour, Christopher Smart.

Smart was not a typical dunce. As a young poet he received a letter of commendation from Alexander Pope himself. The problem began when he left Cambridge for London, and had to supplement his college bursary with some real work. There was no money in sonnets, so penning articles for *The Gentleman's Magazine* helped keep his head above water. Eventually he got the publishing bug, and began to edit (meaning pretty much write in its entirety) a curious journal called *The Midwife, or the Old Woman's Magazine*. Launched on October 16, 1751, this threepenny wonder stood out from the mad Grub Street babble by virtue of its sheer brazen oddity.

The sixteen editions of *The Midwife* catalogue the bottom rung of society, where bohemian writers rubbed shoulders with whores, drunks and panhandlers. This was a milieu roundly ignored by the Augustan elite, but Smart, always a man apart, looked on them with more empathy. Mrs Mary Midnight, the mouthpiece of the disenfranchised, became the magazine's fictional editor, her task to celebrate the strangeness of the world and hold the unconsidered masses up for recognition.

Some of *The Midwife* was reasonably straight. The draconian punishments for debtors sparked a notable crusade in its pages, for example. The rest was completely off-kilter. Mock advertisements promoted The Head Shop, in which old heads could be swapped for new, and a windmill in Guildford that ground old women young, with glowing testimonials from the freshly rejuvenated likes of Mrs Richard Fumbletext and Mrs Philip

Hug-Bribe. There was a prediction of life in 1931, where the people's growth has been stunted to a two-and-a-half-foot average through chronic gin abuse, but *The Midwife* is 'read in all the European Universities and Schools as a Classic'. There was a deeply serious scholarly dissection of a ballad about a cockney butcher shitting himself.[4] Wordplay and weird conceits mocked the certainties of the Establishment. There were no boundaries in the anarchic world of Mrs Midnight.

A great innovation was the inclusion of spoof letters to cultural institutions. The Antiquarian Society was sent a detailed report from Cornwall, where a monolith made of petrified human excrement had been discovered. In issue number three, Mrs M regales the Royal Society with a lengthy description of her Pythonesque cat organ, which enables her, via a keyboard, to play

> ...Cats of different Sizes, included in Boxes, whose voices express every Note of the Gamut, which is extorted from the imprison'd Animals, by placing their Tails in Grooves, which are properly squeez'd by the Impression of the organist's Fingers on the Keys... the Upper Row on which I play Piano, or softly, consists of cats, both of a lesser size, and whose Tails are squeez'd by a much less Degree of Pressure... But the Lower Row, on which I play Forte, or loudly, contains an harmonious Society of banging Grimalkins, and whose Tails are severely pricked by Brass-Pins, inserted in the end of the Key for that Purpose... I have underneath my Instrument a Treddle, like that of a Spinning-Wheel, which I work with my Foot; this Treddle activates a certain Number of Forceps or Pinchers, which open and shut at my Pleasure, upon the Noses and Chins of all the Cats.

After the magazine folded in 1753, it was collected in three bound volumes (a common practice with periodicals at that time), with an engraved frontispiece depicting Smart and his publisher in full drag, next to a chamber pot labeled 'The Jakes of Genius'. It was a fitting send-off for the magazine, though production had ceased only because Smart had become far too busy directing and starring in the stage spin-off.

Beyond the fringe

On December 30, 1751, the guest room at the Castle Tavern in Paternoster Row hosted *The Old Woman's Oratory; or Henley in Petticoats*, 'a Grand Concert of Vocal and Instrumental Musick, by several Eminent Hands… conducted by Mrs Midnight, Author of the Midwife, and her Family.'

The 4' 10" Smart, in shawl and high-crowned hat, introduced a riot of songs, verse, speciality acts and 'dancing in the old British taste'. There was Monsieur Timbertoe, a dancer with a wooden leg. Signora Spoonatissima played delicate refrains on a pair of wooden spoons. Another pair of musicians brought a huge cello case onto the stage with great ceremony, which opened to reveal a broomstick, which they then attempted to 'play' with little success. 'Animal comedians' such as Ballard Mango came close to stealing the show. ('I was astonished at the sagacity of the monkeys' – *The Adventurer*.) Mime artists imitated breaking wind with the help of an off-stage French horn. Prologues were spoken from the back of an ass. Sometimes a short play was chucked into the running order, like *The Adventures of Fribble*. Doors opened at six o'clock sharp and the fun was still going strong well past midnight.

The *Oratory*'s fame spread at tremendous speed. Diarist Hester Piozzi noted 'it was wondrous droll, and what the wags call "funney"', though Horace Walpole was less convinced: 'it appeared the lowest buffoonery in the world even to me who am used to my Uncle Horace.' It transferred to the Haymarket, where *Hurlothrumbo* had been packing them in twenty years earlier, and then to Southwark Fair. Smart's deranged celebration

of the underdog and advocacy of misrule was the talk of the
capital.

Whether through overwork or manic depression, Smart's
mental health took a turn for the worse. He was confined to a
private madhouse in Bethnal Green, where he wrote *Jubilate
Agno*, a mammoth poem of total insanity. ('Let Jahleel rejoice
with the Woodcock, who liveth upon suction and is pure from
his diet… Let Fage, house of Fage rejoice with the Fiddlefish –
Blessed be the name of the Lord Jesus in the fish's mouth.') He
never again returned to the stage or the page as Mrs Midnight.

Mrs Midnight, however accidentally, had become a 'brand'.[5]
The conjunction of magazine, book and stage spectacle was a
new one, which anticipated the 20th-century 'media tie-in'. (It
also anticipated many other aspects of British comedy: the
spectacle of Cambridge graduates in drag, and confusing the
pompous with spoof letters.) At the time, though, Smart's story
represented the dangers of Grub Street's half-mad tomfoolery.
Puritan morality was on the rise, anticipating the staunch
propriety of the Victorians. Smart's brand of liberating madness
would have the best part of two centuries to wait before it could
show its many gurning faces in public again.

5

MIDDLE CLASS REVOLT

British society had been boiling over since the restoration, and the newly minted middle classes watched the pot with mounting concern. The toffs still had most of the money, but were steadily sliding down a spiral of decadence. Cloth breeches were triumphing over silk. The agreeably righteous atmosphere of the coffeehouses provided the perfect conditions for upright debate, aided by the newssheets available for free perusal by the increasingly influential mercantile classes.

In theory, at least. The problem with newspapers was the same as that of Grub Street. Where amongst all the clamour did news end and opinionated rumour begin? There was no regulation, though the incautious editor could find himself in the pillory, as Daniel Defoe (brother-in-law of John Dunton) did after his *Review* courted party political controversy.

Ploughing through the daily piles of posts, mercuries and intelligencers, many of suspicious origin and even more suspiciously short life span, tended to compound a fellow's ignorance rather than dissipate it. *The Court Mercurie*, for instance, was published by John Cotgrave, last seen encouraging young men to wash their hands in molten lead in his *Wits' Interpreter*, while the *Athenian Mercury's* promise to answer 'all the most Nice and Curious Questions' became marginally less enticing after a glance at the editor's name: John Dunton.

Impartial information was hard to find. What was needed was someone with an intellectual scope enabling him to peer

over the parapets of prattle and survey the social scene with
coolly detached judgment. That man – at least, according to
Richard Steele – was Richard Steele.

An army dropout and middling dramatist, Steele saw himself
as a moral reformer, but he also had strong Cavalier tendencies
fostered in London's hearty clubland, and was unlikely to
practice exactly what he preached. In 1708 he was sacked from
his position of gentlemanwaiter to Prince George of Denmark.
In April of the following year, to stave off bankruptcy, he began
publishing a thrice-weekly news and opinion sheet, the *Tatler*.

What Steele brought to the periodical party was a sharp eye
and a broad grasp. He started with a remit to provide reliable
news from home and abroad, mixed with a hefty dose of
moralistic gossip. Steele savaged well-known Londoners without
giving their full names, in the quaint belief they would mend their
ways after seeing their misdeeds broadcast. Pseudonymously, of
course – the *Tatler* claimed, from the off, to be 'the lucubrations
of Isaac Bickerstaff', a cantankerous astrologer spying on
Londoners' comings and goings with wry aloofness.

Steele took a censorious stance, setting himself against the
bone-idle courtiers, those 'whisperers without business and
laughers without occasion,' and aligning himself firmly with the
more respectable and increasingly more powerful middle class.
On the other hand, he also asserted 'the force and efficacy of
well-applied nonsense' in wooing the ladies. Then there was the
Trumpet Club, a fictional society numbering among their rapidly
decreasing membership country gent Sir Jeffrey Notch, Major
Matchlock and the beau Dick Reptile, which would become the
template for a century of whimsy.

Clubbability

The club was a powerful social symbol. Literary life in late 17th-
century London revolved around an exclusive club congregating
at Will's Coffee House. John Dryden, in his armchair by the fire,

challenged the others to come up with witty verses. One contest was famously won by this poem from the Earl of Dorset:

> I promise to pay John Dryden, Esq.; or order, on demand, the sum of five hundred pounds.
>
> Dorset

As time wore on, exclusive cliques-within-cliques formed at Will's – were you a member of the Grave Club, the Witty Club, or the 'Rabble'? Coffeehouse clubs became increasingly high profile – more so than the raucous but seldom intellectually productive tavern gatherings, which turned out little more than self-satisfied, ruddy-faced songs. ('Here is a crew of jovial Blades that lov'd the nut-brown ale!') Men of the middling orders gathered to talk politics, 'toast the great beauties of the day' and of course bandy wits.

Some clubs were renowned. Steele was a member of the Kit-Cat Club, which took its name from one Christopher Cat, a pie shop proprietor whose puddings provided the ideal accompaniment to agreeable banter. Similarly grub-oriented was the Beefsteak Club, actor Richard Estcourt's society devoted to the consumption of rare meat. Estcourt, as secretary, hung a small gold gridiron round his neck ('O resound the Utensil invented for Grilling!') and imitated public figures to the amusement of all.

In January of 1711, Steele packed in the *Tatler*, perhaps fearing the secret identity of Isaac Bickerstaff was becoming too well known among those he'd badmouthed. Tea merchants hungry for fop-baiting gossip didn't have long to fret, though, as March 1st saw the relaunch of daily Whiggish scuttlebutt in the form of the *Spectator*. (Neither paper, incidentally, is related to its modern namesake.) Here Steele was joined by Joseph Addison for yet another high-concept venture, set in another club.

The imaginatively named Mr Spectator introduced himself in the first issue, a walking storehouse of worldly wisdom observing society stealthily from the inside. He was joined at his club by a gallery of old buffers: Captain Sentry, a retired army man; Will Honeycomb, the comic relief fop; and Sir Andrew Freeport, a wealthy merchant and enthusiastic spokesman for 'common-sense'. Most notable of all was Sir Roger de Coverley, a benevolent country squire of the old school whose bucolic adventures contributed greatly to English humour's 'man of the world' homespun mantle, and quite possibly the invention of *The Archers* to boot. 555 issues later Mr Spectator retired, his sober brief 'to enliven morality with wit; and to temper wit with morality' exhausted. Steele's farewell address summed up the *Spectator*'s pseudonymous world:

> It is much more difficult to converse with the world in a real than a personated character. That might pass for humour, in the *Spectator*, that would look like arrogance in a writer who sets his name to his work. The fictitious person might condemn those who disapproved him, and extol his own performances without giving offence. He might assume a mock authority without being looked upon as vain and conceited.

These ephemeral scribblings were preserved in bound collections, which became a standard reference for manners and morals following the paper's demise. Meanwhile, Steele ploughed on. In the *Guardian* (1713) he was 'Nestor Ironside', guardian to the aristocratic Lizard family, with help from the general public, who were invited to pop their letters into the mouth of a model lion's head set up in Button's Coffee House, Covent Garden. The *Englishman* (1713) suggested the idea of Robinson Crusoe to Daniel Defoe, but other scandalous content lost Steele his seat in the Commons. Once bitten, Steele's later periodicals played it safe – such short-lived sheets as the *Lover, Town Talk* and *Chit Chat* (1711-16) appealed to 'the softer affections of the mind'.

The 'Me, too!' Club

By the time Steele retired, coffeehouse periodicals were piling up like mad, most of them modelled on the *Spectator*. For the rest of the century they multiplied and interbred. Here are some of the more influential (or at least bizarre).

The Grub-street Journal (1730) – The satirical proceedings of a fictional gathering of hacks, including Mr Quidnunc (scholar), Mr Poppy (poet), Giles Blunderbuss (historian), Mr Noodle and Mr Numbskull, parodying modern hackery's 'false confused Histories… low creeping Poetry and grovelling Prose'.

The Parrot (1746) – As the titles piled up, opportunistic periodical printers invented ever more desperate 'eye-catching' conceits with which to brand their essays. Hence this short-lived oddity from Eliza Heywood, a rare female presence on the periodical scene, which was narrated by… er, a well-travelled parrot.

The Rambler (1750) – Dr Samuel Johnson turns up to the party, bringing his formidable intellect but also his unremittingly melancholy worldview, which guarantees a heavier read than the *Spectator*, Johnson not being a fan of 'the idle sports of imagination'.

The Covent Garden Journal (1752) – *Tom Jones* author Henry Fielding's last dabble in the periodical trade (posing as 'Sir Alexander Drawcansir') saw the advent, in issue #4, of that toilet book staple, the humorous glossary. ('Author: a laughing stock. It means likewise a poor fellow, and in general an object of contempt.') The *Journal* fought a doomed 'paper war' against the Grub Street mediocrities, particularly John Hill, foppish literary critic and vegetable-peddling quack physician. Fielding's motive was partly righteousness, partly revenge, but mostly to bump up sales. Other writers entered the fray, including Christopher Smart, but Fielding's crusade soon fizzled out, leaving him looking the fool.

The Adventurer (1752) – Johnson contributed to this globe-trotting miscellany, but most of the text came from John Hawkesworth, in the form of sundry tales of accident-prone periwigged fools in social situations. ('At the same time bowing with the most profound reverence, unhappily I overturned a screen, which, in its fall, threw down the breakfast-table, broke all the china, and crippled the lap-dog.')

Have-At-You-All (1752) – Taking the 'paper war' to its limit, one 'Madame Roxana Termagant' unleashed cutting parodies of countless periodicals, including *The Rambler*. About as incestuous as the periodical world got, and indeed could possibly get.

The World (1753) – Editor Edward Moore, as one 'Adam Fitzadam', introduced papers on whist, punning, gardening, turtle feasts, 'Periwig makers in Distress' and pithy observations on Sunday trading. ('We have happily got rid of the religious prejudices of our forefathers, and know but one way of keeping Sunday as it ought to be kept – the lying in bed all that day.')

The Connoisseur (1754) – Introduced by 'Mr Town' and 'Mr Country'. Includes a fine 'art of conversation' essay by the poet William Cowper on 'Tatlers and Swearers'. 'The *Swearers* I have spoken of in a former paper, but the *Half-Swearers* who split, and mince, and fritter their oaths into gad's bud, ad's fish, and demme; the *Gothic Humbuggers*, and those who "nick-name God's creatures", and call a man a cabbage, a crab, a queer cub, an odd fish, and an unaccountable muskin, should never come into company without an interpreter.'

The Idler (1758) – Johnson returns in a shorter, lighter format. A cast of characters includes Treacle, Whirler, Betty Broom and Dick Shifter. The title would resurface twice over the next 230 years, on quite different periodicals.

The Bee (1759) – The first of a series of short-lived periodicals from Oliver Goldsmith, which were mainly remarkable for the various excuses offered for their existence – the author of *The Busybody* (1759) is supposedly passing time while laid up with a broken leg, and the brains behind *The*

Spendthrift (1766) is even more open – he just needs the money. The latter features more fine fop baiting in Hawkesworth's *Diary of a Macaroni*: '*Thursday* – Too ill to go out today. Unlucky to happen on the ball night. Almost perished with ennui. Went to bed early.'

The Devil (1786) – Desperation for novel conceits inspires 'a Society of Gentlemen' to invent a suicidal author talked out of hanging himself by Satan, who persuades him to… yes, start a periodical in his name. Despite the title, the tone is still more Beefsteak Club than Hellfire Club.

The Trifler (1788) – As if to show up the periodical trade as child's play, this was the product of errant Westminster School pupils, in which 'Timothy Touchstone' pronounced 'I shall endeavour to catch "the flying Cynthia of the moment".' School matters alternated with general stuff on swearing and hairdressing.

*Winter Evenings (*1790) – Published all at once as a forty-chapter book rather than a weekly sheet. Vicesimus Knox regaled the reader on such homely subjects as the delights of a really good inglenook fireplace, and tellingly lamented periodicals as having 'lost their grace and power by being so frequently read… and even loathed by the reader, who is apt to yawn over them and exclaim, "I'm sick of this dull dose of daily trash".'

The periodical didn't last long into the 19th century. For insight into character and social satire, readers turned increasingly to novels. For weekly doses of tittle-tattle, the magazine rose to prominence, such early templates as the *Gentleman's Magazine* (1731) boasting 'more in quantity and greater variety than any book of its kind and price'. But the bound volumes lived on as light-hearted, dippable anthologies in respectable libraries (and, no doubt, the statelier variety of smallest room) long after the coffeehouses fell from fashion, and their jocular influence would hold sway over British humour for centuries.

Woman's Realm

Women were largely absent from periodical clubland (despite the appearance in the *Tatler* of one Jenny Distaff). This changed with the publication on July 8th, 1709 of the *Female Tatler*. Edited by one 'Mrs Phoebe Crackenthorpe, a Lady that knows everything', it provided a broadsheet of society gossip thrice weekly. Names, as ever, were changed, but those in the know could quickly put faces to giveaway monikers like Captain Sturdy or Lady Bumfiddle. Though the language approaches critical mass in quaintness terms ('Mrs. Honeysuckle was two hours pleasing herself in a paper nosegay, and Mrs. Delf employed five people to match her grout cup'), the rhythm of breathless gossip is still recognisable:

> The Lady Well-Bred, at Eltham, in Kent, is willing to dispose of a romping daughter, aged fifteen years. Her Ladyship, passing thro' the hall last week to order some whipped syllabubs when a great deal of company was there, saw Miss sit very quietly in the footman's lap to be kiss'd. She took no notice of the matter, but when the girl came into the dining room: 'See me no more this month,' says my Lady, 'you confident thing, to let a nasty fellow who stinks of the stables flop you at that rate. I perceiv'd you, but said nothing, being resolved to shame you before all this company.' Miss star'd her in the face and cry'd – 'Well, what if he did? I like it.' My Lady instead of dashing her daughter, was so out of countenance herself, she knew not which way to look; which, the girl perceiving, made mouths at her, and hoyden'd out of the room. Whoever can like her person with two thousand pounds, may have a full view of her at Eltham-Church, where by her manner of behaviour, she distinguishes herself from the whole congregation.

Mrs Crackenthorpe, whoever 'she' was, soon announced her retirement from tattling, handing editorship over to a 'Society of Modest Ladies', who kept the dainty banter up for another year before the waspish sewing circle finally imploded for good in a cloud of scented wig powder. Other gossip rags followed, including Eliza Heywood's *Female Spectator*, Mrs Penelope Pry's *Lady's Weekly Magazine* (1747) and the less exciting *The Old Maid* (1755) under the aegis of 'Mary Singleton, Spinster', but none lived up to the original *Female Tatler* for catty popularity. No *FT*, no comment.

Character witnesses

These game old amusements may seem hoary now, but one of them in particular, the identification of types of people in short essays, or 'characters', was quite the thing in literature at the time. For a definition of the character, let's consult an acknowledged master of the form, Sir Thomas Overbury.

> If I must speak the schoolmaster's language, I will confess that character comes of this infinitive mood, χαράσειυ, which signifies to engrave, or make a deep impression. And for that cause a letter (as A, B) is called a character: those elements which we learn first, leaving a strong seal in our memories. Character is also taken for an Egyptian Hieroglyphic, for an impress or short emblem...

OK, let's forget Overbury. He's not that much of an acknowledged master anyway. His characters were mostly written by assorted other 'learned gentlemen' and only sold in bucketloads after his controversial death by slow poisoning at the hands of a royal court conspiracy. (Personal tragedy meant posthumous sales then as now.) Let's try an example instead, from a much older source. Characters stretch back to 300BC and the writings of Theophrastus, a thoughtful vegetarian

Lesbian[6] who, when he wasn't looking at interesting stones, was looking into the minds of his fellow ancients and mulling over what separated a grumbler from a gossip, a coward from an idiot. As such, his work seems unusually modern. Here, for instance, is The Gross Man:

> The Gross Man is one who… in a theatre, will applaud when others cease, and hiss the actors who please the rest of the spectators. When the market-place is full, he will go up to the place where nuts or myrtleberries or fruits are sold, and stand munching while he chatters to the seller. Then he will call by name to a passer-by with whom he is not familiar… and will explain, as he stands at the door of a barber's or perfumer's shop, that he means to get drunk. His mother having gone out to the soothsayer's, he will use words of evil omen; or, when people are praying and pouring libations, he will drop his cup, and laugh as if he had done something clever… And, when he desires to spit, he will spit across the table at the cup-bearer.

And presumably says 'Cheer up John, it might never happen!' when Theo and his mates start tutting loudly from the taverna snug bar. This is the vital thing about the best character writing. No matter how antiquated, it has a shaft of perception running through it that sounds surprisingly fresh. Where much of what we've seen so far is in some way overwritten or fustily dry to modern eyes, it's easy to get a grip on a well-written character of any vintage.

Addison and Steele revitalised the character, paving the way for a generation of journeymen to ply their rough-hewn social observations. Chief among these was, yet again, Ned Ward, who in *The London Terraefilius, or the Satyrical Reformer* (1707) presented every London stereotype under the sun. The cantankerous Ward pledged to the reader:

Satyr, at present, is my Tallent: for Stubborn Folly and Habitual Vice must be corrected with Severity, therefore stand off Knave, have a care Fool, fly Hypocrite, hide Harlot, run Libertine, chaw Bully, skulk Bawd, lope Skellum, for I am just now going to lay about me like a Country Cudgel-Player.

Ward carries on haranguing the reader as the metropolitan caricatures amble past. 'Here comes a Neat Prim Fellow for you. Pray observe Captain Cog yonder, Strutting along to the William and Mary...' Sailors, philosophers, printers and a 'Sodomitical Succubus' are among the throng painted in broad strokes and broader language. In a combination of reportage and character writing, Ward's *History of the London Clubs, or the Citizen's Pastime* (1709) gives accounts of the Kit-Kats and Beefsteaks alongside made-up societies like The Beaus Club, The Liars Club, The Broken Shop Keepers Club, The No-Nose Club, The Surly Club and, inevitably, The Farting Club.

Eventually, Charles Dickens brought the character bang up to date in his debut volume *Sketches of Young Gentlemen* and *Young Couples* (1833), with fine cut gems like this:

The censorious young gentleman has the reputation among his familiars of a remarkably clever person, which he maintains by receiving all intelligence and expressing all opinions with a dubious sneer, accompanied with a half smile, expressive of anything you please but good-humour. This sets people about thinking what on earth the censorious young gentleman means, and they speedily arrive at the conclusion that he means something very deep indeed; for they reason in this way – 'This young gentleman looks so very knowing that he must mean something, and as I am by no means a dull individual, what a very deep meaning he must have if I can't find it out!' It is extraordinary how soon a censorious young gentleman may make a reputation in his own small circle if he bear this in his mind, and regulate his proceedings accordingly.

So give a cheer, as literature finally turns a corner, emerges from the antiquarian fog of arcane spelling, fussy sentences and book titles that could have your eye out, takes its jacket off and starts looking more relaxed. But we needn't stop there, as even before 'Boz' was remoulding fiction in his own Puckishly bearded image, a Leicestershire rector was quietly going about inventing observational stand-up comedy.

Is it merely I, or is every thing grossly disagreeable?

For the toilet book purist (should any exist), our story really begins with The Rev James Beresford's *The Miseries of Human Life* (1806). The Reverend set out the book's mission statement thus:

> Nature having made me one of those gossamer, sensitive beings upon whom the breath of Heaven cannot blow without creating more or less agitation, I amused myself last year with keeping a Diary of Vexations... I moreover found that to describe these teasing troubles was to disarm them of their sting, and that one might as quietly contemplate them afterwards as a fine lady might a mouse in a cage.

Beresford's breakthrough was to spot universal truths in the microscopically mundane tribulations of ordinary life that had previously swum under the literary radar. His miseries work like epigrams in reverse: the universal nugget of observational wisdom came not from a lofty peak of wisdom, but from scrupulous observation of the daily grind. Unlike the bone-dry epigram, the small, skulking misery could both make sense and be genuinely funny.

Once the concept was in place, examples flowed in torrents. The shortest and sweetest are the petty physical annoyances: 'Finding an human hair in your mouth, which, as you slowly draw it forth, seems to lengthen *ad infinitum*', 'Taking a step more, or a step less, than you want, in going up or down stairs', 'Waking with the pain of finding that you are doing your best to bite your own tongue off.' Deadpan description of slapstick misfortune was another rich seam: 'In attempting, at a strange house, to take down a large book from a high, crowded shelf, bringing half the library upon your nose,' 'Sitting in a chair on which you do not discover that honey has been liberally spilt, till, on rising to make your bow, you carry away the cushion.'

Beresford employed fictional narrators, feckless wimps and languid snobs to a man. Timothy Testy decries 'the dead, lumpish, tubby tones of the fourth and fifth strings of the guitar'. Samuel Sensitive, meanwhile, brings social calamity on himself, such as 'suddenly thinking of your best argument in a debate, and, in your eagerness to state it, swallowing your wine the wrong way, and so squeaking and croaking more and more unintelligibly, with the tears running down your cheeks, till the conversation has been turned, or your antagonist has left the company.' There's even room for self-deprecating misery: 'Borrowing, on condition of returning it to-morrow morning, a book, consisting almost wholly of short detached sentences; such as *The Miseries of Human Life*.'

Such arse-covering disclaimers proved unnecessary. The book swiftly became a bestseller. Plaudits came in from the great and good – this was one toilet book even the pernickety Sir Walter Scott could get behind. With rather un-miserable speed, Beresford ensured the excitably titled *More Miseries!! Addressed to the Morbid, the Melancholy, and the Irritable*, by 'Sir Fretful Murmur, Knt', followed later that year. Merchandise appeared in the shape of sixteen paintings by John Augustus Atkinson 'inspired' by assorted miseries described in the books, which span off into a coffee-table volume of their own.

Publishing phenomenon status was sealed with the appearance of an unofficial cash-in, Harriet Corp's *An Antidote to the Miseries of Human Life in the History of the Widow Placid, and her Daughter Rachel* (1808). Admittedly this was a straight and starchy novella about the eponymous Quaker widow's drearily pious mission to inform the world that the original book is a trivial distraction and that the only sure antidote to the miseries of human life is a hefty dose of 'experimental religion'. This rather missed the perversely uplifting point of the original, but didn't take the shine off Beresford's book. The original grumpy old rector has been more often in print than out ever since.

6

RUM TRUFFLERS

The British Empire, in all her high majesty, marched forth into a world ill equipped to wedge a defensive foot in the door. Britannia poked a toe into every corner of the world, in a stout spirit of enlightened Christian enquiry. (The presence of easily exploitable natural resources and free labour was a happy bonus.) While their more glamorous pith-helmeted cousins set sail, Empire's land-locked antiquarians directed their expeditions inwards, to the libraries and museums, and foraged after facts. Academics were there already, but just as the spirit of the 'gentleman amateur' opened up exploration of foreign lands to those with enough independent wealth to hire a small tramp steamer, some oversize khaki shorts and an elephant gun, so the Dons were joined, whether they liked it or not, by the quizzical snout of the gentleman truffler.

The gentlemen explorers returned from their voyages with astounding treasures and tales of derring-do. 19th-century curiosity gatherers became showmen too, talking up their tomes of wonder in the manner of sideshow barkers. Titles became emphatic, such as *The Entertaining Companion; Consisting Chiefly of Such Curious Matters as Come Under the Denominations of Miraculous! Queer! Odd! Strange! Supernatural! Out of the Way! Whimsical! Absurd! Humorous! And Unaccountable!* (1805). Authors wanted their books to encompass the entire subject, in a literary manifestation of Empire's desire to colour the entire globe pink.

One of the most colourful of these writers, William Hone, was a man of parts: humorist, political reformer, prototype investigative journalist, permanently broke philanthropist and the proprietor of a three-foot-wide Fleet Street bookshop, which provided crowd-drawing window displays of the latest satirical prints, including those from his own pen, which would bring him face to face with his targets – in court.

Hone was charged with publishing three blasphemous pamphlets, including *The Political Catechism* (1817), which featured a spoof Ten Commandments for corrupt MPs. ('Thou shalt not take the pension of the Lord thy Minister in vain.') Under the guise of prosecuting Hone for blasphemously defacing a sacred text, the government sought to make an example of him and face down the rising tide of reformist satire.

Hone defended himself, spectacularly. Against a prosecution fixated on obscure points of law, he drew on a lifetime of literary foraging to assemble, as his defence, a historical roll-call of Christian texts warped by literary parodists, all of them, from Martin Luther to John Milton, historical heroes of the present Tory government. Taking the argument away from dusty legalese, Hone stole the show. Sheriffs had to be appointed to control the court's fits of laughter. By the time he stumbled exhausted from the third trial, he had given the British cause of free speech its biggest lift since *Magna Carta* on a raft of pastiche and punning.

Victory over draconian libel laws secured, Hone led the satirical charge. In league with young cartoonist George Cruickshank, he published a series of seditious nursery rhymes subjecting George IV and the Tories to new levels of ridicule. He designed a parody of the new and monstrously unpopular pound note. The Prince Regent's highly suspect divorce proceedings against Princess Caroline led Hone to publish that old chestnut, a self-assembly satirical step-ladder, each rung elaborately illustrated by Cruickshank to show a stage in the whole farcical process.

By 1821 the rush of invention and activity became too much. Episodes in which Hone witnessed parts of his own body drift down Fleet Street by themselves suggested early retirement was in order, but the imprudent philanthropist was skint. A solution began appearing in weekly installments from January 1st 1825. Hone's *Every-Day Book* was a sedate collection of historical curiosities with not a seditious couplet in sight. For 27 months, a weekly 32-page pamphlet related cultural titbits organised by the days of the year, ending the run as two bound fourteen-shilling volumes of 1,700 pages each, detailing such arcane nuggets as:

> Drinking, excessive
> Beards on women, superstition about
> Children, pickled and come to life
> Sausages, festival of
> Spit, movement of to music

This bucolic miscellany was Hone's paean to the rural suburbs of London, then being carpeted by a wave of property development. It was also intended, in its own mad way, as a *Reader's Digest*-style 'one-stop library' of condensed knowledge with which lower-middle-class households could supplement their meagre education. So keen was the over-generous Hone to keep the weekly price well within his target audience's means, he forgot to include a profit margin and was soon in debt again.

From debtor's prison, Hone began clawing back the money he owed with the monthly *Table Book* (1827). 'Perhaps,' he wrote in the introduction, 'if the good old-fashioned window seats had not gone out of fashion, it might be called a parlour-window book – a good name for a volume of agreeable reading selected from the book-case, and left lying about, for the constant recreation of the family, and the casual amusement of visitors.' Such modest aims contrasted with its description in his private correspondence as 'a kind of literary kaleidoscope... to annihilate both space and time'.

Eclecticism was Hone's watchword. Obscure play excerpts sat alongside hand-me-downs from the old jest books (labelled 'ancient waggery'). An essay on horsehair armchairs sidled into James Beresford's miserable territory. ('If you try to compose yourself with one of these pretenders, by endeavouring to protect the back of your head with your pocket-handkerchief for a pillow, you either dream that you are under the hands of a surgeon who is cupping you on the cheek, or that you are transformed into your cousin Lucy, and struggling to avoid being kissed by old Mr D-----, who does not shave above once a week.') The compendious index contains many intriguing entries that, oddly, don't appear in the text:

Cabbage-trees, vast height of
Crabbing for husbands
Mice, field, for preventing injuries from
Table book, editor's severe domestic afflictions

This last was no joke. The *Table Book* sold poorly, and it was down to opportunistic publisher Thomas Tegg to pick up all Hone's publishing rights for a song, and pay him to compile the more crowd-pleasing *Year Book of Daily Recreation* (1832). But Tegg's £400 advance wasn't enough, and after an ill-fated attempt to run a coffee house Hone suffered a series of strokes that ended his writing career. Meanwhile Tegg went on to sell over 80,000 copies of *The Every-Day Book* and turn a massive profit. But then the gentleman trufflers were true literary romantics, right down to the complete lack of income.

Are you sitting comfortably?

The ultimately unsatisfactory nature of a book that is, strictly speaking, a haphazard collection of 'some facts' was eventually sidestepped with the creation of a genre: the bedside book. The cosiness of the term wasn't initially apparent – in the 19th century a 'bedside book' was a collection of hymns and prayers for the very sick. This was usurped by the new definition, that of a light-hearted anthology of factual titbits for night-capped, cocoa-swilling readers. (And with the chamber pot stowed unnderneath, the journey from bedside to toilet book was often a matter of inches.) Early somnolent nosegays included Joseph Robert Clegg's *The Hush-a-by Papers: a Book for the Bedside* (1898) and Harold Begbie's disarmingly honest *The Bed-book of Happiness: Being a Colligation or Assemblage of Cheerful Writings Brought Together from many Quarters into this One Compass for the Diversion, Distraction, and Delight of those who Lie Abed, a Friend to the Invalid, a Companion to the Sleepless, an Excuse to the Tired* (1914).

As the word 'miscellany' was to the 17th and 18th centuries, so 'bedside' was to the 20th, which produced nocturnal collections for every subject under the moon, including soccer, saints, sea stories, Cornwall, climbing, clarinetting, bridge, beer, 'bigheads', farming, insults, murder, sexual disasters (Gyles Brandreth's, that one), insomnia and insurance underwriting. No field was deemed inappropriate for the hottie-toting reader. The British booklover had to contend with a singularly crowded futon.

Even fictional characters got in on the act. *Mrs Dale's Bedside Book* (1951) cashed in on the popularity of the BBC radio soap *Mrs Dale's Diary*, presenting the thoughts, observations and handy recipes of the eponymous suburban doctor's wife. *Dame Edna's Bedside Companion* (1982), a self-styled 'brilliantly researched seminal and pivotal work… filling an important vacuum in the literature of the boudoir', encompassed everything from flowerbeds to Tasmanian sex under the aegis of the Moonee Ponds matron. Even satire had a bedside manner, in the form of Jon Courtenay Grimwood's comic trilogy *Mrs T's Bedside Book* (1985), *The Official Royal Bedside Book* (1986) and *Mrs T's Election Bedside Book* (1987). By the end of the century, however, the bedside publications tailed off rapidly. The word spoke of cosiness, infirmity, old age – not the sort of dynamic, youthful image the discerning publisher wanted their product associated with. It all seemed a bit... well, knackered.

Serious ephemera

The first British book with 'trivia' in its title was Logan Pearsall Smith's *Trivia* (1926), a slim volume, not of bite-size facts, but short diary-style paragraphs musing on everyday events. But trivia books had been appearing by the dozen since the previous century. The Victorians loved trivia, they just called it by other names, such as *Notabilia: or, Curious and Amusing Facts About Many Things* (1872) or *Periwinkles: a Collection of Facts and Fancies* (1875). That phrase 'facts and fancies' became a publishers' favourite, signaling a collection that wasn't too dry and serious – facts for fun only. The collation of out-of-the-way intelligence proved irresistible to even the most renowned authors. Sir Arthur Conan Doyle compiled *Round the Red Lamp: Being the Facts and Fancies of Medical Life* in 1895.

The appetite kept up into the 20th century, though by now a flooded market, and the inevitable duplication of facts, meant a little talking up was in order to keep one's trivia collection afloat – as with Frank Hubert Shaw's mouth-wateringly titled *Odysseys and Oddities: a 'Tarpaulin Muster' of Seagoing Facts and Whimsicalities by a Man Who has Tasted Adventure and Swallowed Romance* (1948). And so the market slowly bumbled along, until 1951 when Guinness brewery MD Sir Hugh Beaver got into an argument during a shooting party over which game bird was the fastest in flight. This led, after a few more similarly unsolved puzzles had been suggested, to *The Guinness Book of Records* (1954 -), the central prong in a multimedia assault built around the superlative-stuffed brains of professional fact-finding twins Ross and Norris McWhirter. The McWhirters provided the book's backbone, but marketing was a big part of the phenomenon from the off. The first edition of 1,000 copies was given away free, making an initial loss but reaping long-term publicity rewards. (Guinness are just as canny today, being careful to limit the print run of each annual edition to ensure the book retains its reputation as a sure-fire Christmas sell-out – nothing tarnishes a bestseller's image more than huge piles of the thing still lurking about the shop in January.)

With the TV spin-off, *Record Breakers*, a fixture of children's programming, TV tie-ins were a no-brainer for publishers: ally your selection of facts to such programmes as *Bullseye, Blockbusters, Telly Addicts, Winner Takes All, Ask the Family, Runaround, University Challenge, Mastermind* and *Top of the Form* and the royalty cheques write themselves. Celebrities carried on compiling – some seriously, such as *Isaac Asimov's Book of Facts* (1980), some more lightly. 1979 saw two under appreciated entertainers with gargantuan capacities for pointless facts pitched against each other. Jeremy Beadle, he of the cavernous private library, found a historical fact or two for every day of the year to fill *Today's the Day* (1979), at the same time as Bob Monkhouse illustrated his own *Book of Days: a Whacky, Day-by-Day Guide to History's Strangest Facts* (1979). It was a friendly rivalry of course, Monkhouse sportingly giving his chum's volume a plug at the front of his own book, and the pair liaising to ensure they weren't duplicating each other's periwinkles. But such truces were rare in a cutthroat market.

Others thought outside the trivial box. Hunter Davies's great brainwave in this field was *The Book of British Lists* (1980). Scouring ancient records, official sources and famous friends, Davies served up top tens and twenties of anything that took his fancy, from most hated figures to most populous trade unions, popular crisp flavours to famous bastards. The polar opposite of the Guinness book, its very lack of definitiveness provided its charm. (There were crossovers with other franchises – Roy Castle nominated his ten favourite Guinness records, while Nigel Rees picked twenty examples of graffiti.)

In the 1980s, the trivia market received two boosts. The launch of *Trivial Pursuit* led to an avalanche of 'me too!' fact lists, and publishers were equally quick to leap on the later phenomenon of the pub quiz, the first literary sighting of that notorious phrase being on the front of Corgi's *The Pub Quiz Book* (1987). About the same time, Russell Ash embarked on his own list franchise. *The Top Ten of Everything* is one of those ideas that need no further explanation. The title alone was enough to sell the idea to Aaron Simpson at the Queen Anne Press. Two years of work later, the first volume appeared in 1990. It sold well, and has remained a regular fixture ever since, although Ash has had to shop around to keep the franchise afloat. 'Publishers,' he says, 'tend to be very excited about a new acquisition, but start losing interest a few years down the line.' So over nearly two decades *Top Ten* has wandered from Queen Anne to Headline to Dorling Kindersley to Hamlyn, Ash always aware his work is a 'cuckoo in the nest' of any house's portfolio. Though one third of the book remains more or less constant (rivers and mountains rarely change their dimensions from year to year) the rest needs continual updating. 'A trivia franchise is the Forth Bridge of publishing,' admits Ash. 'There's always something that needs fixing.'

The last of the great revolutions in trivia presentation occurred in 2002, when Ben Schott brought out *Schott's Original Miscellany*. From a textual point of view, there are many reasons to query the aptness of that central adjective. It is, in content terms, nothing new at all. Bed sizes, digits of Pi, 'I love you' in various languages, selected aphorisms from Dr Johnson and entries from *The Devil's Dictionary* – there's nothing here that the trivia industry hasn't seen before. What makes it is the presentation. Schott made use of recent advances in printing technology to craft a densely packed book from typefaces and layouts closely modelled on antique miscellanies. Fussy typographical tricks of the sort not seen since Victorian times add spice to expositions of compass points and atmospheric layers. The busy atmosphere of Old Empire truffling is perfectly evoked. The inevitable imitations (and parodies) followed, but the mould had been broken. It's hard to imagine the market going back to the old yellowing paperbacks with the big-nosed cartoons on the front and the spines that always seem to have been pre-broken at the printer's. With transportation provided by Adobe, Inc., British trivia found its way back home.

7

TO CLARIFY AND CLASSIFY

Trivia buffs of a lexicographical bent had been compiling dictionaries since at least 1538. Before long attention turned to the words some dictionaries, with all due propriety, kept well out of. Richard Head's *The Canting Academy, or, the Devils Cabinet Opened* (1673) collected rough and reprehensible slang terms from the taverns and back streets of the country, for the instruction of the more respectable gentleman.

After Head, the filthy deluge. In 1699 one 'BE, Gent' published *A New Dictionary of the Terms Ancient and Modern of the Canting Crew, in its Several Tribes, of Gypsies, Beggers, Thieves, Cheats, &c.,* which was touted as 'useful for all Sorts of People, (Especially Foreigners) to Secure their Money and Preserve their Lives; Besides Very Diverting and Entertaining.' More authoritatively, Nathan Bailey's *Universal Etymological English Dictionary* (1721), the chief model for Samuel Johnson's famous work, included a selection of 'Canting Words and Terms', tastefully segregated from their above-stairs companions.

Here were the official definitions of Autem-Cackletub ('a Meeting-House for Dissenters'); Beard-Splitter ('a Whore-master'); Bingo-Mort ('a She Brandy Drinker'); Cackling-Farts ('Eggs'); Gundiguts ('a fat, pursy Fellow'); Snudge ('one that lurks under a Bed'); or a Westminster Wedding ('a Whore and a Rogue married together'). Bailey's expert approach meant that entries were itemised and cross-referenced to an almost dizzying degree. ('ARCH ROGUE, the Dimber-Damber Uprightman or

Chief of a Gang; as Arch-Dell, or Arch-Doxy signifies the same Degree in Rank among the Female Canters and Gypsies.') Bailey was also less squeamish than the Good Doctor all round – if you wanted to know what a dildo was, you'd have got no joy from Johnson.

There was another quantum leap when port-bibbing antiquarian Captain Francis Grose published his *Lexicon Balatronicum, or Dictionary For Jesters* (1785), 'a Dictionary of Buckish Slang, University Wit, and Pickpocket Eloquence'. Grose amassed well over four thousand slang definitions from all walks of life. He also ditched the self-righteous posturing of previous slang philologists, having no truck with their priggish 'defence against villainy', instead offering a genuine, unbridled celebration of British free speech, 'arising from, and privileged by our constitution'.

Trawling London's slums and dockyards by night with his trusty companion Tom Cocking, Grose ferreted out such linguistic essentials as Double Jugg ('a man's backside'); Farting Crackers ('breeches'); Fussock ('a lazy fat woman'); and Twiddle-Poop ('an effeminate looking fellow'). He also allowed in humorously suspect definitions ('Butcher's Dog: To be like a butcher's dog, i.e. lie by the beef without touching it: a simile often applicable to married men') and threw himself into some exorbitant etymology:

Boh: Said to be the name of a Danish general, who so terrified his opponent Foh, that he caused him to bewray himself. Whence, when we smell a stink, it is customary to exclaim Foh! i.e. I smell a general Foh. *'He cannot say Boh to a goose'*; i.e. he is a cowardly or sheepish fellow. There is a story related of the celebrated Ben Jonson, who always dressed very plain, that, being introduced to the presence of a nobleman, the peer, struck by his homely appearance and awkward manner, exclaimed, as if in doubt, 'You, Ben Jonson! Why, you look as if you could not say Boh to a goose!' 'Boh!' replied the wit.

In the 20th century, the lackadaisical business of slang notation received a dose of scholarly rigour. Pipe-smoking man of letters Eric Partridge published the first edition of his still-updated *Dictionary of Slang and Unconventional English* (1937), which has since swollen to over 60,000 definitions. The unshakeable don augmented the main event with, among others, *A Dictionary of Forces' Slang* (1948) and *A Dictionary of the Underworld, British & American* (1949).

Later, Jonathon Green took up Partridge's mantle as the Sherlock Holmes of the English-speaking vernacular. On the way to compiling *The Cassell Dictionary of Slang* (1998), which used extreme pedantry as a potent weapon against that enemy of slang lexicographers, the false etymology or *Call My Bluff* syndrome, he produced a sizeable *Slang Thesaurus* (1986), combining academic punctiliousness with a more worldly approach to his sources. Green ventured further into youth subcultures than Partridge had ever dared, shifting the focus from the cloistered whimsies of students and RAF officers to the labyrinthine constructions of workers, gangs and schoolkids.

Which brings us up to date with that *locus classicus* of false etymology, *Roger's Profanisaurus* (2002), a spin-off from Tyneside comic *Viz*, wherein bored DHSS officers submit the most contrived and obscure sexual/digestive euphemisms they can invent. These assorted *cedar burps*, which would otherwise remain confined to the *Scotsman's lounge*, are fully cross-referenced for the leisurely perusal of bored *cable layers* and vicarious *nodgers* alike. Some ended up spreading so far they were eventually picked up by the 'proper' slang dictionaries, in an endless, self-devouring loop, which is what makes the cataloguing of slang as endlessly fascinating as it is ultimately pointless.

The rules of the game

In the ranks of the fascinatingly pointless, games rule supreme. The Victorians were as avid about playing as they were about collecting, and brought the truffling instinct to their pastimes. Card tricks and cribbage rules had long been used to pad out a gentleman's miscellany, but antiquarians could take leisure activities as seriously as high art. In 1750, society whist tutor Edmond Hoyle enshrined a series of card games in authoritative little rulebooks. From then on, scholarship of recreation was the game.

Take the prolific George Frederick Pardon. As 'Captain Crawley', named after the game rogue in Thackeray's *Vanity Fair*, he edited ripping boys' publication *The Gentleman's Journal; The Quarterly Magazine of the Independent Order of Odd Fellows*, and published little books on games related, rather archly, in 'character'. Thus the Captain would spice up a list of technical backgammon terms with a bit of colonial wistfulness: 'The technical terms of backgammon may teach valuable lessons... In the game, it is proper to "get your men to your table", and to effect it as rapidly as possible; that teaches hospitality, brisk as its own champagne.... "Get home as quickly as you can" inculcates the culture of domestic happiness: and suggests a speedy return from even the most festive scenes, in order to light up eyes that such return renders brighter than the tapers by which the loved one waits and muses.' The gnomic aphorisms of Eastern chess philosophers are imported to the fireside – shove ha'penny becomes the Glass Bead Game.

Under his own name, Pardon wrote titles as varied as *The Book of Manly Games for Boys* (1869), *Illustrious Women who have Distinguished Themselves for Virtue, Piety and Benevolence* (1868) and *Dogs: their Sagacity, Instinct, and Uses* (1857). Sometimes this flailing oeuvre hit home. Pardon's *Parlour Pastimes: a Repertoire of Acting Charades, Fire-side Games, Enigmas, Riddles, etc.* (1868) took its place among a flood of collected dinner party frivolity aimed at rising middle-class socialites. Whimsical titles reappeared on the shelves: *Endless Mirth and Amusement: A Capital and Clever Collection of Mirthful Games* (1874); *Cheerful Pastimes for Merry-making Parties* (1830); *Merry Evenings for Merry People* (1859).

For the dedicated recreator, showbiz specialists spilled the technical beans. Angelo Lewis was a barrister who, as 'Professor' Louis Hoffmann, brought conjuring into the parlour with a series of detailed books from *Modern Magic* (1876) onwards. Drawing-room drama attracted the attentions of stage playwrights, who adapted West End plays for the after-dinner amateur troupe, or published learned advice for the tyro thespian, such as one 'Captain Sock Buskin's forthright treatise on *How to 'Get up' Theatricals in a Country House* (1866). The nation was being encouraged to put aside the port and walnuts and do something less boring instead.

Fun house

Home Fun (1910) is a typical gazetteer of indoor levity. Editor Cecil Henry Bullivant and his assembled experts present crash courses in every pre-wireless activity known to man, from charades to ventriloquism, plate spinning to phrenology. It's bursting with quiet enthusiasm and a DIY ethic. Amateur dramatics loom large, with armchair reminiscences of famous home productions such as 'a strong Fennimore Cooper drama in which the top of a shed became a mountain crag'. The tone throughout is encouraging, but always mindful of the calamitous results when Pooters try and do a Garrick. 'Single-piece moustaches are very uncomfortable, and usually come half off at the critical moment.'

Bullivant has a knack for turning a simple game into a full-scale production by sheer force of enthusiasm. Charades, it is noted, are best acted out in front of French windows. But what if your parlour has no French windows? Well then, why not make some false French windows out of hardboard? The opposite question, 'why?' is never asked. There's so much to learn and so little time – acquiring a sense of proportion will have to come later, after we've worked through a chapter on the art of whistling ('Methods of a Famous Siffleur').

There are some activities to which posterity has not been kind. 'Some people imagine that a black face, a pair of large check trousers and a rather dilapidated hat, are all that's necessary to make a nigger minstrel. This is, however, a great mistake, and whoever feels the stirring of ambition to amuse his friends with a nigger entertainment, so popular some years ago, must not be discouraged if he finds the road harder than expected.' So begins a lengthy discourse on the art of blacked-up bawdry detailed in a style so deadpan as to render the process as abstract as any other entertainment craft, which in the average Edwardian household it still was.

The tone is as keen as the rest of the book, filling the amateur in on the basics: you'll need an interlocutor ('usually known as Mr Johnson') and four 'comical corner-men', one in a wig with a 'workable tuft'. It's all determinedly right and proper: the show must go on, and the author signs off with a piece of theatrical encouragement that would raise a few eyebrows in the modern West End. 'Do not be shy; remember in the first place that the black hides all your blushes, and in the second place that nobody is there to see you, but to see a "nigger" who is going to make them laugh. So take heart, and show them all how really well it can be done.'

Something approaching sound advice rears its head in the chapter concerning comedy. Drawing room entertainment is progressive enough here to consider in detail the soubrette or female comedy entertainer. 'The latter charming lady begins at once with a song. This gives the audience time to appreciate her and her frock, which, by the way, should be full evening. Afterwards she comes down to mere talk – child impersonations, stories, and then by way of another song, or whatever it is, to her exit.' There follows a general list of rules of comedy, documenting the state of the humorist's art:

> Don't be facetious. That is, don't try to pretend by your manner that what you are saying is funnier than it really is.
>
> Don't – please don't – make funny faces. If your face is funny it doesn't need them, and if it isn't it can't stand them. Funny faces are so fatiguing to all but their maker.
>
> Don't be racy unless you must. Remember that the more homely and decent your fun, the larger and happier your audience. Or, if you must be racy, don't start too soon. If you do, unless you are to disappoint the few who like it, you will have to go on getting racier and racier, and the majority will dislike you long before the end.
>
> Don't forget that there are a number of things that, though funny once, wore out long ago, and that there are others which never were funny and never will be. It ought not to be necessary to mention this, but it is. At the moment there is a comic song on the market called 'The Undertaker.' Positively! Could anything be more inept or more certain to offend?
>
> Don't forget that topical touches are always welcome, but that if they apply to any one in the audience it should be to some one who will not resent it. When in doubt, choose a fat man for your subject. He can always be relied upon to enjoy it.

Party conferences

After the Edwardians renovated the Victorian entertainment guides, the Georgians knocked them all through into one spacious, all-purpose compendium. Poet Francis Meynell set up the Nonesuch Press in 1922 to print attractive versions of

Dickens and Dante in elegant, Arts-and-Crafts style bindings. But this refined cottage industry would have ground to a halt had they not also produced *The Week-End Book: A Sociable Anthology* (1924). Meynell, a keen metropolitan thrower of country cottage weekend parties, envisioned an all-purpose companion with which everyone – well, everyone in possession of a Cotswold cottage and a gaggle of bright young friends – could add spice to their hebdomadal idylls.

Meynell took care of the poems. John Goss collated the songs, ranging from old standards like D'Ye Ken John Peel to more esoteric ballads like They Were Only Playing Leapfrog, The Wraggle-Taggle Gypsies-O! and I'm a Man That's Done Wrong to My Parents. Children's author Eleanor Farjeon commandeered the games section, supplementing the standard spread of Consequences, Crambo and Sardines with tempting exotica like Up-Jenkyns! and Tishy-Toshy. (Or, for those weekends that really drag, Looking at Your Feet Through the Wrong End of the Opera Glasses.) Here the neat, utilitarian design of the book came into its own – the endpapers doubled as boards for draughts and Nine Men's Morris, along with a handy ruler.

Meynell's wife Vera provided food and drink recipes, with the accent on leisurely preparation. ('Week-end cookery should either be very quick… or very slow, put on before you go off to tennis or to lazing.') Her speciality was finding a thousand and one ways to 'decorate the commoner foods into jolliness,' and she even slipped in a recipe for a homemade aphrodisiac cocktail. More pragmatically, Dr Maurice Newfield presented 'First Aid in Divers Crises Medical, Surgical and Gastronomical,' such as Immediate Relief of the Windy Spasms, hiccup remedies and post-fainting restoratives. ('It is pleasant and fitting that the patient celebrate the first moment he is able to stand upright by partaking of a fluid ounce of brandy.') There was also The Law and How You Break It, A List of Great Poems Not in this Book, and pages 337-369 were entirely blank 'manuscript

pages' for the reader's own poems, recipes, 'favourite inns' and
train times home.

Meynell could tell he had a winner at the launch party: a
recreation of the ideal weekend jaunt thrown entirely by the
book. Frère Jacques was sung, Sardines was played, commoner
foods were decorated, feet were optically reduced and no one
had the hiccups for very long. London's literati lapped it up. HG
Wells was spotted enjoying a few rounds of Tishy-Toshy with
the rolled-up sleeves of fiercely competitive gusto. (This wasn't
surprising: in 1911 he wrote *Floor Games*, a eulogy on the
childhood art of carpet-based mucking about.) Not everyone
was enchanted. Virginia Woolf told Meynell 'The Hogarth Press
[her own hand-cranked literary imprint] may not make any
money, but at least we didn't publish *The Week-End Book*.'
Fortunately for Nonesuch, the public disagreed with her to the
tune of over half a million copies.

British publishing's 1970s Edwardian revival enabled Gyles
Brandreth to resuscitate the weekend format for his *Complete
Book of Home Entertainment* (1974), updated slightly for the
permissive society. ('I would have called it my *Complete Book of
Home Fun* but for the fact that "fun" seems such a simple word
for such a sophisticated age.') Brandreth gamely takes up the
Meynell-Bullivant-Pardon mantle, and tops it off with period
exuberance. Thus we're led through puzzles, tricks, party games
(including a round of 'Authentic Hunt the Thimble') and even
fire eating, sword swallowing and walking on broken glass, all
amiably rattled off in Brandreth's breathlessly enthusiastic voice,
with lashings of emphatic italics. ('Needless to say, I have had a
marvellous time writing this book.')

The quintessential exponent of the novelty book, Brandreth
has claim to some heritage in the field. He recalls: 'My great-
great-grandfather, Benjamin Brandreth, left England in the
1830s and went to the US to make his fortune manufacturing
and marketing "Brandreth's Pills" – they cured everything! As a
tool to promote his products he began creating "novelty books"

and a century on, I followed his example.' Ghosting celebrity trivia volumes became a speciality, Brandreth manning the library for stars as diverse as Michael Caine, John Inman, Frankie Howerd, Derek Nimmo, Dudley Moore and Jim Davidson. But his personal favourite project from that time was slightly lighter on research. 'It was one that Transworld published for Valentine's Day back in the late '70s. It was called *I Love You* and all it contained were the words I LOVE YOU repeated over 64 or 128 pages. I didn't ask for an advance, but I remember earning a useful royalty – for just three words! Those were the days.'

Brandreth was also the 'little man behind the curtain' for *Larry Grayson's Parlour Fun Book* (1980), a collection of vintage entertainment culled from 'Everard's great-auntie's Home Entertainment Handbook' jazzed up with photos of Lal acting the ponce in a paper party hat, and the cartoon menagerie of characters from his *Generation Game* act. It's 'a rollicking feast of home entertainment with an all-star cast including Everard Farquharson, Apricot Lil, Slack Alice, Sterilized Stan and Pop-it-in-Pete', who chip in with innuendoes amidst the cut-and-pasted Dumb Crambo guides ('This is what Mavis does when Stan clinks his bottles!') and sheet music for Jeanie with the Light-Brown Hair. ('Never mind the light brown hair, she needs a light brown ale!') It's an odd book. Lal's interjections make the activities seem silly and unappealing, much the same effect as his bewildered on-screen persona had on those televised cake-icing marathons.

The compendium then laid low for a while, until the same printing advances that helped resurrect the miscellany were applied. A revived Nonesuch republished *The Week-End Book* in 2005. *The Dangerous Book for Boys* (2006) by Conn and Hal Iggulden was an assembly of tally-ho activity inspired by the old compendia, with a heady dose of *Boys' Own Paper* derring do for good measure. Paper planes and treehouse engineering mingled with amateur astronomy and card games, illustrated in clean and cosy *Look and Learn* style. Though ostensibly a children's book, the nostalgia value of the Baden Powell-esque decoration gave it much currency among the upper echelons of masculinity whose scuffed knees never fully healed. The advent of a pocket version and *The Daring Book for Girls* (2007) suggest the revived spare time miscellany has a few more Christmases left yet.

'Merry in the hall, when beards wag all.'

Christmas, so says everyone old enough to recall the days of shillings, steam trains and Trimphones, is no longer what it was. But what *was* it?

> You must understand, people, that the manner of celebrating this great Course of Holydays is vastly different now to what it was in former days: There was once upon a time Hospitality in the Land; an *English* Gentleman at the opening of the great Day, had all his Tenants and Neighbours enter'd his Hall by Day-break, the strong Beer was broach'd, and the Black-Jacks went plentifully about with Toast, Sugar, Nutmeg, and good Cheshire Cheese; the Rooms were embower'd with Holly, Ivy, Cypress, Bays, Laurel and Missleto, and a bouncing *Christmas* Log in the Chimney glowing like the Cheeks of a Country Milk-maid; the Servants were then running here and there, with merry Hearts and jolly Countenances; everyone was busy welcoming of Guests, and look'd as smug as new-lick'd Puppies; the Lasses were as blithe and buxom as the Maids in good Queen *Bess's* Days, when they eat Sir-Loins of Roast Beef for Breakfast; *Peg* would scuttle about to make a Toast for *John*; while *Tom* run *harum scarum* to draw a Jug of Ale for *Margery*: Gaffer Spriggins was bid thrice welcome by the Squire, and Goody Goose did not fail of a smacking Buss from his Worship…

Thus spake – at colossal length – 'Dick Merryman' in his chapbook masterpiece *Round-About Our Coal Fire; or, Christmas Entertainments: Wherein is Described Abundance of Fiddle-Faddle-Stuff* (1740). Pining for the past has been a sentimental necessity during the festivities for as long as logs have roared. A hundred years previously, John Taylor, the Water Poet,[7] penned *The Complaint of Christmas, and the Teares of Twelfetyde* (1646), on the decline of honest festivities: 'this Hall have I seen strewed with rushes, a signe of the soft and kinde entertainment the guests should have… I feare, I am growne so old and dimme, that I shall never see it againe.' No doubt there was some saucer-eyed misery around in 2AD to moan that this year's Christmas wasn't a patch on the last one.

Such wistfulness was part and parcel of the Victorian way of moping. The 19th century saw a heritage reconstruction of mythical Christmases past, with programmes available in the foyer in the form of Christmas books. These were nothing new, as the likes of *Paddy Whiskey's Christmas Box for 1792* demonstrate, but the century's accumulated wealth of truffling spilled over into semi-scholarly works like John Poole's *Christmas Festivities* (1845) and gamesome compendia along the lines of *Christmas Diversions; or, A New Book of Games and Forfeits* (1826). The moral backbone was strengthened with timely selections of carols and sermons, and of course Thackeray and Dickens were perched by the tills with lavishly tooled Yuletide editions of their best-selling fiction, adapted to the mood of the season. Book titles bulging with whimsy at the best of times burst in a mess of festive soppiness. One thinks, unless one can help it, of Abel Heywood's *Mr. Pimpchook's Party; a Series of Tales and Songs for the Merry Season* (1870), Edwin A Tice's *Rumfusticus: a Christmas Budget of Fun and Amusement* (1871) or Ernest Geldart's *A Christmas Faggot* (1884).

Come the 20th century, reviewers wearied of the commercial rigmarole. In 1925's December edition of *The Burlington Magazine for Connoisseurs*, one 'RRT' laments the tide of publications unleashed in late October: 'For nearly a quarter of a century English publishers have confronted us towards Christmastime with masses of illustrated books, such as they would never have dreamt of letting us see, much less review, at any other time of the year. The most interesting Christmas book I can think of,' he astutely reflects, 'would be one containing the history of the Christmas book'. We can safely assume this applies equally to toilet books.

But commerce ruled the roost, ever keen to repackage the same traditional games, ten-bird roast diagrams and the money shot from *A Christmas Carol*. Whether you got your midwinter jubilations via *The Oxford Merry Christmas Book* (1987), *The Reader's Digest Book of Christmas* (1973) or *Gyles Brandreth's Book of Christmas* (1984) was down to personal taste. The odd lump of humorous heresy, such as Jilly Cooper's *How to Survive Christmas* (1986) aside, the Christmas book (in the strictest sense of the term) remains one monolithic, unchanging entity, appearing as regularly as the festival itself, with a fresh jacket concealing the same gaudy baubles that have been fetched down from the family attic for generations. A touching display of cheerful folk tradition or a case of money for the oldest of old rope, depending on how many sherries you've had.

8

A MICROBE IS A ROBE THAT MICS WEAR

The trufflers varied in the degree of humour with which they practiced their dark art. Many solemnly rooted themselves in their interests like cellar mushrooms. Others sifted literature for nuggets of unintentional comedy. In the late 1920s trade magazine editor Cecil Hunt put to his employers the idea of a book consisting of schoolboy howlers, little nuggets of 'found humour' from the pens of eager yet gormless juvenile scholars. The howler was, according to the gentlemanly Hunt, 'a form of humour that is without malice and is alive with humanity', usually verbal cock-ups like 'Lourdes is a cricket ground in London', or 'bees are insects which go from flower to flower collecting pollard.' Some exhibit, under the goofiness, a Byzantine logic it's almost possible to follow. ('The feminine of drake is Queen Elizabeth.')

Howlers (1928) debuted as a small run of paperback booklets at 1/6 apiece. When subscription passed 10,000, people began to take notice. Many sequels later, *Ripe Howlers* (1939) boasted total 'Howler' sales in excess of 150,000 and claimed, in time-honoured jacket blurb tradition: '*Ripe Howlers* is the perfect gift book; welcome everywhere. Anyone who fails to respond to the innocent, inconsequent humour of the howlers... probably needs medical attention. It is sufficient to add that these Howler books are stolen by the dozen from Doctors and Dentists' waiting rooms. All but the short-sighted patients get away with them at the Oculists'.'

Linguistic misfires were nothing new. Sheridan's play *The Rivals* (1775) made a star of the comically clubfooted sayings of Mrs Malaprop, allegedly inspired by the real life strangulated metaphors of Irish parliamentarian Sir Boyle Roche, inadvertent populariser of the 'Irish bull'. Blunders, bulls and bloomers thronged the pages of Victorian works, whether they were intended as instructional correctives as with Thomas Preston's *Dictionary of Daily Blunders* (1880) or more for humour value, as CC Bombaugh intended when he gathered 'Hibernicisms, bulls that are not Irish and typographic errors' for his *Book of Blunders* (1871). And of course the Reverend Spooner was becoming famous for boiling his icicle at New College, Oxford round about this time.

No one, though, had managed to distil the formula so successfully as Hunt. He became 'the Howler man', a title he suffered stoically, even though his 'other books' included some brilliant collaborations with string-and-sealing-wax artist W Heath Robinson, including *How to Make the Best of Things* (1940). But the trickle of howlers before Hunt's first volume was nothing to the torrent that followed. As well as over a dozen collections of Hunt's own, fellow newspaper editor Walter Jerrold compiled *Bulls, Blunders, and Howlers* (1928), and Frank M Richmond turned in a comprehensive *School Yarns and Howlers* (1934).

In later years, one 'Ben Trovato' (Italian for 'well invented') gave Wolfe Publishing a slim *Best Howlers* (1970) for its 'Mini Haha' gift book range, Roger Williams pasted up his *Dictionary of Howlers* (1991) and, of course, Gyles Brandreth was on hand to dispense some *Crazy Howlers* (1998). The professions were mined for stupidity, and yielded rich seams in *Football Howlers* (1951) by Victor Rae, or Roger Brook's *Wake Up, Nurse! Hundreds of Nursing 'Howlers' Taken from the Actual Examination Papers of Many Great Hospitals* (1963), or even *Holy Howlers* (1999) by

Patricia Joan Hunt (no relation). All these books, by their nature, ended up plagiarising each other, and nearly all ultimately fed off Hunt's originals. This was the problem with 'found' humour. If you didn't create it (and the diligent Hunt insisted none of his howlers were by his own hand, as that would be cheating), how could you claim copyright? Russell Ash went some way to redressing this imbalance when, in 1985, he re-released a selection of Hunt's original howlers, fully attributed to the great man and with the blessing of his widow Kathleen, who received half the royalties.

'If the baby does not thrive on fresh milk it should be boiled.'

Authority built on the correct use of language can be knocked flat when sentences prolapse. In this spirit, The Bodley Head, that rarefied publishing house committed to 'stylish decadence', enlisted the Hon. Edward Gathorne-Hardy to compile *An Adult's Garden of Bloomers: Uprooted from the Works of Several Eminent Authors* (1966), a slim booklet in the *Howlers* vein full of excerpts from great literary works where *double entendres* shoulder their way boisterously into view. Jane Austen's '... in winter his private balls were numerous enough for any young lady who was not suffering under the insatiable appetite of fifteen,' from *Sense and Sensibility*, is a typical entry. As the boyishly daring jacket blurb notes, 'If you give [*Bloomers*] to Aunt Edna, she may never speak to you again.'

Denys Parsons established himself as the country's curator of typographical pratfalls with *It Must be True... It Was All in the Papers* (1952), a collection of newsprint howlers illustrated by Ronald Searle, and soon found public demand as great as the professional supply. *True to Type* (1955), *Many a True Word...* (1958), *Fun-tastic!* (1971) – the books kept on for over thirty years, each going through countless reprints. Parsons was aided by like-minded mistake hunters, among their number Patrick

Moore. With *Funny Ha Ha and Funny Peculiar* (1965), Parsons
modified the format by filling even-numbered pages with typos
(for instance 'Experts know that the alcoholic process takes
longer in men, but the end reshult ies the same.' – *Daily Record*),
while the remainder hosted error-free, but nonetheless bizarre,
copy. ('A Portsmouth man believes he has found a way to talk to
hedgehogs – although he does not know the meaning of what
he says to them.' – *Evening News*.) One reason for Parsons's
success was his community spirit, entering into mountains of
correspondence and conjuring up Gobfrey Shrdlu, a sinister-
sounding gremlin haunting the printing presses, an anti-patron
saint of sub editors.[8]

On TV Parsons's baton was taken up by Cyril Fletcher, the
amiable 'odd ode-er' seated in a demure leather armchair to the
right of Esther Rantzen on *That's Life!* In between whimsical
poems based around viewers' tussles with the gas board,
Fletcher recited misprints in a bearishly droll manner, and
enshrined the best in his *Oddities from 'That's Life!'* (1981). A
celebrity agent looking for a swift book for their client to 'write'
happened upon the 'bloomer' canon and saw that it was good,
thus giving traumatic birth to *Barbara Windsor's Book of Boobs*
(1979) – the real legwork was all done by one G Brandreth.
Devotees of Parsons and Hunt would find many of Babs's
trufflings highly familiar, but the Shoreditch soubrette also flings
in unusual epitaphs (along the lines of Russell Ash's 1974
collection *Dead Funny*), quotes from Mrs Malaprop and a 'daft
dictionary'.

'Don't board with the devil if you wish to be fat.'

Babs's dictionary owed a huge debt to Ambrose Bierce, the
American journalist and Civil War veteran whose finely turned
aphorisms had a distinctly sardonic outlook: 'True, man does
not know woman. But neither does woman.' 'Age is provident
because the less future we have, the more we fear it.' Bierce

began paraphrasing figures of speech in bleakly pithy ways in 1869, for a light-hearted column in the San Francisco *News Letter*. His favoured form was the mock dictionary entry: 'WITTICISM, *n*. A sharp and clever remark, usually quoted, and seldom noted; what the Philistine is pleased to call a "joke."' The entries mounted up, until a collection totaling 500 words was published as *The Cynic's Word Book* (1906), with a revised edition, twice the length, appearing in 1911 as *The Devil's Dictionary*. Two years later, the peripatetic Bierce disappeared amongst the chaos of the Mexican revolution, but his dictionary proved a resilient idea.

If resilient ideas are simple enough, they can strike more than once. Russell Ash contemplated a variation on Bierce's theme when director at Weidenfeld and Nicholson during the early '80s, despite being unaware of Bierce's work, just as Cecil Hunt was in the dark over previous howlers. *The Cynic's Dictionary* (1984), styled itself as a 'guide through the minefield of doubletalk, euphemism and deception' of the commercially saturated late 20th century. Taking the form of a phrasebook, Ash's dictionary translated the hyperbole and euphemisms of advertisers ('Refreshing = Transiently thirstquenching.'), publishers ('Complete Book of... = Last word, until the next last word is published.') and personal ads ('Freethinking = Screws around.') Bierce variants have been periodically successful ever since, from Rick Bayan's *Cynic's Dictionary* (1994) to Jonathon Green's *The Cynic's Lexicon: A Dictionary of Amoral Advice* (1984) and Maggie Pinkney's attractively bound *The Devil's Collection: An A-Z of Cynic's Quotes* (2004). Even the necessary celebrity version was a cut above the usual standard, as Leonard Rossiter contributed many definitions of his own to his *Devil's Bedside Book – A Cynic's Survival Guide* (1980).

Ash's next book was pure truffling. Along with antiquarian bookseller Brian Lake, he trawled flyblown bookshops for *Bizarre Books* (1985), a collection of outlandishly titled works taking its lead from the Diagram Prize, an annual competition run by *Bookseller* columnist Horace Bent since 1978, awarded to the most inexplicably named publication of the year. The results included the bewilderingly specialized (*Truncheons: their Romance and Reality*), the mightily useless (*An Historical Curiosity, by a Birmingham Resident: One Hundred and Forty One Ways of Spelling "Birmingham"*) and the flightily saucy (*Let's Make Some Undies*). Ash kept the title going with semi-regular revisions, bolstered by the Parsons method of encouraging readers to nominate their own choices.

Down the pan

Nigel Rees set his literary sights considerably lower in 1979, expanding a strand of his Radio Four programme *Quote, Unquote* on quotable graffiti. We'd been here before, via Mad Sam Johnson's *Bog-House Miscellany*, but *Graffiti Lives, OK* became a rampant bestseller, 'doing for graffiti what Bolognese sauce has done for spaghetti'. Sensibly ignoring the vast majority of personal insult and inarticulate rage in the average gents, Rees went for the wittier end of the wall daubing market, cherishing the bad pun ('Jesus saves – with the Woolwich'), the howler ('Don't let them cut hire education') and the nugget of good-natured nihilism ('Northern Ireland has a problem for every solution'). There's a spot of serious historical context too, tracing the 'OK' ending to the early days of the Troubles ('Provos rule, OK' etc.) and speculating on the identity of the original Kilroy (possibly the foreman at a Massachusetts shipyard who signaled a completed inspection with the words 'Kilroy was here').

A second volume in 1980 proved an easier gig, with readers sending in their own sightings by the ton, including, on a wall in Wells, 'I thought graffiti was a kind of pasta until I discovered Nigel Rees'. A total of five books, plus a compilation, *The Graffiti File*, kept the bandwagon rolling as far as 1987. The bookshelves were fast becoming as crowded as the walls, however, as rival scribble collections muscled in on the racket, the most notable being *Graffiti: the Scrawl of the Wild* (1979) illustrated by the great Edward MacLachlan and compiled by one 'Roger Kilroy', who on closer inspection turned out to be – who else? – Gyles Brandreth. Brandreth's run of spray-can wit clocked up six volumes by 1985, after which the grand master retired from the novelty book scene. Rees, meanwhile, continued upping his game, and now turns out huge, authoritative works like *A Word in Your Shell-Like: 6,000 Curious and Everyday Phrases Explained* (2004) and *A Man About a Dog: Euphemisms and Other Examples of Verbal Squeamishness* (2006), giving him some claim to be 'the lineal successor to Eric Partridge'.

Graffiti scholars championed the free expression of the underachiever. Still further books championed the under-achievements of the underachiever. WA Clouston compiled a scholarly collection in *The Book of Noodles: Stories Of Simpletons; Or, Fools And Their Follies* (1888), cataloguing examples of historical idiocy from the Wise Men of Gotham to Hobson the tailor. Christopher Logue's *True Stories*, a collection of news snippets recounting acts of bizarre misfortune, crossed over from the pages of *Private Eye* to the bookshops in 1973. But it took journalist Stephen Pile to turn failure into a philosophy. Working on the basis that 'I am not the only one who cannot do things and the slightest investigation reveals that no one else can do anything either,' Pile founded The Not Terribly Good Club of Great Britain, a society dedicated to the celebration of disaster in all endeavours. Perhaps it was this conceit – again, an author showing the personal, inclusive touch – that led to the club's 'official handbook' *The Book of Heroic Failures* (1979) to become such a – there's no other word for it – success.

Pile took an authorial tone only slightly less deadpan than the *Guinness Book's* sober McWhirterese to relate tales of the bus service that kept to the timetable by not stopping, a seventy-page book with a 140-strong errata slip and the poetic gems of William McGonagall. The book's second edition merited only a two-page errata slip, which was good going for a compilation of anecdotes which some might have seen as libelous. The only problem was that, by the strict logic of the endeavour, its days were numbered. Thanks to a membership form on the last page of the book (supply name, address, and main areas of incompetence), the NTGCoGB went from a membership of around twenty to a waiting list of over twenty thousand, and newly bestselling author Pile, obeying his society's constitution to the letter, formally expelled himself for acute lack of failure, and wound the society up.

9

ONE FOR THE ANTHOLOGIES

If Victorian society was stifled, Victorian technology, including printing technology, ran riot. In the mid 1850s Edmund Evans revolutionised the popular novel with the introduction of the yellowback, a shilling-a-throw forerunner to the mass-market paperbacks of the 1930s, often to be found on the racks of newsagents and railway station shops. This new proximity of the book to its periodical cousins may have helped to blur the boundary between literature and journalism, but it had never been clear in the first place. Many magazines graduated to books via annual bound collections. These sold well, particularly the regular compilations of short stories from fiction gazettes such as *The Strand*, *alma mater* of Sherlock Holmes, and another publication titled *The Idler*, this one an excuse for Jerome K Jerome and pals to wax wry and drink each other under the table.

The Victorian magazine boom spawned many long-lived publications of note: *Vanity Fair, The Lady, The Bookseller, Tit-Bits* and *Country Life*, to name a few. Thousands more are long-forgotten, but a rummage through your average Victorian newsstand could turn up any or all of the following delights: *Actors by Daylight, Bachelors' Buttons, Bent's Monthly Literary Adviser, The British Controversialist, Celebrities of the Day* (see also *Our Celebrities: A Portrait Gallery* and countless other proto-*Heat* titles), *The Englishwoman's Review of Social and Industrial Questions, Hardwicke's Science Gossip, The Lady Cyclist (incorporating The*

Wheelwoman), The Rational Dress Society Gazette and *Steam: A Boiler Insurance Monthly*. Niche publication had arrived with a vengeance.

By the early 20th-century newsprint was being recycled into books by the ream: cartoon collections, political pamphlets, even – a *Sunday Times* speciality – car maintenance handbooks. But the idea of a miscellany of items branded with the paper's masthead didn't catch on until the Second World War, when *A Daily Telegraph Miscellany* (1940-3), a collection of famous poetry and prose intended to distract domestic readers from their grim plight, and later the likes of *War Poems from The Sunday Times* (1945) established a ready market for anthologies, giving the cream of the national press a second wind.

The *London Evening News* was the first British paper to compile an annual selection of its articles with *Late Extra: A Miscellany by Evening News Writers, Artists, & Photographers* (1952). Editor John Millard introduced the illustrated collection (sample articles: Cricket for Thrills, Old Gilpin's Garden, What Has Happened to the Oak?) in a slightly apprehensive tone: 'It is, we believe… the first miscellany of its kind… we are, to be frank, keeping our fingers crossed. Well… if the readers of this bedside sort of book enjoy reading it half as much as we… enjoyed compiling it, we shall be most amply rewarded.'

The *Manchester Guardian* launched its first anthology, *The Bedside Guardian*, that same year, and unlike the *Evening News*, the franchise still exists today (with a mid-'90s purge of the homely word 'bedside'). By the 1960s colour supplement glamour usurped grubby newsprint, leading to coffee table reprints such as *Encore: The Sunday Times Book* (1962), in which William Rees-Mogg's learned editorials on the Profumo scandal sat snugly alongside sophisticated lifestyle bumf like 'My Monte Carlo System' by Ian Fleming. But the publication that really blurred the boundaries between periodical and book publishing was also, for better or worse, one that came to define several generations of British humour.

The polite bureau

A divided nation, rent by mass poverty, disease and an urgent need for social reform, might not seem the ideal launch pad for a periodical of whimsical musings, droll cartoons and what one contributor later termed 'easy, conversational verse well-fitted to deck-chair reading,' but the turbulent early Victorian period proved the perfect cradle for *Punch*. Journalism at the time was either trustworthy and stolid like *The Times*, or full of scurrilous muckraking and partisan abuse. The time was right for a satirical paper that steered nimbly between the two extremes, and on July 18, 1841 a loose club of writers including Douglas Jerrold, Henry Mayhew and William Makepeace Thackeray made it a reality.

In its very early days, *Punch* was crusading and idealistic. It was still acceptable in a family publication to lay into politicians, which *Punch* did with typical abandon. Social problems were earnestly addressed in poems like Thomas Hood's famous invective against labour conditions, *The Song of the Shirt*. But gradually the tone shifted, and the *Sunday Times* approvingly noted its freedom from 'grossness, partisanship, profanity, indelicacy and malice.' *Punch* was the outpouring of a merry crew of wits, who often called round each other's country retreats for an idyllic, and tellingly childlike, knees-up:

Dinner, if there be no visitors, will be at four. In the summer, a cold quarter of lamb and salad, and a raspberry tart, with a little French wine in the tent, and a cigar. Then a short nap – forty winks – upon the great sofa in the study; and another long stroll over the lawn, while the young members play bowls, and tea is prepared in the tent. Over the tea-table jokes of all kinds, as at dinner.... The crowning effort of this memorable evening was a general attempt to go heels over head upon haycocks in the orchard, a feat which vanquished the skill of the laughing host, and left a very stout and very responsible editor, I remember, upon his head, without power to retrieve his natural position. Again, after a dinner party under canvas, the hearty host, with his guests, including Mr. Charles Dickens... indulged in a most active game of leap-frog, the backs being requested to turn in any obtrusive twopenny with the real zest of fourteen.

Blanchard Jerrold,
The Life and Remains of Douglas Jerrold, 1859

Running gags were introduced to help the regular reader feel part of the clubbable fun, including frequent pops at bellicose Tory grandee Colonel Sibthorp. Invective against social injustice was matched pound-for-pound by theatrical reviews. Bad plays were amusingly savaged in deadpan fashion. There were drunk jokes, spinster jokes, jokes about sailors vomiting, jokes about servants being awkward and ungrateful. Puns predominated. Bad puns. Chronic puns. Puns in ancient Greek. You wouldn't expect a weekly periodical to wear well over the course of a century and a half, and in *Punch*'s case you'd be bang on the money.

Money was what the magazine, with rotten distribution, initially lacked. Spin-off books swelled the coffers, starting with the annually published *Punch's Almanack* in 1842. A calendar crammed with jokes, cartoons and mock prophecies, this soon became a Christmas gift staple, reaching a circulation of 90,000 copies. Themed *Pocket Books* padded out the range. Merchandising helped the magazine rise with the middle classes, and regular dinners (later lunches) round the Punch table, into which staff and esteemed guests carved their initials in overgrown schoolboy fashion, became grand affairs. By the end of the century, blissful contentment set in at the magazine's Bouverie Street offices.

Roll call of ribaldry

The danger of the *Punch* writers' club was stagnation. Every so often, usually when proprietors Bradbury and Agnew came round with a sales graph resembling the down escalator on the north face of the Eiger, the mixture was shaken up, only to quickly settle into the same old pattern with a few minor changes.

But small changes were all that was needed for new talent to slip between the covers. Founder member Thackeray scored a hit with his character portraits of snobs, collected in book form as *The Book of Snobs; by One of Themselves* (1848). These studies of the social type who 'meanly admires mean things' were full of breeziness:

> What I like to see, and watch with increasing joy and adoration, is the Club men at the great looking-glasses. Old Gills pushing up his collars and grinning at his own mottled face. Hulker looking solemnly at his great person, and tightening his coat to give himself a waist. Fred Minchin simpering by as he is going out to dine, and casting upon the reflection of his white neckcloth a pleased moony smile. What a deal of vanity that Club mirror has reflected, to be sure!

Elsewhere, ever more variations on a theme. The pastiche of school textbooks that would give rise to WC Sellar and RJ Yeatman's masterful wallow in half-remembered history *1066 and All That: A Memorable History of England* (1930) was there from the early days, but 1066... added that distinctive voice of unflappably confident ignorance. ('The Norman Conquest was a Good Thing, as from this time onwards England stopped being conquered and thus was able to become a top nation.')[9] Scenes of comic domesticity were common, such as Shirley

Brooks's matrimonial breakfast table battles *The Naggletons;* and *Happy Thoughts*, Francis Burnand's domestic tribulations of a middle-class gent, which generated a series of hardcover spin-offs including *Happy Thought Hall* (1872) and *The Happy Thoughts Birthday Book* (1888).

The easy, familiar comedy of the drawing room took over from the pun as *Punch's* stock-in-trade. At its worst the determined jocularity, the in-print nudge under the ribs to convince the reader of the fine old time he was having in the magazine's pages, became comedy's gurning replacement, in aimlessly jovial features such as *Mr Punch's Table Talk*. ('Anchovy on curried toast is very much to the purpose!') But the comfortingly familiar, exclamation mark-strewn hullabaloo was lapped up by readers.

Innovative ideas still managed to seep in, the most popular of which became books. RC Lehmann parodied popular literary styles in *Mr Punch's Prize Novels* (1892). F Anstey's *Voces Populi* (1892), a collection of short conversational snatches overheard by the author, drew complaints for being too documentary, and too newfangled in general, but proved a durable idea, with more recent copies including Nigel Rees's *Eavesdroppings* (1981) and *All Ears* (2007), a spin-off from the *Guardian Guide*. Former lawyer AP Herbert's tales of the courtroom tomfoolery of one Albert Haddock were collected in many volumes beginning with *Misleading Cases in the Common Law* (1927), some of which were quoted by magistrates presiding over real court cases, particularly the notorious 'negotiable cow', the account of Mr Haddock's payment of a tax bill with a cheque written on the hide of an angry-looking heifer.

Further up the literary deep end, George and Weedon Grossmith's *Diary of a Nobody* (1888) was another long-term paperback favourite which began its washstand-painting lower-middle mockery in *Punch*. PG Wodehouse was an occasional visitor, and AA Milne became assistant editor, plying his Edwardian gentleman of leisure, 'Saturday afternoon on the cricket field' trade and giving his childhood paean *When We Were Very Young* its first airing, leading to allegations that the paper was 'going all whimsy'. (Milne kept his radical politics well to the back of the bus in *Punch*.)

And so it went on, deemed clapped-out by the cognoscenti, relegated to an infamously seldom-thumbed pile in the corner of provincial doctors' waiting rooms, but still undaunted for all that. After World War II, it was also unwrapped in sitting rooms every Christmas morning in the form of the annual anthology *Pick of Punch*. Becoming less relevant by the day, *Punch* became a reactionary cubbyhole for contented wits, a sort of comedic flywheel. Out of its time, it dug in its heels. But, as the staff would say, revolution and fashion are best left to the world's beret wearers and beret makers. The comedian's job is not to drive the social charabanc on, but to supply a waspish commentary from the back seat.

10

THE SEVEN 'C'S OF WRY

One undervalued area of British comedy is the humorous newspaper column. America had James Thurber, S.J. Perelman and, of course, Groucho among their wisecracking men of letters. We had Arthur 'Coo-ee!' Marshall. But then the American image of the writer is altogether more romantic. Their humorists are cigar-drawing, bourbon-swilling hilarious Hemingways dispensing sly observations about hat blocking or the Irish sweepstakes. What competition the fusty Old Harrovian in the corner with his Humorous Thoughts on Bicycle Clips? But the very humility that denies the column its rightful recognition provides its power. Here are seven elements of the British humourist's arsenal which, taken to excess, are sure to stink the place out, but when handled intelligently form the essence of British comic prose.

Characterisation (1)

Tarry awhile in the vales of English whimsy and you'll bump, sooner rather than later, into Beachcomber, a pen-name for an assortment of writers for the *Globe* and *Daily Express* of whom JB Morton was the most important. Beachcomber 'edited' *By the Way*, a motley assortment of social news, melodramatic serials and literary parody, peopled by a rep company of baroque characters, their names a violent clash of Anglo-Saxon syllables. Mr Justice Cocklecarrot, Mountfalcon Foulenough, Dr Alf

Spoddoes – the Oxford English Dictionary collapses in on itself, taking common sense with it.

Beachcomber's columns plunge, with no ado whatsoever, into opening lines of matter-of-fact madness. ('It is not generally known that in her wild youth Mrs Wretch was the girl who stood on the elephant's back in Wugwell's Mammoth Circus.') Stories tail off, switch to wild tangents, or never get started in the first place, due to the stubbornness of the participants (Cocklecarrot in particular has frequent circular arguments in court with a platoon of red-bearded dwarfs). The result is a series of dispatches from a fantasy newspaper co-owned by Swift and Lewis Carroll, at the same time exotically bizarre and as English as bread sauce.

If this sounds like an acquired taste now, it was even then. *Express* owner Lord Beaverbrook had to take its hilarity on trust. George Orwell rounded on Morton during the war, attacking his reactionary stance. But even those for whom one Tinklebury Snapdriver is one too many can't deny the column's influence. There's a direct lineage from Dickens and Carroll to *The Goon Show* that goes right through the heart of Beachcomber. *Private Eye*'s cast of shabby characters mirror Beachcomber's at many points. Richard Ingrams, Michael Frayn and Barry Took adapted the older columns for printed collections and radio. A humorist's humorist perhaps, but Beachcomber laid the ground rules of polite dementia on which later whimsical columns were built.

Circumlocution (2)

The arch verbosity of the Beef-Steak Club proved shockingly durable. Dickensian heartiness and a stockpile of chucklesome catchphrases remained the default setting for British comic prose, long after the last man to really talk like that died of consumption in the Garrick. In *Scoop* (1938) Evelyn Waugh poked fun at the style via William Boot's overcooked Nature

Notes column. ('Feather-footed through the plashy fen passes the questing vole…') At its worst, it's as if the writer has just swallowed a Home Counties snug bar, a fact acknowledged in Stephen Potter's history of comic prose *The Sense of Humour* (1954). Potter calls this unhappy trait the English Reflex:

> 'How are you?' There, at the bar, is my solid friend G., the ornithologist. 'Jolly D,' he says. 'Well played,' I say. No smile, of course: it is something less than being facetious, even… We shake jokes, as it were, instead of shaking hands, to show that there is no hostility. It is as automatic as the cough reflex for clearing the throat… It is true that most of these preliminary parries, these chewings of a worn-out old cud, are a symptom of a decadent tendency to live-off-the-land in the world of humour, without putting anything back.

This National Trust idea of English comedy is decidedly unhealthy. *Punch* went through lean periods regarding innovation and freshness, but there was never any danger of the 'collapse of stout party' tendency fading away. Even modern comic creations like Alan Partridge wallow in the easy delights of agreeable joviality as much as they snap at its legs: Partridge's grotesque 'hail fellow well met' vocabulary is crafted with the unnerving accuracy and perverse relish of writers who've caught themselves talking like that more often than they'd like to admit.

Stephen Fry's collection of columns, *Paperweight* (1992), is riddled with what Fry's old tutor referred to as 'sixth-form words' and unabashed use of fogeyish expressions such as 'that inestimable phrase'. But Fry turns his baroque, sesquipedalian style in on itself, mocking his own desire to show off in hearty prose. Nevertheless, it's still there. He may wear those threadbare slippers with a knowingly apologetic shrug,[10] but there's no denying how comfy he looks in them. He also proves there's nothing inherently Conservative about the style, laying into the Gulf War and Section 28 in the same giddy manner. The hearty style can work in your favour, but you must keep your wits about you.

Cleverness (3)

Ivory-tinkling topical wit Richard Stilgoe's Aunt Sally status was down to good old English distrust of precocity. In the small hours of 4 May 1979, he rounded off the BBC's election coverage with a lengthy piano ditty detailing the night's losses and gains. 'Commander Boaks got twenty votes/There were more for Hatters-ley/And Tam Dalyell did awfully well/So he can't blame that on me!' Live, it smacked of showing off. In print, it's easier to swallow. *The Richard Stilgoe Letters* (1981) detailed the adventures of a host of characters made from anagrams of Stilgoe's name, Giscard O'Hitler and Dr Gloria Ethics being the most infamous. Just as precocious, but without the jolly piano flourishes the 'smug' label was less likely to stick.

There was more wordplay in the books based on Frank Muir and Denis Norden's radio programme *My Word!*, a parlour game in which a popular phrase is mangled with a sledgehammer pun, and a rambling piece of mock etymology is retrofitted around the mutilated proverb. The first spin-off title – *You Can't Have Your Kayak and Heat It* (1973) – illustrates the principle perfectly. Muir had an extensive solo writing career poking a sardonic stick into a variety of topics in the *Frank Muir Goes Into...* radio programmes and books. He also acted as *de facto* curator of humorous prose, editing several anthologies for the OUP.

Away from the smart set, some columnists mined a vein of unworldly clumsiness. The Third Baron Glenavy, under his workaday alias of Patrick Campbell, was the master of the elaborately recounted gaffe. In his columns for *Lilliput* (collected in 1949 as *A Long Drink Of Cold Water*) and the *Sunday Times* (see 1963's *Brewing Up in the Basement*) he's an outsize donnish klutz, forever coming off an amusingly gauche second to whatever people or objects he encounters. Barbers, coffee percolators, even spoons become sources of everyday horror. The stories are precisely cut to column length, looking like haphazard rambles but constructed with devilish precision. Incidents such as the one where Campbell locks himself out of the house, with a running bath and a senior stew on the hob, may not be revolutionary comedy but are perfect one-man miniature farces. Like Paddington Bear, Campbell allied an inquisitive eye to a clueless hand, via a permanently bewildered brain.

Capriciousness (4)

The humorist with a weekly deadline leads a butterfly dance from subject to subject, which can seem like desperation disguised as eclecticism. Between the wars, when *Punch* was frequently in the doldrums, this became derided as the 'weekend essay', a chunk of dull observation on whatever crossed the writer's mind, dressed up in archaic circumlocution and a liberal sprinkling of those literary deelyboppers, the dreaded exclamation marks.

The best columnists avoid self-indulgence while seemingly writing to please nobody but themselves. Paul Jennings's *Observer* column, running from 1949 to 1966 and collected many times from 1950's *Oddly Enough* onwards, quietly revolutionised the form. He wrote in an un-fancy, 'thinking aloud to myself on the 8:45 from Esher' manner, which clicked with commuters nationwide. His subjects were suitably suburban as well. The Jennings world existed alongside our own dull sphere, occasionally glimpsed through portals found in such unlikely places as trams, lost property offices and council bye-laws.

Any mundane item could induce a Jennings reverie. A job ad for 'an experienced rotary mud flush driller'. A trade journal article on the National Paper Bags Renovation Industry Co-operative Union. An office door marked 'Activated Sludge'. One tiny kink in the workaday world and Jennings is off on a stream of consciousness with its own warped internal logic. John Betjeman's humdrum home counties are, it transpires, powered by an unfathomably weird hidden system out of Heath Robinson by way of Ludwig Wittgenstein. Metroland is mental, and Jennings has volunteered as its uncertified psychotherapist.

Many columnists took up the Jennings baton, to be startled by the commonplace effluvia of subsequent decades. Miles Kington laterally glanced his way around the country for thirty-odd years, via *Punch*, *The Times* and the *Independent*. Kington borrowed from the best: his 'unusual jobs', such as a photographic stand-in for the book jacket shots of shy authors, use the Jennings method of hopelessly uninformed (but keen!) speculation. But his original creations include *Let's Parler Franglais* (1979-87), a series of mock language lab dialogues enhanced by, but not dependent upon, the slovenly intrusion of misapplied O-Level French *mal mots*; and a miniature airline novel to read during the part of the flight where 'the plane stops, everyone stands up and nothing happens for ten minutes'.

Comment (5)

Hungarian journalist George Mikes was sent to London to cover the Munich crisis and ended up staying put, forging the vast bulk of the cultural anomalies that had struck him into the playfully snappy *How to be an Alien* (1946). Mikes claimed to have been 'bitterly disappointed' at the British public's positive verdict, but he was only half-joking – the book was also serialised by Romanian radio as anti-British propaganda. Caught between two cultures, Mikes appreciated this galumphing irony.

Mikes's old Budapest pal André Deutsch published his musings on the indigenous population's attitudes to the weather, tea, queuing, buses and sex. ('Continental people have a sex life,' Mikes famously wrote, 'the English have hot-water bottles.') *Alien* reached its third reprint in as many weeks, setting Mikes on

a long writing career that perennially returned to his *How To...*
formula. By this time Mikes was a naturalised Briton, but the
titles were still a giveaway. *How to be a Swell Guy* (1959), *How to be
Inimitable* (1960), *How to be Decadent* (1977), *How to be God*
(1986)... no Englishman would have dared to slap such
forthright titles on the front of his books.

In *How to be a Guru* (1984) the 72-year-old Mikes has moved
far away from the humour template. Five lines in he's quoting La
Rouchefoucauld and proffering observations a million miles
from the usual snug bar comfort zone, like 'those who hate
homosexuals with an uncontrollable fury are only too often
suppressed homosexuals,' or that the working classes are trying
to do 'two things at one and the same time: to despise the middle
classes and to join them.' It's not immune from the occasional
descent into folksiness, but a lot of *How to be a Guru* is oddly
close to philosophy. But why should that be odd? Philosophy
and humour are mutually dependent, not exclusive. And think
how much more appealing Nietzsche's *Ecce Homo* would have
been with a few cartoons by Larry.

Before he wrote for the stage, Michael Frayn wrote a thrice-
weekly column for the *Guardian* and *Observer* called, with an
almost daunting lack of boundaries, *Miscellany*. Frayn employed
Beachcomber's ' cast of characters', but the big game hunters of
old had been superseded by more swinging stereotypes: smug
NW1 couple Christopher and Lavinia Crumble; Rollo Swaveley,
PR guru; Ken Nocker, up-and-coming satirist, and marketing
agency Harris-Harris, fuelled by an apocalyptic desperation to
manically sell everything from Frungles cereal to Shakespeare's
As You Like It. ('Ye sauceyest piece since ye Decameron!')

Later packed into three volumes, *The Day of the Dog* (1962),
The Book of Fub (1963), and *At Bay in Gear Street* (1967), Frayn's
Miscellany belonged to newspaper tradition, but offered
something new. Like Mikes, Frayn knew that the humorist
needn't relegate himself to a trivial world of socks lost in the
wash. Satire reared its charming head in columns such as his

Rules of the International Union of Disarmament Industry Workers. ('5. The Union shall maintain friendly fraternal contact with armaments manufacturers, members of the armed services, espionage and counter-espionage agents, and members of any other profession whose objectives are in harmony with the aims of the Union.') Frayn modestly claims he was overtaken in the satirical field by *TW3* and the *Eye*, but this is just a tacit admission that he was once way out in front.

Cadence (6)

There was always room for poetry in *Punch*. Beachcomber penned song lyrics and pastiched AA Milne. But the best comic prose sounds more poetic than most whimsical poetry, as that hearty wordiness is put to good use in the name of timing. The good column is light but strongly built, with verbiage deployed along elegant lines that are also instrumental in keeping everything together, like the chains in a suspension bridge. The advanced humorist can choose to secure these with a selection of fancy literary knots, such as:

The multi-syllable euphemism – venerable great uncle to the *double entendre*. 'It is easy to be rude on the Continent. You just shout and call people names of a zoological character.' – George Mikes, *How to be an Alien*.

Surrealist bathos – build up a dramatic atmosphere, burst it the next instant with the deployment of nonsense. 'But on the footplate of the Silver Monster, all unheeding, Ingeborg Maelstrom, the first Norwegian woman renegade politician to cross the Rockies, was braising carrots.' – Beachcomber, *By the Way*.

Pastiche – the strolling manner of the humorous column implies that the author is operating on a different wavelength to the world. As such, any other style can be adopted in order to show up its panicky absurdity, as long as the rhythm's faithfully reproduced. Here's Michael Frayn reworking an excitable *Daily*

Mirror women's section review of the year for men: 'Did you...
go wild about iced popadoms? Wear a ginger wig for smart little
Chelsea dinner-dates? Clean your false teeth with one of the
new easy-to-use butane gas denture scourers? Go gay with a
tumbler of pep-you-up port for breakfast?'

The Googly – The author takes a long, slow, build up to this
delivery, moving in his usual measured, loping strides until, at
the last possible moment, he bends the wrist sharply from the
normal writing position and sends the sentence spinning off in
a totally unexpected direction, wrong-footing the hapless reader.
This should only be attempted by the seasoned expert. 'In the
event, however, EM Forster was in Lytton Strachey's bath when
Foskett called and sprang at the young visitor with such force
that Lytton, two rooms away, fell off the milkman.' – Alan
Coren, *The Cricklewood Diet* (1982).

Coren (7)

The heyday of wry humour ended with the rise of those polo-
necked iconoclasts at the end of the 1950s. But the rearguard
action continued under the generalship of Alan Coren, *Punch*'s
deputy editor throughout the '70s and *capo di tutti capi* for most
of the '80s. Coren ruled his benign dictatorship from behind a
bureau in Cricklewood, the ideal deceptively humdrum base for
a deceptively humdrum man. A Yale-educated plumber's son
who hob-nobbed with Princess Margaret, Coren was never that
close to his assumed average English origins in the first place,
but the tweeds were ideal camouflage.

Worlds of accidental strangeness were Coren's forte. The
odd word conjunctions on spines of a set of *Encyclopaedia
Britannica* inspired reviews of fictional masterpieces like *Napoleon
Ozmolysis*. At his best, Coren works on the same level as
Perelman and Woody Allen, and his Moses, desperately casting
about for a plot for the book of Genesis, could even be written
by Allen. 'You spend a couple of pages setting the scene then

right away, boom! You bring on a couple of naked people, they fool around a bit, then there's a murder, that's the kind of thing people go for, then there's some disaster stuff, a conflagration maybe, a flood, something like that... I tell you, this book is going to be very big!'

'Are you still going to be writing little pieces about people called Norman Foskett when you're sixty?' asked his wife once, and Coren's blood froze. All humorists are haunted by the fear that time spent lightly is ultimately time wasted but Coren's playfulness endures. Anarchy sometimes wears a sports jacket. In 1975 Alan Coren's publisher advised him the three most popular subjects for books were golf, cats and Nazis, leading to him titling his next column collection *Golfing For Cats*, complete with subtle swastika on the cover cartoon. The bluff old fogey in the herringbone tweeds could subvert with the best of them.

II

THE MAYFAIR PLAY

Toilet books can arise from the unlikeliest situations. No one would have predicted that the Christmas lightweight hit of 1947 would arise from highbrow BBC radio station The Third Programme, but on September 27th, 1946, the Third's first ever programme, at 6 PM sharp, was *How to Listen* ('including How Not To, How They Used To, and How You Must'). The *Radio Times* explained: 'Special Double Number for the Third Programme by Stephen Potter, with selected examples, by Joyce Grenfell, of Third Class Listening.'

Listeners were treated to forty-five meandering minutes of wireless deconstruction: technical 'noises off', interviews with 'typical listeners' and digs at wireless obsessives who fit sets inside cocktail cabinets. Genteel by today's standards, it nevertheless caused one critic to label it 'brutal'. This was something new in the world of comedy, and the man behind it was co-writer, producer, former English Lit don and ex-Coldstream Guard Stephen Potter.

Potter's defining moment occurred on 8 June 1931, during a doubles tennis match at Birkbeck College between two undergraduates and two lecturers, one S Potter and future *Brains Trust* panelist Dr Cyril Edwin Mitchenson Joad, an archetypal eccentric who turned up with an outlandish metal racket and baggy trousers tied up with string. This rakish gear, Potter noted, wrong-footed the undergrads, scrupulously turned out in whites. But victory was sealed by what Potter termed 'Joad's Gambit':

after a not-at-all dodgy line call, as Potter was returning service Joad called to the opposition 'Kindly say clearly, please, whether the ball was in or out.' This cheery suggestion put the students off their game completely, and they never recovered. They were made to feel, in Potter's words, 'that something has gone wrong, however slightly', and the dons won the game 'without actually cheating'.

In Potter's middle-class, metropolitan world of country house weekends and highly competitive London clubs, this kind of trick (or 'ploy', in Potter's coinage) was rife. It was how one 'got on'. And Potter, a suburbanite in awe of the upper classes, was an inveterate social climber. ('Meet more Lords,' went one New Year's Resolution.) At the Savile Club, haunt of many BBC alumni, competition was fierce indeed. Potter and fellow members endlessly discussed sporting minutiae, often straying waggishly onto the topic of how to bend the rules.

Pottering away in the dark

These *bons mots* would have remained within the club's Mayfair walls had it not been for the fuel crisis of 1947. During a bitterly cold February, with BBC broadcasting suspended to save energy, Potter found himself at a loose end. No radio to produce or write for, too cold for golf – what to do? In lieu of anything more constructive, he began to jot down those Savile Club discussions. On scraps of paper, backs of fag packets, anything that came to hand (even sheets of shiny Bronco austerity toilet roll), his treatise on *Gamesmanship* slowly took shape. Gradually the pile of scrap witticisms grew to some 30,000 words, about the length of a short book, the type that traditionally appears in the shops in time for Christmas. Why shouldn't this go to print too? After all, as Potter himself put it, there were '500 books on how to play games, but none on how to win'.

One of these 500 books bequeathed Potter its heroically over-serious tone. *The Isthmian Book of Croquet* (1899), a breathless tome of rules for the ultimate Victorian society game, was deliriously self-important. It mired itself in jargon and reminisced dewily over the game's great characters ('everyone will remember the occasion when Colonel Streeter said "There's nothing for it but to go for it" and hooped diagonally across the lawn'). This overpowering solipsism was the perfect form for Potter to recount the immortal antics of C Joad and friends.

Gamesmanship was rounded off with a deft line in footnotes which wrong-foot the reader and muddy stagnant waters still further, and a set of appendices that fly off into pure whimsy, musing on the authenticity of WG Grace's beard. But that Isthmian solemnity steadies the tone throughout. There's none of the winking, chortling playing up from *Punch* that had become so prevalent between the wars. In a climate of unrelenting drollery, where humourists offered up their 'sideways looks' at the world with after-dinner ebullience, Potter, always disapproving of 'writey-writey' authors, pared everything down to a deadpan minimum. Those years of editing scripts to strict BBC time limits helped.

The final element in the book's deadpan artillery was the illustrator. Standard practice at the time would be to commission one of a small pool of 'name' cartoonists from *Punch* or the national press. This would look wonderful, but would scream 'comedy!' – not *Gamesmanship*'s style. Potter's obsessive networking solved the problem by turning up Lt-Col Frank Wilson (Ret'd), a regimental illustrator who, though in on the joke himself, contributed brilliantly stiff and straight diagrammatic depictions of Joad's Gambit and tactically overloaded golf trolleys which perfectly complemented Potter's spurious seriousness. That the Colonel came a great deal cheaper than David Low was a happy coincidence.

Salesmanship
The Theory & Practice of Gamesmanship; or The Art of Winning

Games Without Actually Cheating was published in October 1947 by newly independent publisher (and father of Adam) Sir Rupert Hart-Davis, who took a risky punt during a paper shortage by printing 25,000 copies. Reviews were mixed. One CEM Joad enjoyed it enormously, while the *Times Literary Supplement* sniped: 'It is impossible not to admire Mr Potter's tenacity in turning a joke into a book.' Initially, the book sold only moderately well, but the ideal publicity was on hand. Christmas Day saw the broadcast of *How to be Good at Games*, dramatising much of the book's material. Thus plugged, the book became a bestseller, and requests for themed *Gamesmanship* articles began to come in from magazines and newspapers – all of which would yield material for the sequel, *Some Notes on Lifemanship with a Summary of Recent Research in Gamesmanship* (1950).

Lifemanship improved on its progenitor's impenetrable mixture of Savile in-jokes and croquet manual parody. It's a more sophisticated, more unified and, importantly, funnier book, opening out Potter's world, most notably with the debut of the Lifemanship College at Station Road, Yeovil. Potter moved away from sporting in-jokes towards life in general. We're introduced to conversation-winning gambits such as the notorious Canterbury Block, in which any knowledgeable colleague can be silenced mid-flow with the interruption 'Yes, but not in the south.' The characters of *Gamesmanship* line up to demonstrate ploys, some as real as a croquet Colonel (C Joad and J Grenfell make appearances), others invented: the downbeat, devious H Gattling-Fenn demonstrates Writership (subdivided into Newstatesmanship and Daily Mirrorship), and the outlandish G Cogg-Willoughby impresses womenfolk with his lucid yet made-up nature knowledge (a favourite game of Potter himself).

Lifemanship was a roaring success, selling 100,000 in the UK and over 70,000 in America. The US fell for Potter instantly. This testifies to the universality of Potter's observations as much as to American audiences of the time being less alienated by 'Ingerlish yumor' than English humourists like to make out. But Potter didn't do himself any damage by courting the Ivy League set. Exhaustive lecture tours of the nation's colleges promoted the book, and Potter's clubbability came into play as he appointed various newfound friends rankings in the International Lifemanship League. Potter found himself in talks over a US television series, and was courted by Cary Grant over a possible film of the books. By the time Democratic hopeful Adlai Stevenson coined the word 'brinkmanship' to describe the Eisenhower government's aggressive foreign policy, a transatlantic cult had been created.

How to start a franchise without actually repeating

In October 1952, *One-Upmanship: Being Some Account of the Activities and Teachings of the Lifemanship Correspondence College of One-Upness and Games Lifemastery* arrived – longer but no less funny than *Lifemanship*, and only slightly less successful. The critics continued to snip, but one-joke Potter was still OK by the public. He wasn't OK by Potter, though, and the author tried to move away from the suffix with which he'd reluctantly become identified. *Sense of Humour* (1954) was an interesting dissertation on the history of comic prose which critics labeled 'too dry', missing the 'Potter touch' they'd supposedly been tiring of two years previously.

Potter finally caved in and wrote *Supermanship, or, How to Continue to Stay Top without Actually Falling Apart* (1958). Chapters on Reviewmanship and 'When to Use Spidery Handwriting' retained some of the old spark, but sales were barely a fifth of the all-conquering *Lifemanship*, and the knives were out. ('Please may we have a new joke now?' – *The Observer*.)

In 1960 the film arrived. *School for Scoundrels or How to Win Without Actually Cheating!* was a fine attempt (by Peter Ustinov, among others) to squeeze Potter's rambling, footnote-festooned lectures into a ninety-minute narrative. After many false starts, Potter finally made it to TV on August 21st 1963, presenting *The British at Play*, a forty-five minute wry look at games and sport for Associated-Rediffusion.

1965 brought a rent-paying volume, *Anti-Woo: The Lifeman's Improved Primer for Non-Lovers*, a business-as-usual treatise on 'How not to be in love without actually thwarting'. It was a thin piece, almost living up to the *TLS*'s mean assessment of Potter as 'making the same joke in the same way without any sense of strain or sign of indifference.' *The Complete Golf Gamesmanship* (1968) was the Great Gamesman's last throw of the dice, a familiar series of sporting in-jokes forming a sort of superior 'bedside golf' anthology, though that's not saying much. Illness and depression were now closing in. On December 2nd 1969, a bout of pneumonia finished the job.

Though he worried throughout his life about not fulfilling his potential (whatever that actually means), from this distance Potter's legacy is impressive indeed. Besides the books, the first three of which at least are classics, there's the enduring film and, most gratifyingly for a man obsessed with etymology, he lives on in the dictionary with the various '-manship' suffixes. It's a testament to Potter's sharpness that he could tease out a Mayfair club in-joke into a universal and unique comic style, and a lasting monument to human pettiness.

Lawmen

Post-war society, as it reconstituted itself, began poking about in its nooks and crannies to find out what made it tick and, most importantly, what made it go wrong. Talk was of systems and models. Like turning over an ant's nest, the curiosity became a compulsion. What *was* going on down there?

Humorists were as well placed as analysts to figure society out. Even before the war, the world of commerce had been codified sideways by 'Mark Spade' (that is to say, novelist Nigel

Balchin) in a series of *Punch* essays collected as *How to Run a Bassoon Factory* (1934) and *Business for Pleasure* (1935). (He also published a leisure-oriented volume, *Fun and Games: or How to Win at Almost Anything* in 1936, which may or may not have influenced Potter.) 'Spade' dug into Georgian corporate concerns with cheery matter-of-factness. On the crucial matter of the business lunch, he suggests:

> When he asks (as he certainly will) whether you like a big lunch or a light one, there is no alternative but to reply, 'Oh, light – very light.' Then explain quickly that you can't bear these heavy solid grills and things and that you have an essentially French stomach, preferring a very little of each of six courses to a big dull steak. That in itself will show him that you are a seasoned lunchee.

Naval historian Cyril Northcote Parkinson took a long, hard look at the British civil service in an essay for *The Economist* in 1955, originating Parkinson's Law, which states that 'work expands to fill the time available for its completion.' Two years later came the book *Parkinson's Law: The Pursuit of Progress*, a dense tome full of invented equations to demonstrate the inherent wastefulness of the rapidly expanding public sector. The Law passed into common currency, and Parkinson turned out several variations on his theme, including *The Law and the Profits* (1960), *In-Laws and Outlaws* (1962) and *Mrs. Parkinson's Law* (1968).

More laws-cum-books followed. Dr Laurence J Peter enshrined his rule of managerial hierarchy – i.e. that 'every employee tends to rise to his level of incompetence' – in *The Peter Principle* (1968). Most famously of all, Murphy's Law, the famous dictum that 'anything that can go wrong, will go wrong', was compiled by Arthur Bloch in several volumes from 1977. These books could be said to embody a law of their own: the more complicated professional society gets, the bigger the

Christmas market for volumes of wry professional cynicism.

The S-Factor

> Our aim in this book is simply this: to show you the road
> to success. We present for your consideration a new code
> of ethics. It is a code which leads neither to salvation nor
> to Utopia; it is a code – or, more plainly, a method –
> which leads to success.

So begins *The S-Man* (1960), in the hype-fuelled, cod-evangelical
style of the self-help manuals that sold in bushels to timid post-
war punters eager to buy their way out of the doldrums with a
slim volume of easy answers. But in this case, the author (the
ominously named Mark Caine) had come to ridicule the
prophets of upward mobility, not to join them. So closely did he
mimic their patronising wise guy manner, however, that it took
a while to spot the parody.

Caine takes the reader into his confidence, laying down the
arcane law on how to get ahead in society at all costs. As he goes
deeper, the reader realises something's amiss. Promising to keep
the lecture jargon-free, Caine starts bunging down neologisms
like *success-potential*, *inhibition barrier* and *motivation ratio*, phrasing
obvious observations to make them seem like new discoveries,
raising questions on the reader's behalf in order to dismiss them,
and slowly racking up the sense of claustrophobia as life is
reduced to a simple trek up and down the greasy pole.

The businesslike tone turns brutal. ('A sign of stagnancy is to
do the same thing again for the same amount of money. This is
the Prostitute's Fallacy.') Precocity is urged in all departments,
even sex. ('When you are in bed with a man's wife it is as well to
have your school cap on display in the hall.') A wife is important,
but only as a means to an end – *the* end. ('You too believe in love,
but… you are too tender to offer woman marriage until you can

give her all this and heaven too. But especially all this.') Everything is reduced to a grim realisation of that 'success-potential'. ('We believe only in *things*.')

The book was the pseudonymous work of two upwardly mobile twentysomethings. The idea was hatched by Tom Maschler, editor-in-chief for Jonathan Cape, and executed by the young Frederic Raphael, who would carry on the theme in two big British films, *Nothing But the Best* (1964) in which cynical Denholm Elliot coaches outsider Alan Bates in the rules of success, and *Darling* (1965) in which social climbing It-girl Julie Christie takes the fast track to a life of emptiness.

To publicise *The S-Man*, Maschler appeared on TV as Caine, face covered by a large hood. The *Observer* unmasked him soon after, noting his day job and lamenting 'the practice of publishers publishing publisher's books seems to be growing out of hand'. It found the book itself 'curiously humourless', while an unimpressed Richard West dismissed it in the *Guardian* as 'a remote and donnish joke… altogether this is an F-book and at times B-irritating'. While the joke is as dry as it is overstretched, a glance through the book today shows how well the theme was chosen. The chinks of darkness in the light-hearted world of Stephen Potter have widened to engulf everything, and there's no way out but to endlessly chase the nebulous prize of success. As 'Caine' himself says, in signing off:

> We have not been playing with words. We have invented no game for snobs or highbrows. We have explained the logic of our time, the logic of the Age of Success. We have said what we have said. We are not joking.

Just for men

The magazine trade has always enjoyed a symbiotic relationship with the less literary end of the book industry, with a free exchange of ideas, and fads flowing between the two. At this point in the story, one homely subsection of the former is worth considering for its influence, both witting and unwitting, on its perfect-bound cousins. By the 1960s, women's magazines outnumbered those for men by ten to one but, due no doubt to the publishing industry's strong male bias, the manly publications had the greatest effect.

Pocket-sized miscellanies were aimed firmly at the go-ahead pipe-man in the street. *Lilliput* (1937-60) was the most famous, started by Hungarian émigré Stefan Lorant, who fled Nazi Germany and ensured his publication kept up a vigorous criticism of all totalitarian political systems, along with short stories by reputable authors like HE Bates. But what really drew the punters were the retouched nudie photo stories. *Lilliput* enjoyed its imperial phase in the 1950s under the aegis of pipe-smoking countryman Jack Hargreaves, who brought out bound Christmas compilations such as *The Bedside Lilliput* (1950).

Its main rival, which eventually swallowed it wholesale, was *Men Only* (1935 -), a thicker, gutsier and altogether more blokey affair. 'We don't want women readers,' proclaimed its masthead, and the contents made good on its word, packing the small format pages with everything that was anathema to the fair sex. Bathing beauties featured in glossy photos, alongside more and broader cartoons than *Lilliput*. Where *Lilliput* ransacked 17th-century medical books for laughs, *Men Only* went for photos of boxing cats. It also leapt on the nascent craze for fashionable menswear with its 'style conscious jottings'. ('Knitwear still holds firm with some bold styling along Italian lines. Thick husky sweaters continue to make headway among all men who like messing about in boats, TV studios and class-conscious pubs.') This was exciting new territory, where manly success and reliability mixed with casual elan. Responsibility met excitement. The pipe met the cardigan. It couldn't last, and it didn't.

The '60s put paid to the genteel men's magazine. In 1971, strip club entrepreneur Paul Raymond bought up the ailing *Men Only* and turned it into the straight-up soft porn publication we know and feign ignorance of today. Another dashing mag, *Man About Town*, tried to swing along with the new crowd when it was taken over by equally dashing young businessman Michael Heseltine, who shortened its name to *About Town*, and then just *Town*, but still failed to pilot it through the turbulent decade unscathed. The urbane cardigan-'n'-slacks gent was an anachronism, and the Stay-Prest bottom fell out of his market.

The men's mags became a source of visual material for the next generation to poke fun at. Those brusque, earnest adverts for male corsetry were ripe for parody. ('Inches off your waist instantly with the Manly. Only the Manly will instantly pull in your waistline the moment you put it on. Extra detachable supporter included free.') Equally infra dig were slogans that, though barely a decade old, suddenly seemed as antiquated as Chaucer. ('When you find that things go wrong/Fill your pipe and smoke Tom Long.' 'Free as a bird in Aertex shirts. Always cool – however warm the waltz!' 'Always use Energol. The oiliest oil.') The magazines that mattered now were the newspaper colour supplements, whose lavish layouts would prove unexpectedly influential on the toilet book trade, leading its proponents to make their work look – and read – more like a magazine than ever before, and one particular inky, low-gloss rag which took its place in the vanguard of a seismic shift in English humour.

12

HO HO, VERY SATIRICAL

Everywhere we see the dreariness of man. We see the squat-bottomed pipe-smokers ensconced in pubs discussing the day's rugger… What is more, we can envisage them in 40 years' time. And what will they be doing? You can bet your bottom dollar that they will be squatting in suburban pubs talking about the day's rugger.

So ran a 1959 edition of *Parson's Pleasure*, a student periodical emanating from University College, Oxford. Its undergraduate writers were lamenting the dullness of the archetypal reader of *Men Only* – in much the same way Pope and Swift had lambasted the small-mindedness of 18th-century commercial journalism. Fellow satirist Jonathan Miller made the link explicit when he excitedly invoked 'the final overthrow of the neo-Gothic stranglehold of Victorian good taste.'

The magazine's motley staff were young fogey Richard Ingrams, young lefties Paul Foot and Christopher Booker, and 'fat cartoonist' Willie Rushton. The comic inspiration was *Beachcomber*. The circulation was tiny. But things move fast in the student publishing, and Balliol College's Peter Usborne started the glossier *Mesopotamia*, a sturdier vessel for the Ingrams posse. Added to the team was John Wells, who doubled as the physical model for Little Gnittie, a timid suburban ingénue who was cast adrift in the fleshpots of Oxford in one of Rushton's cartoon strips.

The varsity years ended, the gang broke up, and that would have been that but for Usborne's discovery of offset litho, a new printing process available at very reasonable rates from an outfit in Neasden. The team regrouped at a secret location (Rushton's mum's house at 28 Scarsdale Villas, Kensington) to put together the first issue of *Private Eye*, all pasted up in rough and ready fashion and launched onto the streets on Friday 25th October 1961. As a statement of intent, the new magazine fingered *Punch* as its Bore of the Week.

A year into its life, the magazine slipped between hard covers. *Private Eye on London* (1962) took *Mesopotamia*'s Gnittie adventure (the poor sap was now the magazine's mascot, an impotent version of the *Daily Express* knight) and relocating it to a decadent London on the verge of swinging change. Rushton's able pen guided the gullible Gulliver from urban type to urban type, taking in royal watchers, advertisers, Wimpy bars, kitchen sink filmmakers and pornographers. This sixteen-shilling wonder was produced at great speed, but with meticulous attention to detail, after a deal was struck over drinks at the Ritz with George Weidenfeld.

So neatly was the job done that Gnittie's odyssey seems all of a piece, even though many of his encounters were repackaged hits from the *Eye*'s first year. These included the Peter Cook-mocking 'Jonathan Crake' strip, Great Bores of Today (featuring a 'liberal intellectual' closely resembling Booker) and a parody of Heseltine's *About Town* which, when it originally appeared, led to the team being wined and dined by Heseltine, keen to start a pull-out satire section in *Town*. He didn't get his supplement. In the minds of the *Eye* lads, *Town* was distinctly pipe-and-rugger dull.

Eye compilations became annual affairs. Assorted publishers and formats were tried out. December 1965's pocket softback *Penguin Private Eye* was a more conventional anthology, banned from Smith's due to the chunderous antics of Barry Humphries's comic strip Ocker Barry McKenzie. Regular columns appeared on the bookshelves, though sometimes not for long. *Mrs Wilson's Diary* had 12,000 copies of its 1965 compilation recalled as the diaries' authorship was considered 'unclear'. The parody of the Labour PM's wife was so accurate it risked being taken at face value and must be banned: the ultimate backhanded compliment. Some successes arose from the magazine unbidden, like *Colemanballs*, a collection of media inanities initiated by reader W Sadler, available in regular editions from 1975.

By the start of the 1980s, the magazine's literary sideline was ticking along at a healthy six books per year, most prominently stocking blockbuster *Dear Bill: the Collected Letters of Denis Thatcher* (1980), which spawned a stage show and sold 125,000 copies in total. Distributed by various companies but always organised by the in-house staff, the *Eye's* publishing arm became a solid cottage industry. But other thrusting young satirists took the *Eye* boys' ball and ran with it. The conservative *Eye* team unwittingly found themselves, reluctantly, in the vanguard of a dynamic movement.

Roy Kinnear's fly buttons bring down the cabinet

In a blaze of televisual publicity not seen since the Queen was fitted for a new metal hat, satire arrived at the BBC at 10.50PM on Saturday, 24th November 1962, with a programme that began with a brassy jazz number about the falling price of tea, *That Was the Week That Was*. Rushton and Booker were involved, but the show's figurehead was a Cambridge alumnus whose consummate knack for self-advancement suggested he'd been taking Raphael's *S-Man* at face value.

David Frost was no comic genius, but he was a greasy pole-vaulting champion, playing the success game with tremendous tenacity. According to Rushton, he was often accompanied on his transatlantic travels by a folder marked 'airport quips', containing an A-Z of spontaneous wisecracks with which to greet reporters on arrival. The contrast with the *Eye's* 'gentleman amateur' approach couldn't have been greater.

As the second (and, as it turned out, last) series geared up for transmission in September 1963, a couple of cash-in books were flung Smithswards. *The BBC Book of That Was the Week That Was* sounds authoritative but reads otherwise. Kenneth Adam, Director of Television, scribbles a blandly jovial foreword. ('I think it would be unwise to try to write a witty foreword; the competition later on is too hot!')

The hot competition comes from one George Campney, with a few hundred words of rubberised PR fluff. 'Not to have an opinion about the programme was like not having an opinion about cats, spinach or the government.' The folk behind the most modern show on the box are introduced with the corniest of flippant clichés. Producer Ned Sherrin 'was born in Dorset, where the cider apples grow.' Bernard Levin's interviewees 'must feel a little like batsmen facing Freddie Trueman.' And fans of Frost are treated to 'the five faces of Dave.'

In fairness, the photos do provide a blurry account of Levin's notorious on-screen punch-up, rakishly laid out (unlike the swift-ducking Levin) in the spare style of *Town* with Bauhaus-y typography strewn in between. They're the only reason for paying the five-shilling admission, aside from the thrill of watching the publicity machine undergo the occasional kooky misfire, as when Millicent Martin becomes 'the girl whose voice sounds like a corncrake complaining to its MP about the shortage of nesting boxes.'

True fans of the programme would have shelled out a few shillings more for WH Allen and Sons' *That Was the Week That Was*, a big heavy hardback edited by Frost and Sherrin, and featuring material from most of the writing team including such embryonic luminaries as Dennis Potter, Keith Waterhouse, John Bird and Bernard Levin, along with in-house cartoonist Timothy Birdsall, to whom the book is dedicated after his untimely death that summer.

The bare-bones style of the programme's half-rehearsed skits on bare sets, with studio paraphernalia intentionally on view, is gamely transferred to the book. Frost glowers from the type-free cover, snapped in the middle of the famous sketch where he conducted massed sound effects of modern warfare like a superpower Semprini. Inside, genuine screengrabs from the programme, each of their fuzzy 405 lines glowing proudly, apply a modern sheen to what's otherwise a fairly staid-looking book. One exception to the straight presentation is an elaborate *Reader's Digest* parody, complete with small ads for condensed Bibles, but otherwise it's a *Pick of Punch* for the NW1 set.

Indeed, about half the material is *Punch*-able stuff. Caryl Brahms and others contribute poetry that wouldn't be out of place in a 1940s 'intimate' West End revue. Sketches are represented by scripts, often converted into the 'humorous dialogue' form familiar to *Punch* readers, adorned with cartoons or converted into photo stories (then becoming popular in American satirical magazines like *Help!*) In one of the better ones, Millicent Martin spies on Roy Kinnear's furtive Soho activities: 'Over to *Sun Lover's Paradise* at the Berkeley. Out at 5.30 and over to a Wimpy for a Whippsy and a Wimpy and back to *Naked as Nature Intended.*'

By now satire was more commercial property than social insurrection. Leslie Frewin, publisher and anthologist extraordinaire, dedicated a series of his topical 'Books of Our Time' to a 'homage' of *Private Eye*'s photo-plus-speech-balloon covers. *The Harold Wilson Bunkside Book* (1965) led the charge, putting droll sayings into the pipe-smoking premier's mouth. Then came *The Big Ben Bunkside Book* (1966) (sample gag – Wilson: 'Can't stop – my chauffeur's working to rule!'); *The De Gaulle Seineside Book* (1968) by 'Jean Bidet' ('Can't you take "non" for an answer?'); *The Ted Heath Bunkside Book* (1971) ('Thinks: Good grief, not Barbara Castle in hot pants?'); *The Snowdon Slideside Book; The Prince Philip Throneside Book...* you get the idea. In three short years the sights had lowered from skewering the government's defence plans to giving Uncle Alan a small chuckle on Boxing Day morning. The buck was the only thing that didn't stop here.

Even the pioneers weren't above a knock-off. *David Frost Prescribes How to Live Under Labour – or at Least Have as Much Chance as Anyone Else*, a 10/6 Heinemann paperback, appeared in November 1964, a mere four weeks after the Labour election victory seemed to have nailed the satire boom's coffin lid firmly shut. Frost gurns from the cover as Harold Wilson, complete with Gannex raincoat, unlit pipe and bottle of HP sauce. Inside Booker and future Labour MP Gerald Kaufman assist him with a parody manual for disillusioned Tories run to ground by the new regime. 'Life in Tory Britain: Everything on HP. Life in Labour Britain: HP on everything.'

There's a self-aware dig at the impending fizzle of the satire boom with a note for insurgent conservatives to avoid watching TW3's underpowered sequel, *Not So Much a Programme, More a Way of Life*. 'There's no room for that kind of destructive malice any more.' There was still room of course, but as with previous satire booms – the early years of *Punch*, for instance – acceptance and dilution were inevitable and swift. Nobody thought much of this particular effort, though.The *Guardian* surmised: 'Mr Frost is once more trying to put over, in print, the sort of humourless, laughless nonsense that he specializes in on television… the rest of the book is on the same level, if you can call it a level.' From university quad to prime time BBC1 to Christmas stocking reject before they'd even opened the Post Office Tower. Shurely shome mishtake?

13

SMASHING TOMES

With satire having routed government complacency and social injustice forever (citation needed), time to celebrate with a spot of decadence. A city enlivened by a mass influx of rubberneckers from all over the world, London was the town where everything swung (with the possible exception, due to tourist overcrowding, of cats). Straight-faced guidebooks were no longer what the turned-on crowd required to get about. Something hip was needed, and fast.

But to go Mod we must first dip back into the past. Ned Ward's *London Spy* appeared in 18 monthly parts from November 1698 to May 1700. There had been literary tours of the capital before, but the incorrigible Ward broke the mould in chatty style, imbibing plenty of ale and 'stately Cheshire Cheese' as he perambulated about the town. There are serious episodes, most notably a grim tour of Bedlam, but the general tone is detached amusement verging on disdain. A young fop with 'a Wheel-Barrow full of Periwig... stunk as strong of Orange-Flower-Water as a Spaniard does of Garlick.' On the wild side, 'the Night-Accidents, the Whims and Frolicks of Staggering Bravadoes and Strolling Strumpets' are documented with worldly disapproval.

No activity slips beneath Ward's earthy gaze. Covering the Lord Mayor's annual precession, Ward is less interested in the parade itself than the activities of the bored crowd waiting along Cheapside for the carriages to pass, who amuse themselves by filling a blacksmith's apron with shit and lobbing it at some women. He puts himself at the centre of the action, making the events as much as reporting them. In a coffee house, he takes against 'a very Gaudy Crowd of Odoriferous Tom-Essences' and smokes them out of the place with tobacco pipes. The most unreliable of guides perhaps, but Ward's is a livelier picture of late 17th-century London than any other, and the collected *Spy* was a library staple for centuries to come.

Ward pioneered the author-centric tour guide, paving the way for whimsical wanders such as Pierce Egan's *Real Life In London: Or, The Rambles And Adventures Of Bob Tallyho, Esq., And His Cousin, The Hon. Tom Dashall, Through The Metropolis* (1821) and *Bill Adams in the North; or, Doing the Trossachs Without Leaving Your Own Drawing-room* (1892), right up to today's blockbusting efforts of Bill Bryson and his numerous imitators.

But back to the sixties, and *The New London Spy* (1966), publisher Anthony Blond's attempt to rewrite the 'merry jaunt' gazetteer for the Carnaby generation. Editor Hunter Davies split the task of cataloguing 'the pleasures of London' between a team of trusted experts. Meanwhile, an author usually preoccupied with spies of a different stripe, Len Deighton, did the same mere months later, in *Len Deighton's London Dossier* (1967), an even groovier-looking slice of insider knowledge from which Twiggy peered out through a peek-a-boo keyhole cover.

The two volumes have many similarities, beginning with Jane Wilson, who wrote for both. She's best in the *Dossier*, waxing wry on the vexed subject of the capital's Mod community. ('Mods don't go to bistros, they prefer the Golden Egg type of restaurant. Wherever you see gigantic orange light fittings and décor that looks like one huge fruit machine, you will know that the Mods are inside eating square meals in round buns.') Things explode into living Technicolor on Carnaby Street. 'It's PVC Bermuda shorts one week, and Hebridean tweed culottes the next... Boys try on trousers two inches too tight from every angle in merry little pink and orange pagodas... there is only the occasional pair of two-tone trousers (mauve at the front and pea-green at the back).'

Both books act nonplussed at the thrusting new culture, rather than apprehensive. Fleet Street may have been busy whipping up fear of the youth explosion, but these books are for the outsider who fancies himself as an insider: it's one eyebrow raised in quizzical amusement, not two in outright panic. This detachment also works in the other direction. *Spy* laments the poor reception still afforded to London's women, warning them against entering pubs alone ('no-one will believe that you have just dropped in for a pint of mild') or wandering about Soho 'at any time of the day or night with an available expression on your face'. By dipping a tentative toe into the zeitgeist rather than jumping in with both feet, they spot areas where the water's still running cold.

But lapses into journalese are never far away. The tone often sounds forced, like Rank's *Look at Life* cinema newsreels. ('At six o'clock in the morning, the Billingsgate bell goes clang!' 'A lot of bus conductors are Jamaicans, and very sunny fellows they are.') Sometimes the topics aren't quite swinging enough. ('Shove ha'penny is hardly a game poised on a razor's edge of sin and depravity, but you may learn something.') Sometimes they're all too contentious. *Dossier* referred to the cheapo Rowton Hotels as 'grim places, echoing with the cries and coughs of defeated men.' Unfortunately Rowton's chairman also happened to be a QC, and took Deighton and his publishers to the cleaners.

The underworld is a huge voyeuristic draw. In *Dossier*, Eric Clark gives expert advice on penetrating the small back rooms of Soho porn shops ('Try wearing spectacles; managers do not expect to see policemen in glasses'). *Spy* goes even further, delving deep into prostitution. ('Avoid like the plague the bedroom with a wardrobe large enough to conceal a ponce waiting to nip out and grab the wallet the moment the trousers are laid aside.')

If these books seem arch now, they were considered arch even then. The *Observer* ran them head-to-head, giving Deighton's collection (considered smart, but seldom 'unbearably so') the nod over *Spy*, which was 'snobbish and self-congratulatory, and the poor quality paper won't stand up to much thumbing'. Useless now as guidebooks to London, they remain valuable as guidebooks to the past, giving a vivid sense of a time full of contradictions, opportunities and Chips with Everything, where camp was king, pubs were manly, and the Savoy bar still did free cheese footballs.

Paint it black (two coats, one afternoon)

Books from within the social revolution were harder to come by in the High Street. America produced anarchic nosegays such as Abbie Hoffman's Yippie bible *Steal This Book* and William Powell's bomb-making, banana-smoking gazetteer *The Anarchist Cookbook* (both 1971). Europe gave rise to the odd controversial tome, such as Danish free love primer *The Little Red Schoolbook* (1969), but when turned-on Brits slipped between the covers, the results were slightly more down to Earth.

Nicholas Saunders was an academic dropout who monitored the country's alternative culture from his modified flat in Edith Grove, where he slept in a papier-mâché cave and gathered information from the assorted heads who'd drop in to feed the ducks or just stare at the bubble machine. This he corralled into a self-published bestseller, *Alternative London* (1970), whose groovy cover belies a practical turn of mind. Much of this book wouldn't be out of place in a consumer guide, or DIY manual. There's a page about Rawlplugs, for instance. Well, squats won't build themselves. Saunders makes a survey of the Big Three supermarkets (Sainsbury's, Safeway and MacFisheries) and finds them largely wanting, although he wholeheartedly recommends Safeway's Hungarian jam ('the communist countries excel at jam, if nothing else.') The golden rule, as ever, is don't be afraid to complain. ('When I last complained about my pork pie being clammy, a straw-hatted Wall's representative came round with a giant fresh one.')

Humdrum basics dealt with, alternative life can begin. Saunders takes in the counterculture in all its mad forms. Political organisations are listed without prejudice: Anarchists, Communists, the Black Panthers and ARSE (Architects Revolutionary Socialist Enclave) all getting equal billing. Communes are recommended, from the forty-strong Eel Pie Island set-up to the Chapel of Isis – four non-violent transsexual anarchists in a flat with a black and white telly. For six shillings, the greenhorn hippie could do a lot worse. 1972's bright pink third edition expanded into chapters on DIY divorce and India overland trekking. Saunders thanked his many contributors with a slap-up Sunday lunch of organic risotto and apple juice.

In 1975 he toured the country in a battered Transit van for *Alternative England and Wales,* celebrating the thriving alternative press of Rochdale but finding little worth mentioning in Liverpool. The enterprise came to an end shortly after an inattentive meditator let a candle gut the Edith Grove Shangri-La, and Saunders upped sticks to Neal's Yard to inaugurate the wholefood movement.

One of the few countercultural artifacts Saunders feels compelled to shout down is *Oz* magazine. ('There's sex and more sex of an aggressive nature. The word "liberation" is bandied around quite a bit while they express their cramped ideas about how to live.') Richard Neville, prime mover behind the candy-coloured outrage rag, made his own attempt to bring the counterculture to the straight world with *Playpower* (1970), a stream-of-sub-consciousness ramble in which paragraphs overtake pages and sentences overtake paragraphs – all the better to satisfy the hemp-shrunk attention spans of the turned-on.

There's a whirlwind tour of pop from Bill Haley to The Who,

and an exhaustive run-through of the international underground press. Here's the *Berkeley Barb*'s agony column: 'Dear Dr Schoenfeld, a couple of weeks ago me and my girlfriend got loaded and we were making love... What she did was to stretch my scrotum out tightly, then she took a pair of finger nail scissors and cut a small hole in the sac... Next she stuck a small plastic straw into the hole in the sac and started blowing air into it... My sac got bigger than a baseball, but surprisingly didn't hurt much and felt kind of good... What I want to know is could this practice cause me any harm?' The good doctor's answer: 'Yes'.

The counterculture's attitudes to race and gender were an improvement on straight society, but it was still primarily a man's game. The Hell's Angels and the Black Panthers hold no fear for Neville (or if they do, he diplomatically keeps shtum about it) but militant feminist organisations such as SCUM (Society for Cutting up Men) and WITCH (Women's International Terrorist Conspiracy from Hell) induce a verbal crossing of legs. Germaine Greer, at the time holed up in Cambridge hammering out *The Female Eunuch* on a battered typewriter, is quoted purely as a groupie, getting hot flushes over the sight of Simon Dupree's sweaty underpants at the BBC. When the exclusive press area at the front of the crowd for the Stones' Hyde Park Concert gets crowded, the girls are the first to be ejected by force. ('There isn't enough room for everyone, so chicks will have to leave... Angels, get rid of them.') Perhaps the denizens of the squat had more in common with the blokes in those woman-wary pubs than they cared to admit.

14

'THAT REMINDS ME...'

Autobiography lies beyond this book's scope. Boasting a proper narrative, it demands attention spans longer than our admission rules allow. Fortunately it's the anecdote to the rescue, whittling the big events of a star's life down to little chunks that, after countless interviews, after-dinner engagements and afternoons at the Garrick, become honed enough for their curator to bung down in a book. The traditional biography turned into something bitty and superficial enough to be considered for the toilet round about the publication of David Niven's *The Moon's a Balloon* (1972). In Niven's nostalgic chamber pieces, the genteel purr of the narrator is accompanied by the clangorous percussion of several hundred carelessly dropped names.

Better yet, do the rounds of your celebrity muckers, prod them for a wry story each, and tally the results in a clubbable compendium. *Howlers* compiler Cecil Hunt took to the circuit for *Fun with the Famous* (1929), setting the format in stone. A mixture of backstage informality and due reverence reigned. *Pass The Port: The Best After-Dinner Stories of the Famous* (1976) may have boasted that its pages let 'an archbishop rub shoulders with a football star, a comedian take precedence over a judge', but it still pulled out all the stops for a foreword from Prince Philip. Similarly, *Stories Out of School* (1986), a Save the Children fundraiser sponsored by a leading school dinner firm, may have broken showbiz boundaries by pairing Arthur Marshall and

Alvin Stardust as the intrepid duo charged with wresting scholastic reminiscences from everyone from Thatcher to Lulu, but caps were still doffed for Princess Anne to top things off with her own contribution (livening up school barn dances by inventing 'the Paul Jones', whatever that was). Rank could be relaxed, but not pulled.

Actors are a primary source of anecdotes, and countless volumes replicate the conviviality of a post-triumph dressing room. Donald Sinden's *Everyman Book of Theatrical Anecdotes* (1987) and *Ned Sherrin in His Anecdotage* (1993) are hot water bottles in paperback. The next logical step is to write about anecdotage itself. Richard Briers pursued this line of thought in *Natter Natter* (1981), a paean to the art of polite conversation written in the cosy manner you'd expect, and then some. Slipping between its pages is like drinking a mug of Radox after a long Horlicks bath, right from the very opening sentence. 'If you're sitting comfortably, then I'm delighted.'

The Origin of the Speeches

Literary appetite for the words of the famous was stoked by television from the off. *What's My Line?*, the BBC's imported vocational parlour game which began in 1951, created Britain's first national star in Gilbert Harding. Looking less like Hollywood material than an especially browned-off Surrey stockbroker, Harding stole the rather bland game show with a bracing line in rudeness unheard of in broadcasting. Within days of telling a contestant he was 'tired' of looking at him, Harding hit the headlines, and stayed there.

By 1953 his fame demanded literary support. *Along My Line* was a standard memoir, but it was accompanied by a slim stocking filler, *The Gilbert Harding Treasury of Insult*, an anthology of barbed quotations ranging from Charles I to Billy Bunter, collated by 'the rudest man in Britain... an angry man clad in a shining armour of virtuous rage... Harding the actor thunders against the *poseur*… Harding the journalist sears the pages of the whimsy magazines, and remembers with delight only his Swift, Shaw and Johnson.' To boost the brand further, this 'highly amusing and highly infuriating gift book' was masterminded by the newly formed Gilbert Harding (Exploitation) Ltd.

After a discreet break Harding reversed the charges with *Gilbert Harding's Book of Manners* (1956), a canny attempt to recast the irascible wine-bibber as a defender of old British etiquette, though that crowd-pleasing brusqueness is never far away.

> When I asked my mother why my penis was different from that of the boy with whom I had been swimming, she told me about circumcision and what it meant. If that shakes you, Mrs Addlepate of The Firs, Bloxham-on-Thames, then take this book back to the library now.

Harding had found his niche – respectably blunt, arrogantly proper, shaking up middle class living rooms just enough for that frisson of moral outrage, without troubling the fabric of society. Next came *Master of None* (1958), another *What's My Line?* tie-in which revisited – even repeated – much of his auto-biography, this time jumbled up with random musings on an assortment of jobs. By his own admission, this work was largely dictated and written up by hands unseen, and Harding was increasingly disillusioned with his shallow achievements. 'The big question-mark that hangs over my future is not "How much longer will the public stand me?" but "Just how much longer will I be able to stand *you*?"'

The answer wasn't long in coming. Harding's chronic asthma and increasing alcoholism, exacerbated by his clandestine homo-sexuality (something he could never be frank about with the Bloxham-on-Thames set) wore him down. Surprising, then, to see *A Book of Happiness* (1959), an anthology of uplifting literary snippets hosted by Harding 'in his mellowest mood'. The irony of this cuttings job became apparent the following year, when John Freeman's terse interview programme *Face to Face* saw Harding burst into tears on camera, confessing to his overwhelming despair. A few weeks later, he succumbed to an asthma attack on the steps of Broadcasting House.

As a test pilot for national celebrity Harding crashed spectacularly, but the anecdote gift book had taken wing. Robert Morley, not a man to share a sleeping compartment with at the quietest of times, leaped into the market with both feet with *The Book of Bricks* (1978). A walking *faux pas* in a velvet waistcoat, Morley encouraged his fellow stars to contribute memorable social gaffes. The contents page groans with toilet book perennials: Frank Muir, Denis Norden, Bill Tidy, Miles Kington, Jilly Cooper, Clement Freud, and publisher George Weidenfeld. A more straightforward bit of comedy, *The Book of Worries* (1980), turned up among the sequels.

Diana Rigg similarly passed the hat round when compiling *No Turn Unstoned: the Worst Ever Theatrical Reviews* (1982), but also supplied a scholarly survey of the bad review in history, tracing it back to 650BC, when Thespis's invention of the humorous impersonation was crapped on by Solon the Lawgiver. But in the wake of *Heroic Failures*, anecdotes were turning calamitous all over the place. Gyles Brandreth's *Great Theatrical Disasters* (1982) was followed by maverick author Willie Donaldson's shameless *Great Disasters of the Stage* (1984). Alongside fulsome accounts of his own hopeless outings as West End impresario, Donaldson cribs unapologetically from other books ('What seem to me to be the most amusing bits of this book have been lifted clean as a whistle and without so much as a by your leave from Christopher Logue's *True Stories*'). At the end the mask slips, as Donaldson can't resist signing off without slagging off his fellow anecdotalists: witness 'The Most Unsuccessful Theatrical Anecdote in a Memoir by Peter Ustinov', and the Brandreth-baiting 'Most Disastrous Use of the Word "Inimitable" in a Book of Theatrical Anecdotes'.

Wits' academy

Sometimes, though, these damned anecdotes can't half drag on. Some of them run for an entire page! Time to cut back the chaff even more, and remould the epigram in the image of the celebrity. The epigram's revival centred on John F Kennedy, who gathered quips contributed by his staff in a handy folder marked 'HUMOR', a PR tip noted by David Frost. In the wake of Kennedy's assassination, *The Kennedy Wit* (1964) sold 120,000 copies. Not so remarkable, perhaps – anything to do with JFK flew off the shelves in America that year. But when Leslie Frewin published a British edition for the first anniversary of the shooting, it sold out in ten days, and a new genre was born.

Frewin's *The Wit of Sir Winston* was a similar hit, and so, allowing for seasonal adjustments, were *The Wit of Oscar Wilde, The Wit of Peter Ustinov, The Wit of Prince Philip, The Wit of Harold Wilson, The Wit of Women* and *The Wit of the Jews*. Malcolm Muggeridge scrutinised the first batch of Frewin's collections, and found no discernable stylistic differences between the wits of JFK and the Duke of Edinburgh. Worse still, Muggeridge noted 'the peculiar sort of laughter which greets such utterances, shaking the shoulders and straining the face into a distended, mirthless grin! Rolling helplessly from side to side, slapping the thigh, and then a sudden cutout to give the next quip, looming up relentlessly in the distance, time to come in and make its impact'. These were books for star-struck sycophants, Muggeridge claimed, a cheap way of feeling closer to the great and good by memorizing a few of their zingers.

Kenneth Williams agreed, but was more forgiving. 'The nice thing about quotes is that they give us a nodding acquaintance with the originator which is often socially impressive,' he notes in the introduction to *Acid Drops* (1980), a collection of theatrical bitchery compiled with the help of Gyles Brandreth and ranked alphabetically from Acrimony to Zany. Leonard

Rossiter followed suit with *The Lowest Form Of Wit* (1981), 'a treasury of biting *bon mots* and stinging retorts... the definitive guide to the kind of wit that may be the lowest, but also the most *satisfying.*' Adding sauce to the genre, Richard Hugget knocked out *The Wit and Humour of Sex: A Treasury of Filthy-Funny Jokes (*1975), which opened with that giveaway mock-deprecating account of a meeting with the publisher: '"It'll do well at Christmas," I said hopefully. "These books always do."'

No-nonsense Barnsley boy Michael Parkinson found even the 'wit and wisdom' format a flabby extravagance, and explored new realms of utilitarianism with the Spartan *Michael Parkinson's Confession Album* (1973). The premise: Parky compiles desultory list of dull questions. Parky posts it off to assorted celebrity mates. Mates fill them in, and post them back. Parky swaps filled-in forms for large publisher's cheque. But this isn't just anyone doing it, so you'd expect the questions to be something rather special. And, indeed, they are...

> Favourite Colour. (Lord Longford: 'Mauve'.)
> Favourite Amusement. (Mary Quant: 'Sex'.)
> Favourite Qualities in Men. (David Niven: 'Courage'.)
> Favourite Qualities in Women. (Kenneth More: 'Lack of scholarship and cooking'.)
> Favourite Flower. (Eric Morecambe: 'Lionel Blair'.)
> Favorite Author. (Ernie Wise: 'Me'.)
> Present State of Mind. (Spike Milligan: 'Utter confusion'.)
> Greatest Happiness. (John Betjeman: 'Looking at churches'.)
> Greatest Misery. (Patrick Moore: 'Eating beetroot'.)

Some celebs act clever – John Lennon answers 'Yoko' to every other question, Jimmy Savile scrawls 'I am a machine with no favourite anything' – but Parky's thought of that, providing several blank forms at the back of the book for readers to fill in themselves to redress the imbalance created by grumpy old

Bernard Levin, who responded: 'Dear Michael, Many thanks, but I'd rather be dead.'

Top drawers

Its pages may bulge with wit and bonhomie, but a gift book won't shift from the shelves unless it catches the punter's eye. For decades, the big name cartoonist provided the eye-catching décor, influencing the development of the gift book immeasurably, in some cases more than any writer.

Before the war, things were simple. Humorous books were illustrated by Nicholas Bentley. Except for those that weren't, which went to David Low. Well, it wasn't quite that simple, but soon the field began to open up, and a wealth of new names and styles leapt forth from art schools, magazines and newspapers onto book covers with alarming ferocity. Ignoring, for the sake of space, those who stuck to their own cartoon collections (Giles, Mac, Steve Bell) and those who wrote as much as they drew (Rushton, Monkhouse, Harris) here are some of the most influential post-war pen folk.

Ronald Searle

Though he's best known for illustrating two scholastic literary franchises – *Molesworth* and *St Trinians* – Searle's spindly brand of Victorian dilapidation spread through a plethora of books, mags and ads, ensuring the otherwise sleek post-war British graphic tradition always had a catapult peeking out of its immaculate top pocket. Despite the nostalgic subject matter, Searle's folk were forward-looking, craftily evolving into the optimum physical shape – a gangly colonel curled up in a wing-back chair becomes an agglomeration of tweedy limbs and newspaper corners, while schoolchildren adapt with Darwinian swiftness to the evolutionary challenge of getting a jar of sweets down from a high tuck shop shelf.

Alex Graham

The prolific Glaswegian cut his teeth at the pennywise comic house of DC Thompson, and became a household surname via the canine nice-chapmanship of the *Daily Mail*'s Fred Bassett, but his two-legged creations dotted gift books – often with a golf theme – throughout the '50s and '60s. That era was neatly summed up by Graham's Concorde-nosed, short-back-and-sides suburban everyman, forever glumly removing his hat and mackintosh in apprehension of the minor domestic tragedy about to unfold over his shoulder.

Trog

Do jazz and cartoons mix? Looking at those interminable abstract bebop animations that used to pad out wet afternoons on BBC2, no. Looking at Wally Fawkes, pen-tugging satirist by day and Humphrey Lyttleton's right-hand clarinet by night, yes. His solid lines have covered innumerable books but they're most widely associated with the picaresque adventures of weird hedgehog-pig-thing Flook, the *Daily Mail*'s cartoon homunculus with a penchant for turning into barometers, variously scripted by Humph, George Melly, Barry Norman and Barry Took. Melly and Trog even created an autobiography, *I, Flook*, in 1962.

Martin Honeysett

Honeysett's domestic scenes have a stooped 18th-century queasiness about them, but the look is entirely contemporary – the shabbier end of contemporary, admittedly. In fly-blown front rooms decorated via a joint venture from Laura Ashley and Upton Sinclair, worn-down women in shapeless housecoats and haywire perms confront nervous, lip-biting men who appear to be smuggling a hundredweight of spuds in their trousers. The grotty touches draw you into the page, which, if touched, might give you crabs. In a Honeysett cartoon, the only progress being made is by gravity. His resolutely unsentimental style was perfectly encapsulated in his mockery of the coffee-table nostalgia market, *The Not Another Book of Old Photographs! Book* (1981).

Mel Calman

The much-maligned Calman pared cartooning back to his Zen-like 'little man', a depressed, big nosed and usually balding individual forever on the horns of an existential dilemma. (Either that or he's just not getting any.) Opinion divided between those who felt he livened up countless books and magazines over two decades, and those who deemed it money for old mope. This may have sprung from tales of Calman starting work at *The Times* at 6PM sharp to watch the news, dash off a rough sketch for the front page and lob the half-done result on the editor's desk on the way out half an hour later.

Marc

The dandyish figure of Mark Boxer contained a good dozen people, one of whom was a cartoonist. By day, he was the gregarious editor of the *Times, Tatler* and countless other. By night, he favoured a louche, looping line of ink for the delineation of assorted members of the upper-middle NW1 set, epitomised by his Alan Bennett-inspired couple Simon and Joanna String-Along. This wine bar Matisse was as comfortable on the covers of Miles Kington's *Franglais* books as he was on the front of the *Guardian*. The man's considerable legend is only slightly sullied by the broadly held suspicion he nicked most of his gags from George Melly.

Gerald Scarfe / Ralph Steadman

No slight is meant by unceremoniously bracketing together these two strangers to the ink blotter, but the former alumni of East Ham Tech, though occasionally at professional loggerheads, are forever confused, perhaps because the chasm between their style and everyone else's dwarfs the differences between them. They have a common ancestor, conceived one tumultuous night when Francis Bacon shared a scotch with Ronald Searle, but each refined their butchery in different directions. Scarfe mutilates his subjects along baroque lines, while Steadman's corpses decompose into a less elegant form of fleshy architecture, along the lines of an NCP car park. Steadman spurts where Scarfe squiggles. Simple, really.

Michael Heath

Heath came to prominence in the '60s via *Punch*, contributing masterfully cynical point-by-point guides to Carnaby Street fashion, the brain drain and similar unswinging topics. His emaciated eggheads stumble around a cubist maze of dingy backstreets, acting out painfully contorted diagrams of world-weariness. This spiky angularity and general gloom made him the prime choice for the more introspective Christmas book (Robert Morley ahoy!), and his scratchy ennui-scapes have illustrated works by Jeffrey Bernard, Kingsley Amis and Keith Waterhouse.

Norman Thelwell

A handful of cartoonists stake out their territory so completely the surname is enough to conjure an image. With Thelwell, it's a nervous, stumpy-fetlocked Shetland pony being fearlessly led into adventure by a carefree, cherubic schoolgirl in full riding gear. And though he drew that iconic equine pair (Penelope riding 'Kipper', for the record) for the best part of half a century, he did take in just about every other aspect of human and animal life. 'The unofficial artist of the English countryside' used Constable-ish atmospheric effects as a fine bucolic setting for tales of underage gymkhana meltdown.

Edward McLachlan

Bulbous, curlicued and flared at the ends, MacLachlan's strain of the bemused British public seems positively pneumatic at times, making him the ideal candidate to chronicle the 1970s, that rubberiest of decades. His trademark 'nonplussed mousta-chioed bloke in cap' pondered fruitlessly on the meaning of the wall slogans featured in Gyles Brandreth's *Graffiti* books, while his wistful cartoon *Simon and the Land of Chalk Drawings* brought monochrome daydreaming to a generation of children. Most infamously, his giant hedgehogs and rabbits wreaked terrible revenge on motorists throughout the decade. He's carried on ever since, demonstrating a gift for sublime visual gags that never seems to dull.

Bill Tidy

The Northwest runs through Bill Tidy's work like the boiled egg through a gala pie. Such left-of-Pennine strips as tripe dynasty soap opera *The Fosdyke Saga* and lurid folk-dancing expose *The Cloggies* introduced the rapid-fire draughtsman's amiably daft take on clag-happy parochial foibles to living rooms nationwide, bolstered by a torrent of sketches embellishing other people's publications. The industrious Tidy also ran up a corporate entertainment empire, presented a live cartooning-themed children's TV gameshow, and designed the strange modernist metal spike presented to winners of *It's a Knockout*.

Larry

This list is in no particular order, but if there were to be a victor, then for sheer output and instant recognisability, Terence Parkes would probably walk it. Exhibiting a wobblingly rangy line similar to his colleague Bill Tidy, 'Larry' tore ahead of the competition through a combination of extraordinary industry and indefinable popularity. Larry's main character, the balding everyman with the big nose and the bothered expression as he gazes uneasily at the latest looming wrinkle in life's badly laid stair carpet, went everywhere. From the world of sport (*Colemanballs*) to the groves of philosophy (*How to be a Guru*) Larry's wriggly-outlined salt-of-the-Earth men and women apprehend some strange new aspect of the working day and furrow their brows a bit, but with neither horror or amusement, just another mark added to their mental tally marked 'Hmm.' Perhaps Larry's everyman is the humorist incarnate: Rodin's Toilet Book Author.

15

THE CELEB INTRUSION WILL BE TELEVISED

After Gilbert Harding's premature exit, the TV celebrity colonised the land, evolving new varieties by the day. Two decades on, the manifold species were ripe for analysis. *The Media Mob* (1980) is a collection of star portraits drawn by Barry Fantoni for *The Listener*, augmented with shrewd anthropological annotations by George Melly. Cataloguing what Melly calls 'the aristocracy of the warm cod's eye, the cognoscenti of the idiot box,' Fantoni's solidly shaded monochrome caricatures are distorted yet instantly recognisable faces. Melly's words do the same for their personas, comparing the media bandwagon to a Roman gladiatorial contest where, while 'Simon Dee bleeds to death in the sand, Jimmy Savile parades year after year around the arena in triumph.'

Melly shows a grudging sympathy for Bruce Forsyth, which at the time was as much sympathy as Brucie could expect. He admires Michael Parkinson's professionalism but deplores the 'frightful saloon bar leer' he turns on for young Hollywood actresses. Reginald Bosanquet 'plays Falstaff to [Richard] Baker's Henry IV'. Patrick Moore and Magnus Pyke are TV's 'licensed loonies'. ('I have never read a kindly word about either of them but I doubt it worries them as they lope to the bank.') Melly's final verdict: the Media Mob could do with a lot more people in it like Basil Brush.

Six months before Melly's frontal assault, the fortresses of the stars endured a covert attack from Jonathan Meades. *This is Their Life* (1979) looks, on first inspection, like a collection of chirpily harmless mini-profiles culled from the pages of the *TV Times*. The young drudge saddled with this unpromising commission, however, has other ideas, and warps the cornball format to suit his own subversive ends. Under cover of homely tabloid blandness, he slips in critical curveballs all of his own. Meades dubs David Bellamy 'the Arthur Mullard of natural science'. He notes Michael Barratt's 'characteristic mixture of rude charm, rudeness and gruff, no-nonsense, direct mawkishness' and vouchsafes that 'away from the stage, Pam [Ayres] enjoys cycling, country life and litigation.' Hardly vicious stuff, but in the stiflingly correct world of '70s showbiz journalism, the giddy sense of release was palpable, as when a delinquent choirboy loudly blows off during vespers.

Meades displays a sharp eye for the shockingly incongruous fact. Dickie Davies began his showbiz career clad in the suits of murdered New York gangsters. Hattie Jacques spent World War Two welding bridges. Reginald Bosanquet's dad invented the googly. If John Cleese grows another inch, he will medically qualify as a giant. James Burke lives on hard-boiled eggs. The familiar world of celebrity is revealed as stranger than the reader could ever have imagined. Both these books, along with other contemporary triumphs such as Clive James's *Observer* TV column, wallow in a kind of appalled fascination, a sceptical worship of the freaks and cot cases who have been elevated to television's ramshackle electronic Valhalla, and can do nothing but laugh in horror at the results.

'Price 1 pound 95p, from all good bookshops.'

They may be glaringly absent from the programme itself, but for a paperback TV or radio tie-in, ingenuity and invention are employed by the ton. If you can put it on the TV screen, it seems, you can put it onto the page. The word 'adaptation' is woefully understated for this transfigurative craft, which operates on one of five, increasingly sophisticated, levels:

No-nonsense (1)

At the bottom of the tie-in food chain are books that do what their parent programme says on the credits, like *The Pebble Mill at One Book* (1985), a 'compilation of original and exciting chapters' on cookery, embroidery, renovating old furniture, 'microwave magic' and Bill Oddie in the Seychelles. All very useful and defiantly glamour free, unless you count Paul Coia's giddy showbiz tales of Gene Pitney staining his crotch and Lorraine Chase trilling 'Sorry love, I've got to go to the tinkle house'.

A more self-aware elevation of trivial detail to heroic prose occurs in Paul Heiney's *In at the Deep End* (1986). A phenomenally popular BBC programme featuring Heiney and Chris Serle as hapless laymen given a week to learn the basics of a professional skill, the show owed its success more to its presenters' winning expressions of bemusement in the face of impending disaster than to any lids lifted on the arcane worlds of sheepdog training or haute cuisine. Heiney recasts each of his episodes as miniature novels, each tiny incident conveyed in knowingly tense prose, such as this blow-by-blow account of giving Jilly Cooper a haircut:

> Jilly's hair and I are making music. Two fingers grasp and clench a section of hair with one smooth upwards movement where before a comb and fist would have been called into help, each slice with the scissors is now done with enough flourish to make each cut a balletic movement in itself.

The format loosens up further when the programme's less formal in the first place, as with the 'play along at home' edition of dictionary-derived panel game *Call My Bluff* (1972), a tall, narrow and strange book in which team captains Frank Muir and Patrick Campbell flummox the reader and each other with hoax definitions. As on the TV version, the interest lays not in the words themselves but the players' extra-curricular mucking about. Campbell bemoans

Muir's arch banter. ('We'd better get used to it now. The Muir
BOYISHNESS. Off with the glasses and on with this SAGACIOUS,
QUIZZICAL, OMNISCIENT, ****** [censored] style... on and on and
ON...') Muir quickly gets bored with the game and starts drawing
schoolboyish pictures of hairy legs and bishops falling over. It's all
disgracefully pointless, and really quite magnificent.

Behind the scenes (2)

One step up are the books which 'lift the lid' on your favourite
shows. Radio programmes, despite having fewer scenes to get
behind, benefit from this sort of treatment. John Timpson's *The
Lighter Side of Today* (1983) is whimsical, corny and monumentally
self-indulgent – just how the *Today* programme's listeners like it.
Most interesting for scholars of ephemera are the descriptions of
the dodgy furniture in the *Today* green room, and the clandestine
on-air battles between Timpson and Brian Redhead to sabotage
each other's jealously guarded comedy links.

It's a catalogue of early '80s current affairs effluvia:
palindromes, hedgehog tunnels, people who can talk backwards,
people who can play tunes on their teeth or under their armpits.
('Even more painful was the RAF sergeant who played 'Rule
Britannia' by hitting himself on the head with a nine-inch
spanner.') There are Chinese restaurants with funny names,
irascible vicars, streakers and jokes at the expense of EEC fishery
ministers and the mighty bulk of Cyril Smith MP (who could
always be relied upon to enjoy it).

The insider's guide (3)

Once you've admitted it's all a façade, why not go a stage further
and deconstruct this topsy-turvy business we call show?
Desmond Wilcox and Esther Rantzen are the Woodward and
Bernstein of the off-camera cock-up in *Kill the Chocolate Biscuit: Or,
Behind the Screen* (1981), a book intended 'for the bedside table, the

long journey or even the loo (or are we the only couple in the world that keeps a supply of books in the loo?)'. Des 'n' Est revisit classic moments from *Man Alive* and *That's Life!* Like the time Esther's undercover report on Soho's white slave trade was blown when her audition in front of a Mr Taki Bengali was interrupted by a phone call from her mother! Plus the lowdown on Annie Mizzen, the mad little old lady who tasted sheep's eyes and caviar from Esther's tray on a Fulham street corner every week for what seemed like decades. All anecdotes guaranteed to end with a permutation of: 'we both thought to ourselves, how did we ever get into a lunatic job like this?'

Promising more in the way of 'old pro' analysis, *Tarbuck on Showbiz* (1985) turns out, disappointingly, to be another collection of anecdotes from the gap-toothed feller heavily larded with neatly dropped names. 'One year, Faberge made an advert called Henry Cooper's Christmas Party…' 'The first time I saw Des [O'Connor's] perm was in Tramps one night after I had been doing a Michael Parkinson show.' 'One night Harry [Secombe] broke wind – to put it mildly.' Seven of the tales revolve around Kenny Lynch. More promisingly, Willis Hall and Bob Monkhouse united for *The A to Z of Television* (1971), an alphabetized trawl through the medium's bewildering technical aspects ('Granadaland; subliminal advertising; repeat fees; puppets, glove'). Amongst the gags are bits of proper inside knowledge ('The discriminate use of the cod dry by a skilled farceur is an art worth watching.'); a handy cynic's dictionary of comedian's fallback lines ('"The next line was a beauty but the producer cut it out!" = My scriptwriter couldn't think of a finish for that gag'), and ten cartoons, *apropos* of nothing, involving a pantomime horse. ('See R is for Running Gag.')

'And this is me' (4)

How best to promote a star in book form without penning a proper memoir? Ronnie Corbett went the self-deprecatory route in his *Small Man's Guide… or How to Aspire to Greater Heights* (1976), a rambling discourse on the state of shortarsery pinned together from years' worth of his armchair monologues On the title front, neither Michael Parkinson nor Katie Boyle could resist titling their chummy rambles *Parkinson's Lore* and *Boyle's Lore* respectively (both 1982).

It helps if you've already got a bit of audience interaction going. Take Terry Wogan, whose highly involved two-way radio relationship with the massed ranks of TWITS (the Terry Wogan Is Tops Society) was easy to distil into *Banjaxed: Varicose Utterances by Himself, with Selected Responses from the Listening Audience* (1979). A year's worth of impenetrable in-jokes is strewn across ninety pages. Fighting the Flab, Vitas Gerulaitis, the great 'porridge on the gallop' controversy, Jimmy Young ('Wouldn't it be kinder to have him shot?') and people mishearing 'renewed vigour' as 'a nude vicar'. It's all no doubt hilarious to those who were there, but arcane to the point of stupefaction to those who weren't. Perhaps with this criticism in mind, sequel *The Day Job* (1981) began in typical style. 'There's not a bit of use diving for cover behind the chaise-longue, Hermione, he's got another one out… It's not as if his first effort went well – I know for a fact that he's got 20,000 unsold copies of the thing in his garage.'

'I think the BBC is a load of crap!' The presenter-audience relationship reaches its zenith with Barry Took's *Points of View* (1981). This collection of viewers' letters, many unforgivingly reproduced in facsimile to highlight the author's asylum scrawl, has no reason to exist as a book whatsoever, but carries on doing so undaunted. BBC viewers know what they like. ('When watching last Wednesday's Parkinson Show, I was disgusted to see Dudley Moore playing a Japanese made piano…') They demand perfection. ('My brother and I think *Star Trek* tonight was a waste of time. Grown-ups kissing each other and saying sloppy things ugh it was dreadful please give us more fighting.') But get it right and they'll love you forever, as demonstrated in a verse panegyric to Bazza from GME Wood of Eastbourne:

We are so very proud and fond of you
And your evening programme *Points of View*,
Your image in blue suit and tie of red
Entertains us well before time for bed;
We like your beardless rotund countenance…
… and so on.

Frank Bough's Breakfast Book, 1984 (5)

Out in a category all by itself, this mould-breaking concoction is three books in one, at least. Asked by Weidenfeld and Nicholson to come up with something to celebrate the first year of BBC morning magazine *Breakfast Time*, Bough jumped at the chance. This was no standard fag packet tie-in. Here, after all, was a man whose autobiography ended with the distressing words: 'Tell me, is it too late? What should we all do next?' Frank Bough, as the media were still fortunately yet to prove in graphic terms, didn't do ordinary.

We begin with a potted résumé of Frank's career and those of the *Breakfast Time* team. (Mike Smith 'shows DJs can be cerebral as well as noisy'.) But that's not all. There's also a history of breakfast TV. A history of the breakfast. A sub-history of the British Rail breakfast. A selection of readers' letters. A selection of *Breakfast Time* presenters' recipes, including Selina Scott's Steamed Eggs. A discourse on the revolutionary televisual power of the pullover (Lech Walesa spotted in a diamond-patterned pully in Gdansk – surely no coincidence?) and the sofa ('Ere long, viewers were able to compare Sarah Kennedy's knees with Selina Scott's').

Best of all is a blow-by-blow account of Bough's ideal breakfast, an operation of military precision. ('Two large spoonfuls of coffee into cup. So far so good. Kettle beginning to hum ominously, but toaster still safely at depressed position.') When it all comes together, however, Frank assures us the results can be heavenly, in some of the most disarmingly unselfconscious prose ever published by a British celebrity.

> But what joy to achieve a simultaneous gastronomic orgasm, so that coffee, marmalade, toast and the Daily Mail are started together, closely followed by The Times and the Guardian and the second cup of coffee. The day has started well.

Read the book, buy the toaster

In 1906, Edith Holden, 35-year-old daughter of a prosperous Warwickshire paint manufacturer, decided to keep a nature journal. A dab hand with watercolours, she sketched each season's flowers and birds and made notes on the weather. Nothing remarkable, a hobby many middle-class women indulged in, like sewing a sampler. The diary completed along with the year, it was put away in the loft and forgotten about. In 1920, while gathering chestnut buds at Kew, Holden fell into the Thames and drowned.

And that would have been that, but for Holden's great-niece Rowena Stott, who rediscovered the book in 1975 and smelt publishing gold. She contacted tiny Exeter book packaging firm Webb and Bower. Richard Webb saw promise in the faded yellow sketches surrounded by fat, neat handwriting, and took the diary to a publishing fair in New York. Publishers Michael Joseph came away with the rights, and in June 1977, after much technical wrangling, 75,000 copies of *The Country Diary of an Edwardian Lady* hit the nation's bookshops.

The result was insanity. The run sold out in short order. Another run was printed. These sold out even faster. The *Sunday Times* bestseller list soon had a new champion, which wouldn't be dislodged for the rest of the year (and was still to be seen skulking around the lower regions some two years after that). Christmas 1977 was Edwardian all the way. Tales abounded of stoic grannies smiling ruefully as they unwrapped their seventh copy on

Christmas morning. A million copies were shifted in the UK, 300,000 in the US. German, Swedish and Dutch translations, all painstakingly rendered in Holden's girlish script, were commissioned. There was talk of a Russian edition. The Japanese, predictably, went nuts over it. Rowena Stott bought herself a Porsche.

And then, the merchandising. It was tasteful at first, the publishers not wishing to be seen milking a cash cow. Postcards, gift stationery, calendars, that sort of thing. Oh, and records, tapes, plates and tapestries. Oh, all right, some packets of seeds as well. And a *Country Diary of an Edwardian Lady* cookware set. And a *Country Diary of an Edwardian Lady* kettle. And a *Country Diary of an Edwardian Lady* toaster. When Richard Webb sold the West German jigsaw rights for a four-figure sum, envious jokes were made in the quality press. Victoria Wood claimed to possess a *Country Diary of an Edwardian Lady* bullworker. Stott made a big deal of turning down a *Country Diary of an Edwardian Lady* toilet roll holder, but no one was mollified.

Family attics all over the country were raided for copycat whimsies, such as *Muriel Foster's Fishing Diary* (1980), but the original continued to dominate. By the end of the decade, it had accrued £13 million in gross profits, and garnered the snide title of the most bought, least read book of the 1970s. It could have been pointed out that the 'most bought, least read' book of the 1960s concerned another Edwardian lady – Lady Chatterley – but the derision was total. 'I have seldom, if ever, read a journal so free of any intellectual or emotional response,' sniffed *The Times*. Others questioned the morality of publishing someone else's private diaries in the first place, but no one was listening. Holden's flowers eventually faded back into obscurity, but kept on selling – a hundredth anniversary edition in 2006 enabled a terminally nostalgic populace to go collectively nuts over watercolour lupins once again.

16

'A TRIFFICALLY GOOD BOOK'

By the end of the 1960s, comedy publishing was in a rut. Collected columns from newspapers, *Punch* and *Private Eye* still ticked along, but nothing new was happening in print. Geoffrey Strachan of independent publishers Eyre Methuen was one of the few who noticed the widening gap in the market.

'Between the wars, Methuen had a great tradition of publishing comedy books, from AP Herbert's *Misleading Cases* to *1066 and All That*,' he recalls. 'By the sixties, the paperback rights to these had been hived off to Penguin, and all we had comedy-wise were Ronald Searle cartoon books. I was into revue in university, and I loved radio comedy. I knew the really funny writers in this country weren't writing for *Punch* any more, they were writing for radio and television. I wanted to get people who could write well for performance to write books. It seemed to me the Monty Python team were ideal.'

It was a bold move for a publisher. The first series of *Monty Python's Flying Circus* had been treated shoddily by its progenitor, the BBC: the first series in 1969 was dumped in a regional opt-out slot on Tuesday nights and perennially interrupted by *The Horse of the Year Show*. Despite this, the sheer originality of the programme won out, and a second series in autumn 1970 was both treated with respect by the Beeb and lauded by critics and audiences. Strachan approached the six-strong troupe about a publishing venture early in 1971.

At least half the team – Michael Palin, Terry Jones and

animator Terry Gilliam – was opposed to the idea of spin-offs. In Palin's words, 'Python is a half-hour TV show and cannot easily be anything else.' However, with record and film deals also on the table, ideology gave way to practicality, and Python Productions Ltd was formed to oversee the team's growing comedy empire. Strachan's motives were eventually judged to be above board. 'The Pythons were not unknown of course, but it was never the idea just to do a tie-in to a successful show for the money – I'm a terrible cultural snob! The English have as great a genius for comedy as they have for tragedy or drama. Whether you're looking at *Three Men in a Boat* or *Python*, there's a rich tradition of verbal humour that's consistently undervalued. It's this I wanted to get down in print.'

What form *Python* would take in print was unclear. 'I wanted something that would stand alone as a book,' insists Strachan. 'A book of scripts and photos was not what we wanted. Scripts are very hard to read. In some ways comedy scripts are harder to read than serious drama.' In the absence of much interest from the rest of the team, Eric Idle took on the role of editor. His proposal happened to suit Methuen perfectly. Strachan recalls, 'they wanted to do a large format book, a kind of skit on a children's annual. And we had quite a lot of experience in producing large format children's illustrated books.

'Then it was really a question of getting down to brass tacks. We budgeted for 30,000 copies and 64 pages, and we were aiming for a low price of £1.50. We said, "this is the print run, this is the budget and this is what you can spend it on. You can have 8 pages of full colour and the rest in two colours or 16 full colour, 12 two colour and the rest black and white".' Inevitably, the Pythons queered the budgeting pitch. 'They wanted to have a hole in one page. [A keyhole through which could be viewed a Gilliam-created topless hermaphrodite police constable.] We said, "OK, you can do that, but that's handwork, that's expensive. That means six fewer pages of colour".[11] We were as straight as could be with each other. They didn't want any publisher's bullshit. We worked on it together. It was a learning experience for me as much as them.'

By May, Idle, relishing the 'sleeves rolled-up' design aspect, was stuck into *Monty Python's Big Red Book* (the cover was, naturally, blue). As designer, he picked Derek Birdsall, whose impressive portfolio spanned Penguin books, Pirelli calendars and *Town* magazine. Birdsall worked as overseer and 'design guru', the detail being taken care of by Katy Hepburn, Royal College of Art student, *Spare Rib* magazine illustrator, sister-in-law to Terry Jones and assistant to Terry Gilliam.

'I was working on the television animation before the book,' she relates. 'It was extraordinary at my age to be involved with *Python*, but a lot of work: four minutes of animation a week meant plugging away all night. It was a steep learning curve. I was on my own quite a lot to get artwork prepared, blacking edges so they didn't show under the camera. When it came to the book, Terry Gilliam was too distracted by the animation to become involved. Also, he'd worked a lot in magazines before and had broken off from that. The story arose that I was sent to his house to steal artwork for the book, which was a slight exaggeration!'

As with the programme, parody was key to the book's visual style. 'Sketches like The Piranha Brothers were done as skits on television presentation,' says Strachan. 'Eric's idea was to transfer these spoofs into print.' Book and magazine parodies filled the pages, four of them, containing a *Radio Times* feature on the Upper Class Twit of the Year Show, printed on authentically smudgy newsprint.

Katy Hepburn took charge of the specifics. 'Every sketch is different. If you've got a magazine spoof, you've got to make that look like the magazine. It's like having the right costume in a sketch. Some parts are a bit compromised. The Batley Townswomen's Guild was meant to look like a poster, but it's more half-and-half. If you're trying to make a layout look mediocre it should be clearly dull. The greater the pastiche, the greater the joke. I was obsessive in the detail, and so were the

Pythons. That's what it was all about.'

Pinned up on the cork wall of Birdsall's kitchen, the finished pages of camera-ready artwork finally became a book – uncomfortably late – in mid-November. 'Nobody knew how it was going to do,' says Strachan. 'We serialised it in the *Observer* colour supplement the day before publication – four pages, like a teaser advert, only they paid us! There were queues outside bookshops on Monday morning. The initial run sold out very quickly, so we ordered another 20,000, which we just about managed to get in a week before Christmas.'

As with the TV series, there was professional resistance. 'Some of the sales reps hated it,' Strachan recalls. 'When it came to a paperback version, they said, "Don't throw good money after bad," but I didn't listen.' The crunch came with the paperback's cover, bearing the legend 'special hardback edition'. Marketing director Michael Turner expressed his concern: 'Please don't confuse the book trade.' Idle responded: 'We've got the usual competition between salesmanship and a joke… and the stupidity potential of your booksellers should be overcome in some other manner. You could easily get printed a series of warnings for them that "THIS IS A JOKE".' Provided they can read of course.'

'Don't read it. You'll love it.'

On February 9th 1973, Methuen celebrated sales of 100,000 paperbacks with lunch at Rules restaurant. Over sugar Gumbies and chocolate Spiny Norman hedgehogs, plans were hatched for a second book. Like the second *Python* series, this would have more money and support, and with the rest of the team significantly keener to contribute, *The Brand New Monty Python Bok* (1973) was altogether more ambitious.

Katy Hepburn was this time fully in charge, moving from Birdsall's kitchen to a cavernous spare office in Methuen's New Fetter Lane headquarters. 'It was this mad, huge room which became the Python studio,' she recalls. 'That was a great big space to lay the pages out. It happened thick and fast. The thing was carried off in the end by the amount of hard work.'

The *Bok* featured two inserted miniature pamphlets, some new Gilliam cartoon strips, a pasted-in school library sticker and a mock airline safety card. The varied paper stocks were out, due to a paper shortage. Sex, however, was in. An erotic Biggles adventure, a Gilliam-designed sex aid catalogue and a startling appearance by Graham Chapman promoting 'The Right to Mast' pushed the risqué content further than ever. A clearly worried Palin noted, 'I was relieved that the vast amount of sexual content in the writing was arranged so that the book didn't appear totally one-track minded.'

Once again, the cover baited the book trade. The stark black-and-white dust jacket came complete with grubby fingerprints, supposedly from being fingered by one of Gilliam's raincoat-clad flashers. Booksellers sent them back, only to receive more soiled copies by return of post. Shops refused to display the items, but the option of displaying them without the dust jackets was thwarted by the inner cover: a parade of vintage nudes under the title 'Tits 'n' Bums: a Weekly Look at Church Architecture'.

Potential obscenity and libel charges were keenly anticipated. Letters flew between lawyers for Methuen, the book's printers and the Pythons, full of wonderfully deadpan concerns worthy of the *Bok* itself. ('Pages 63, 67 and 90: References to Mr Des O'Connor which, taken together, might be seen to attack his morality... The article entitled "How to Become a Segas Employee" worries us a little, mostly because we do not know what it is supposed to mean.') The Pythons' solicitor injected a note of sanity, pointing out that the book was clearly parodic, and regarding obscenity charges, social attitudes had moved on: 'Bare breasts have been overtaken by pubic hair'. With only one alteration (the word 'penis' removed), the *Bok* went on sale on November 1st with advance orders of over 105,000, and took off from there, with only one customer sufficiently outraged to return his copy to

Methuen bearing the scrawled legend: 'UNFIT FOR HUMAN CONSUMPTION'.

Sales may have been astronomical, but reviews were sparse. Clive James gave the thumbs up in the *Observer*, but otherwise the press felt the *Python* books beneath their consideration. But by being so original, and so popular, they couldn't fail to set the benchmark for comedy tie-in books for the next two decades. Eric Idle may have exaggerated when he claimed that *Python* 'invented the Christmas book market,' but it certainly gave it a new, and unbeatably silly, lease of life.

'Kids' book!'

The *Python* books' success opened up new commercial avenues for TV comedy merchandise, accompanying the customary LP of songs and sketches. Next came *The Goodies*, a demented pseudo-sitcom starring *Python* contemporaries Graeme Garden, Bill Oddie and Tim Brooke-Taylor. A wafer-thin premise – the three ran an odd-job agency offering to do 'anything, anywhere, any time' – allowed all manner of madness to be shoehorned into each episode, with a heavy emphasis on visual comedy and elaborate special effects. Popular memory has bracketed the show as 'kids' *Python*', recalling the giant kittens and forgetting the black humour of many episodes such as the dark (yet still manic) *Earthanasia*.

A *Goodies* book would inevitably be tarred with the same 'little brother' brush, but this was no bandwagon jumping. 'I think the main influence was the development of printing technology around that time,' says Graeme Garden. 'Magazines like *Oz* and books printed in all manner of styles on high quality paper in full colour. Comedic influences ranged from *Punch* to the *Beano*. I had been art editor of a Cambridge student humour magazine called *ffobia*, and we'd already done some parodies there. I got Bill to draw some little cartoons for it.'

Their first publishing excursion didn't augur well. 'We had a

Goodies Annual produced in 1973 by World Distributors, who did comic annuals,' Garden recalls. 'It was a cheap spin off: coarse paper, limited colour, low concept and an embarrassment, really. We had virtually no input, and it was the naffness of this that provoked us into finding a proper publisher, Weidenfeld and Nicolson.'

The Goodies File (1974) was a collection of spoof brochures, magazines, legal documents and backs of fag packets loosely linked by the story of the team's cleaner Edna Tole (Mrs) attempting to slander their good name in return for a million pound advance from W&N. This storyline, though it arose almost by accident, gave things the feel of an extended *Goodies* episode. Garden notes: 'For TV, Bill and I would write half the script each, but we all three collaborated on the books. They were much more complex, and the technical demands were very different. Instead of working out action sequences, the visual input was on the page. We were very involved with the look of the books.'

Entrusted with the visual side was designer Anthony Cohen, working with the team as closely as the BBC special effects department did on the series. 'I would have regular meetings, at least once a week, to show them illustrations and photos that I had commissioned and rough layouts of the pages as they shaped up,' he remembers. 'They were difficult to deconstruct if there were any corrections – many of them relied on skilled airbrushing by a remarkably talented craftsman called Dennis Hawkins – so I usually showed fairly accurate roughs before committing to final artwork. The Goodies were intimately involved with the visuals, including scripting the photo shoots and vetoing artwork.'

Among Cohen's tasks were the creation of an authentically gaudy 'home-made' Goodies brochure (published by Tatty and Cheap, 'prunters'), an emetically cute 'Things to Do' children's book, and illustrations of the trio's trandem cycle by Da Vinci and Picasso. 'Both Bill and Graeme are visually creative and contributed sketches and, in Graeme's case, accomplished paintings or illustrations.' The variety of these effects – there's a drastic change of style every other page – meant a great deal of design work. 'Anthony was very patient and tolerant,' says Garden. 'He found ways to do most of the things we wanted, and he used our own artwork and made it look good!'

The polished result sold plenty, paving the way for two more, *The Goodies' Book of (Criminal) Records* (1975) and *The Making of the Goodies' Disaster Movie* (1977), for which the bar was raised. 'The first book was fairly basic but very successful in publishing terms,' confirms Cohen. 'As a result, the budget for the subsequent two books was generous, and I was able to commission whatever was required to get the effect we wanted. This sort of book relied on variety, so many different artists and photographers were involved; it certainly wasn't cheap, but the publishers realised the extra expense would be worth it.'

Accuracy was important when it came to visual pastiche, says Cohen. 'The mock "Carry On Christ" poster that appeared in the third book was produced (at considerable expense!) by Arnaldo Putzu, an artist who did the original *Carry On* film posters, and the Baden Powell scouting illustrations were drawn by Arthur Ranson, a leading comic illustrator with a very good eye for that style of drawing.' This combination of off-the-wall variety and on-the-nose visual likeness defined the TV comedy book at its best.

'Special washable edition!'

The Pythons had split by 1974, but the books kept coming. *Bert Fegg's Nasty Book for Boys and Girls* was – seemingly – a children's cyclopaedia edited by the dubious, bloodthirsty Dr Bert Fegg. The cover sticker gave things away: 'A Monty Python Educational Product'. So, if you were shopping at WH Smith's in Kensington High Street shortly before Christmas, did the sight of Michael Palin self-consciously counting unsold copies.

Palin and Terry Jones's first post-*Python* book for Methuen was a melange of subverted adventure stories, spot the difference competitions and diagrams of the West Bromley fighting haddock, a woozy tribute to the respectable, character-building *Look and Learn* literature of their youth. 'And,' as the cover blurb insisted, 'Eyre Methuen say "pooh!" to those who allege that the *Nasty Book* is nothing more or less than a collection of Terry Jones and Michael Palin's old scripts. "Pooh!"'

Not to be mistakenly filed in the children's section was *The Rutland Dirty Weekend Book* (1976), a spin-off from Eric Idle's ITV series *Rutland Weekend Television*, which presented the shoestring programming of the country's smallest ITV region. The idea behind the TV series was both elegantly simple and accountant-mollifyingly cheap. The book, however, was anything but.

Derek Birdsall once again oversaw the technical side, with Anthony Cohen as art director. The *Bok*'s false cover gimmick was revisited and reversed – this time, a risqué wraparound 'bottom inspection' dust jacket concealed 'The Wonderful World of Prince Charles'. 'Eric was a lot easier to work with than the Goodies,' recalls Cohen, 'as there was a lot less of him! He was also, like them, very visually aware. It was easy to discuss ideas and show visuals to Eric. Where there were gaps Eric was more than ready to fill them, he was remarkably funny and the ideas just flowed.'

Idle's bulging contacts book came in handy for contributions. Annie Leibovitz lent her photo of Nixon for a *Rolling Stone* parody, Ralph Steadman illustrated 'Fear and Loathing in Leicestershire' and Michael Palin wrote a guest page on Accountancy and Sex. But technical tomfoolery, even more so than in the *Python* books, took centre stage. (In his diaries, Palin recorded a conversation around this time wherein Idle, then avidly devouring the work of media pundit Marshall McLuhan, propounded the theory that, for comedy books, form was more important than content – the medium was the message.) Parodies of the *TV Times* and *Rolling Stone* were printed on authentic paper stock (waxy paper and yellowing newsprint respectively). A *Who's Who* section was printed on thick brown wrapping paper, and a sealed libel section had to be broken open by the reader.

'It's true that a lot of these books were very elaborate and rather costly,' Cohen admits. 'It's certainly expensive to produce pastiches properly. If they're done poorly the joke is devalued, so the spoof ads in the *Rutland* book – After Eight mints and Badedas – had to be shot with models, locations etc., with no expense spared. The spoof "Rutland Stone" logo had to be recreated accurately, as did the ant exam paper and the "Rutland TV Times". Derek Birdsall was a director of Westerham Press, the printer of the book, and used his influence to get the different paper stocks brought in. This would have been difficult in normal circumstances if a publisher's production manager was involved.'

By now the format was established enough for mainstream appropriation. *The Morecambe and Wise Special* (1977) took the Goodies' template further into family acceptability with what amounts to a live action *Beano* annual. *Film Fun*-style comic strips and puzzles rub shoulders with the format's traditional book club and credit card parodies, as well as an entirely straight selection of ancient Eric and Ern memorabilia.

As a representation of an act that was 90% about the performance, it's as disappointing as you'd expect. Palin's misgivings over *The Big Red Book*'s potential creative poverty had come home to roost by the decade's end. Publishers were happy with their easily turned out new format, but originality was once again slipping away. Fortunately a new generation, and new working methods, would soon give the comedy book a much-needed shot in the spine.

'Is the Shah really dead?'

Comedy's next wave had a difficult birth. 'Political sensitivity' caused the screening of a 1979 BBC2 sketch show pilot, *Not the Nine O'clock News*, to be postponed during the run up to the vote which would return a government on which satire could thrive. One shaky opening series and many alterations later the programme, and cast members Rowan Atkinson, Mel Smith,

Griff Rhys Jones and Pamela Stephenson, took off. A Christmas literary spin-off seemed almost obligatory, but producer John Lloyd wanted more than a quick cash-in.

The *Python* books provided the blueprint. 'They were the great works of my generation,' enthuses Lloyd, 'we adulated *Python.*' *Not!* was kept free of the more characteristic *Python* trademarks – the silly names, the dragging up – but Lloyd acknowledges that 'similar principles were at work'. What appealed to Lloyd was the density and endless variety. 'It appeals to that slightly Aspergers-y schoolboy mentality, that same sort of warm feeling you got opening the *Eagle* Annual at Christmas.'

Lloyd was adamant spin-off books had to be worth doing in themselves. 'You *don't* just knock out a book of scripts,' he insists, 'you take the spirit of the TV show and translate it to print.'[12] Accompanying the third series in 1980, *Not!* combined reworked sketches and brand new material, recast in the mould of *Now!,* a glossy magazine recently launched by James Goldsmith, 'a sort of *Paris Match* for an English audience' as Lloyd recalls.

Not! replicated *Now!,* down to spoof adverts, bridge columns and a *Radio Times* letters page. Initially it seemed a technical nightmare. 'I went for dinner with some tweedy publishers, who said the lead-time would be about a year and a quarter. I said, "That's ridiculous! You want us to write the book in three months, what are you doing the rest of the year?" They said, "Well, there's proofreading, printing, conferences, catalogues, all that stuff." I said, "This is a topical show. In a year and a quarter the news will have changed, people will have died: it won't work. It's got to be fresh."

'So we got talking to BBC Publications. We said, "Well, how do magazines do it? Surely they don't plan a year in advance." They said, "Of course not, they're totally different." "In what way?" "Well, just… different." We didn't really see why that should be. So the idea came to do the book as a magazine. I can never see the difference, personally, apart from the hard cover, but that just enabled them to grasp the concept.'

The book's crammed nature demanded plenty of manpower. 'Not! had about sixty writers,' Lloyd estimates. 'Anyone could contribute, and the royalties were fairly shared out. It meant no one got amazingly rich, but you need that much effort. If readers sense it's a potboiler, there'll be remainder piles six feet high in Smith's. People know if you're churning it out.' Among the many hands were Richard Curtis, David Renwick, Nigel Planer, Rory McGrath, Clive Anderson and Douglas Adams.

The book's production was frantic, but self-governed. 'We were largely left alone by BBC Publications,' says Lloyd, 'but I remember they changed one word in the book, without our permission, which made nonsense of the spoof small ad in which it appeared. The word was "dildo" which, due to some sudden mad attack of prudery, they changed to "rhino".' Not! passed the quality test, selling the best part of a million copies by the end of 1980. Two years later, however, a reprint bombed dismally, confirming for Lloyd the format's transitory nature. 'It becomes like yesterday's paper, it just no longer sells.'

If ever a comedy book was of its moment, it was 1981's *Not the Royal Wedding*. Modelled closely on Pitkin's *Official Royal Wedding Souvenir: the Wedding of Prince Charles and Lady Diana*, it eventually overtook it in the bestseller lists. 'That was the proudest moment of my professional career,' says Lloyd. 'A souvenir book isn't very long, so the spoof didn't have to be long. It's also a single subject with a lot of picture reference, which means there's less work already. So Sean [Hardie] and I basically wrote the whole book ourselves, with a few others. That means you don't have to spend half your day making phone calls and re-writing other people's stuff. And of course you've got this huge archive of royal pictures to play with.'

It was joined on the shelves by *Not! 1982*, a doorstop-thick day-by-day bog paper calendar, crammed with jokes right up to its British Library catalogue details. Both it and *Not! 1983* (1982) mixed photo captions, ancient gags and amusing misprints with the likes of The Skinhead Hamlet ('I'm fucked. The rest is fucking silence') and entries from The Oxtail English Dictionary, which would acquire a life of their own. 'The calendars were horrific to produce,' Lloyd remembers. 'We squandered material on them.'[13] Or, as the calendar itself has it:

> You are a disagreeable bleeder, aren't you? I mean, you spend £3.95 on this calendar, realize you've been ripped off and so you sit there in your office criticizing the content… Do you know I sat up all night to write this page and it gets bloody cold at night here in Nassau. I can tell you… you'd soon grumble if you had to spend half your time sorting out royalty cheques like I have to. I'm really glad you wasted £3.95 on this calendar, I'm not a vindictive millionaire but God, I think you're…

Not the General Election (1983) was, like *Royal Wedding*, organised by Colin Webb, a one-man book packager, which made production even quicker. Lloyd recalls, 'we'd just go to his office, photograph Pamela in a silly costume, and if we wanted a meeting, we'd be instantly talking to the bloke in charge.' But by this time the franchise was stalling. 'It started to get a bit thin on the ground. Sean and I tried to write it ourselves, and oddly enough, it's not a big enough subject. Material ran out very quickly. It didn't sell very well, and wasn't very good, to be perfectly honest. That was when it all ran out of steam and we went our separate ways.

'The books became a victim of their own success. The first sold a million copies, Royal Wedding about half a million. Not surprisingly, the talent starts saying, "Well, hang on a minute, if you're doing two books a year, it's not very fair to have our faces on the cover if we're not getting paid for it." We said, "Well, you're famous, you can all do ads. We still have to make our living writing jokes." But it started to decay to the point where we were just left with Pamela.' But Lloyd wouldn't be out of the comedy book game for long.

Rubber thingies

While the first series of *Not* was filming, two men in a disused London chapel were vulcanising Charles Dickens. Peter Fluck and Roger Law were magazine cartoonists who had moved into three dimensions. Their grotesque sculptures of politicians and celebrities appeared in the pages of the *Economist*, the *Radio Times* and the *Sunday Times* (oh, and *Men Only*), and the duo had internationally syndicated their clay effigies of Jimmy Carter, and the royal couple devouring a roast corgi.

The niche was substantial, but not big enough. A conventional cartoonist could turn out an image a day. To get a solid equivalent sculpted, painted, dressed and lit took Fluck and Law a week at the least. Their rates were consequently higher, but not high enough to make the business work. One solution to this was their lavish, illustrated version of *A Christmas Carol* (1979). Another, put to them over a momentous business lunch by ITN's graphics man Martin Lambie-Nairn, was *Spitting Image*.

If anything, *Spitting Image* took longer to put together than *Not the Nine O'clock News*, again under the production eye of John Lloyd. Lloyd had previously tried to convince Fluck and Law to add their caricatures to *Not,* but the new programme would have more money and, importantly for Lloyd, independence. '*Spitting Image* was one of the first truly independent British production companies. We owned all the rights.' By the time the third series sealed the programme's status as the nation's bespoke purveyor of, in tabloid parlance, 'latex lampoonery', Lloyd's attention turned again to print.

With little interference from either Central Television or publishers Faber and Faber, Lloyd gave *The Appallingly Disrespectful Spitting Image Book* (1985) two front covers, an entire newsstand worth of magazine parodies, from *TV Times* to 'Paunch' ('Alan Coren takes an amusing sideways look at what might happen if Dickens found himself in a nuclear shelter with only Paunch to read'), a hideous Prince Andrew centerfold and a 'genuine but rather obvious publicity stunt'.

Inspired by greensward-knackering hippie picture quest *Masquerade* (1979),[14] Lloyd featured a parody of that puzzle book's impenetrable picture clues, which allegedly pinpointed the whereabouts of the Golden Walnut, a 'life-size replica' of Ronald Reagan's brain in 22-carat gold. But this was the truth – almost. Lloyd explains: 'The puzzle was real and the code could be broken. We were going to bury "Reagan's Brain" on Thatcher Rock, which is a small, uninhabited island near Torquay. Sadly, with the book at the printer's, when we went down there to bury the thing, we found the island was private, and completely out of bounds. The finder was told to take along a Geiger counter to find it. (I seem to remember the idea was to put it in a container covered in radioactive luminous paint.) Eventually two girls, I think, did manage to crack the code and sent us their answer, so we gave them the prize.'[15]

Only occasionally did censorship intrude. A proposed spread featuring a row of Princess Margarets as smoking lab rats was nixed. For the follow-up, *Thatcha: the Real Maggie Memoirs* (1993), a version of the show's well-worn image of Ronald Reagan and Thatcher in *One Man and His Dog* mode, with the latter taking notable interest in the former's backside, was embargoed from the cover, despite having been broadcast on the programme to little controversy. Other merchandise included Margaret Thatcher teapots (easily smashable), the *Spitting Image Book Of Rubber Johnnies*, which incorporated a miniature bellows that inflated condoms depicting world leaders. Satirical publishing hadn't been this 'hands on' since the days of Hone and Cruickshank.

17

HOW TO BE A COMPLETE AUTHOR

In 1985 advertising copywriter Mark Leigh struggled to the end of an especially bad working day. That evening he ran through the sorry details to old college chum and fellow advertiser Mike Lepine, the sole highlight of his litany of professional woe being the tiny fillip he received after doctoring a compliment slip to an especially irritating client to read '*without* compliments'. Noting the inordinate amount of satisfaction Leigh had taken from this immature, futile act, the pair concocted a book on Lepine's kitchen table of similar items – insulting letters, offensive documents and spoof official papers – with which the reader could effect his own mischievous revenge. Virgin Books published *The Complete Revenge Kit* in 1985. Since then, Leigh and Lepine have been behind dozens of books, operating according to the following rules:

Find a celebrity collaborator
For the follow-up to *Revenge Kit*, Lepine conceived 'The Diary of a Complete Bastard', a celebration of anti-social behaviour. 'We pitched it to Virgin Books,' remembers Leigh, 'and they suggested a collaboration with Ade Edmondson.' Then at the height of post-*Young Ones* infamy, Edmondson got on well with the pair, and over many pub meetings they fleshed out *How to be a Complete Bastard* (1986). The book was unashamedly juvenile; the biggest collection of knob and fart gags then seen in print.

Naturally it sold well over half a million copies. Leigh and Lepine split half the royalties from the book, its sequel, and spin-off games and calendars. Not all of their celebrity partnerships were as sound. 'When we wrote a book with Des Lynam, we had one half hour meeting,' recalls Leigh. 'Then it was, "Right chaps, I'm off to France to present the World Cup," and off we went to write the book. Still, he smiled well on the cover and earnt his fifty percent.'

Find a theme

The key is to pick one related to the celebrity's 'brand', while not legally trespassing on existing properties. *Bastard* (and, to a lesser extent, its distaff follow-up, *How to be a Complete Bitch* (1987) with Pamela Stephenson) is a perfect example, being a distillation of Edmondson's popular *Young Ones* persona, but with the copyrighted Vyvyan gear handily evoked rather than expensively licensed.

Is it a funny use of a page?

'The golden rule for all comedy book gags,' says Leigh.

Nothing is sacred

Good taste is the first thing that goes out of the window. Leigh and Lepine courted controversy from the beginning. 'The *Revenge Kit* was the subject of litigation after someone's house sale allegedly fell through due to one of the mock letters in the kit, which says, "your property is in the path of a planned motorway",' says Leigh. 'It was settled out of court but word got out to the *Evening Standard*, and Virgin Books told us to "lie low for a while". Those "not for use on the gullible" disclaimers were no help to us.'

Bastard raised questions in the House of Commons. 'There

was this buffoonish, rent-a-quote Tory MP called Geoffrey Dickens,' recalls Leigh, 'who called for *Bastard* to be banned from Smith's.' Dickens's main reason was an illustration on page 32 of Edmondson helping Sarah Ferguson over a puddle, Walter Raleigh-style, with his knob. No ban occurred.

One book caused a diplomatic incident. 'When we published *The Really Rough Guide to the World,*' says Leigh, 'the Jordanian Embassy got hold of a copy and called for it to be withdrawn.' The embassy's protest centred on the nomination of Queen Noor of Jordan as 'most shaggable monarch'. This was, as Leigh pointed out, meant as a compliment, though references in the text to sucking golf balls through hosepipes, failed to placate the Jordanians. 'What was really annoying was the speed it came off the shelves,' says Leigh. 'They left no time for Mike and me to run round buying up the unsold copies!'

Anatomy of a comedy book

Large format, glossy, full of random graphics and mild swearing, a new assortment of TV-derived hilarity appeared in bookshops every autumn throughout the 1980s. They quickly developed their own grammar. Flick through a random comedy floppy and you'll turn up any or all of the following essential elements.

The fumbled introduction

'Dear Monty Python Reader, I am extremely pleased that you have decided to buy this book as I personally think it's the best book in the world with one or two exceptions,' claimed ITN newsreader Reginald Bosanquet at the start of *Monty Python's Big Red Book,* adding a hasty 'Is this alright? (Incidentally, I thought the book a bit long – can you cut it a little, or a lot? Looking forward to your cheque.)' So began a generation of publisher baiting: a sillier, sharper version of the humour book's traditional 'Will this do?' introduction. 'Weiden, Feld and

Nicolson' ('A song, a smile and amazing stunts with a grapefruit') opened *The Goodies File* with a startling admission. 'On reading the file, you may find it boring. More to the point, it *is* boring.' *Spitting Image* unwisely enlist the dyslexic Susan Hampshire for a foreword, while *The Lavishly Tooled Smith and Jones Instant Coffee-Table Book* (1986) promises the reader will be mailed 'all the subsequent Smith and Jones books which will be published at the rate of one per month for the next twenty years'. Perhaps most brazenly honest of all is *Janet Lives with Mel and Griff* (1988), which lists a few 'Attitudes you might find useful' to adopt while reading the book, including 'Of course, it's all been done by *Monty Python*'.

The photostatted correspondence

The Big Red Book's to-and-fro of senior anchormen set the visual template for a flood of bespoke letterheads, comedy solicitors' names and scrawled memoranda on crumpled fag packets. The style peaked with Geoffrey Atkinson's *The Creation Memos* (1983), the story of the creation of the world told via a series of letters, brochures and telex messages supposedly salvaged from a filing cabinet along with the Dead Sea Scrolls, revealing 'God' to be little more than an absent-minded creative consultant acting as the middleman between Amalgamated Worlds Pty. and unreliable building contractors Cosmic and Universal Construction. Inevitably, the end result is late, bodged, looks smaller than it did in the publicity pictures and soon starts emitting a nasty brown fluid.

The listings magazine parody

Before deregulation of the market in the 1990s, the two magazines produced by the BBC and ITV – *Radio Times* and *TV Times* respectively – were the only reliable weekly TV guides in Britain, and thus multi-million-selling institutions, familiar to everyone and ripe for parody. The spoof TV listing became a comedy book staple, beaten only in popularity by the spoof cigarette ad. Eric Idle's *The Rutland Dirty Weekend Book* featured a complete twenty-page nose-to-tail *TV Times* parody, The Rutland TV Times. Nothing was spared, from the big period drama on the front cover ('The Pink Panzer... Further exploits of the Naughty Nazi, as he gaily romps through Poland, Czechoslovakia and France') to the traditional back page army recruitment ad ('Any other questions? If you have any just send them to us. It's not easy to write ads like this that'll fool the unemployed school leaver.') with holiday ads, tacky 'once in a lifetime' souvenir offers and of course the listings ('8.15 – Misprint Theatre presents The Wife of Christ') in between.

Station loyalty was, on the whole, rigidly adhered to. *The Thoroughly Disrespectful Spitting Image Book* also purloined the fat chunky typeface of the *TV Times* for sarcastic purposes ('8.30 World in Action – This week, the award-winning team investigates the growing unrest on Monday nights at 8.30, when there's only this and PANORAMA on the other side.') *Not!*'s spoof *RT* letters page featured identikit Calman cartoons and psychotic rants about 'bleeding bloody Esther bleeding bloody effing bloody Rantzen bloody woman'.

The parody of other loo books

Ever since the *Big Red Book* offered a subscription to the Python Literary Guild (plus free tub of dung), publishing foibles were a ready target. *The Goodies Book of (Criminal) Records* riffed on the 1970s craze for 'unsolved mystery' trash lit with Tim Brooke-Taylor's *Was God an English Astronaut?* ('It will shock, it will astound, but above all it will sell your newspaper.') For every publishing sensation, there was swift comic retaliation. *Spitting Image* pastiched the rising tide of 1980s 'sociological phenomenon' books with *The Lone Ranger Handbook* (by Peter State and Anne Thebleeding-Obvious). *Radio Active Times* plugged Paula Yates's *Rock Stars on the Toilet*.

Nigel Rees, predictably, suffered more than most. In *Bestseller!: the Life and Death of Eric Pode of Croydon* (1981), a joyful paper version of Andrew Marshall and David Renwick's pioneering Radio Four sketch show *The Burkiss Way*, Rees (a *Burkiss* cast member) plugs 'the ever popular "Things Scrawled on Walls" at only 95p in paperback'. *Not!* advertised *The Nigel Rees Book of Frank Muir Jokes About Stephen Pile by Gyles Brandreth (as Told to Robert Morley)*. Finally, Leigh and Lepine had Adrian Edmonson's *How to Be a Complete Bastard* spoof *Not!* ('INSIDE: nearly nude pictures of Pamela Stephenson! She's not very funny but she's got a nice pair of tits!!'), then in the Pamela Stephenson sequel *How to be a Complete Bitch* (1987) laid into *Bachelor Boys: the Young Ones Book* (1984). ('Poo Hole, Nob, Farty Breath, Snog, Wee Wee, Thatcher, Bottom, Big Jobs, Matey Boy.')

The Small Ads Section

Obvious, really: a page of quickie gags, wrapped up in a busy-looking parody of a newspaper's classified section. Sometimes it was a neatly themed gag, as with *Spitting Image*'s one-page Falkland Islands Yellow Pages. More often than not it was just an excuse to gather up a load of one-liners. *Bestseller!* went out on a limb by siting its small ads page in Big Tentacle, 'the magazine for the dominant squid'. ('Calling all paedophile starfish! "Asterisk Monthly" caters for *your* tastes!')

The blank page gag

To redress the balance of concentrated gags elsewhere in the book, many comedy tie-ins featured at least one page free of content. *Bok* had the heavily signposted Page 71. *Not!* left a page blank 'to attract readers of the *Daily Mail*'. *Janet Lives with Mel and Griff* divided its blank page into smoking and non-smoking halves, while *Who Dares Wins...* 'blank page' consisted of a large photo of *Points of View* presenter Barry Took. Who says new wave comedy dispensed with tradition?

Toying with the format

Infinite variety could be bestowed upon the content, but the comedy book format remained constant for years. The cut-and-paste design ethos reigned supreme too, though often budgets lagged way behind those of the 1970s behemoths. *Bestseller!* had its ambitious comic content either stymied or charmingly offset, depending on your point of view, by a kitty so tiny many of its magazine parodies had to be represented by crude line drawings – even the customary fag packets and discarded solicitor's letters.

Bachelor Boys legitimised the 'home made' feel by adopting the form of a fanzine penned by the scumbags themselves, with off-kilter Letraset and marginal scribbles – ironically designed by Neville Brody, then art director of style bible *The Face*. The text was the responsibility of the show's writers, Ben Elton, Rik Mayall and Lise Mayer, knocked into shape by Terence Blacker. Blacker had co-written the first *Young Ones* spin-off, *Neil's Book of the Dead* (1984), with Nigel Planer, who portrayed the dissolute, out-of-time hippie in the show. Designed by Katy Hepburn to resemble an *Oz*-style underground fanzine, it poked a sharp stick into the woolly mindset of the beautiful people, aided by genuine quotes of lunacy from John Peel, and chunks of unreconstructed crassness from Richard Neville's *Playpower*.

For *Bachelor Boys*, Blacker took a more editorial role. 'It was one of those very happy accidents because they were very keen, but knew nothing about writing a book, and I was there with the knowledge to put all the bits together. Ben, Rik and Lise really were a good team; they were coming out with reams of stuff. We ended up publishing under half of what was written. Some of it was brilliant, some wasn't, but they had this astonishing energy. So firstly one can edit down, which is always a luxury. Secondly they didn't want to write a book that was just an extension of the TV series. That's what makes a really good book – it should have its own integrity other than as just a spin-off.'

Job done, Blacker faced the Thatcherite bullyboys of marketing. 'When it was decided this was likely to become a big Christmas book,' recalls Blacker, 'I remember having a big negotiation with WH Smith's on how many swearwords we were allowed to put in. We sat round this boardroom table: the authors on one side, Smith's representatives on the other. The discussion was bizarre: "We'll give you two fucks if you drop a couple of bollocks," that sort of thing. At one stage we were told the book was right up there... at number two. So we said, "well, who's number one, then?" It was *Wicked Willie*. We couldn't believe it! We'd been cutting out all those "fuck"s to make way for a talking penis!'

The book of Channel Four revue *Who Dares Wins...* (1987) makes the most of its bog-paper format by masquerading as a library copy of Throbbing Torment by Althea Ballard, a Mills and Boon-style romantic paperback, which has been vandalised by one 'Joe Orton', who has pasted the random clippings which constitute the book's sketches in between the pages of the bodice-ripping pot-boiler just as the real Orton famously doctored library books with cut-out pictures of musclemen. *Radio Active Times*, another Radio Four spin-off (this time from *Radio Active*, the condensed output of a fictional local radio station featuring Geoffrey Perkins and Angus Deayton), sacrificed variety for slickness and parodied the good old *Radio Times* – perfectly – throughout its sixty-odd pages.

One of the oddest variants was the first spin-off from Mel Smith and Griff Rhys-Jones's sketch showcase *Alas Smith and Jones. The Smith and Jones World A(t)las* (1983) – published shortly *before* the first series of the programme aired – is an A-Z of countries of the world, crammed with fascinating facts and written in the same wry style of the later *Rough Guides* and *Lonely Planets*. ('With this book by your side you need never stir from the safety of your lavatory.')

John Lloyd provided the book's punning title. 'It's a very well written book,' he says. 'The problem was, it was two books in one. There were funny photo captions [e.g. under 'Poland', an x-rayed skull captioned 'the only known photograph of General Jaruzelski smiling'] with silly jokes, and the articles on each country were extremely well done. But what was the market? The people who liked the television show found nothing in it for them at all. It was a very *QI* book – in many ways the first *QI* book.' The two more conventional *Smith and Jones* books were more successful, the only formal innovation in either being *Lavishly Tooled…*'s suggested conversion into a coffee table with four screw-in legs (though that joke had previously appeared in the *Brand New Bok,* and would crop up elsewhere in the future, most notably on an episode of *Seinfeld*.)

The comedy tie-in family gathered in 1986 for *The Utterly Utterly Merry Comic Relief Christmas Book*, a charity compilation overseen by Douglas Adams and comedy producer Peter Fincham. *Private Eye*'s Lord Gnome and *Yes, Minister*'s Sir Humphrey Appleby provided forewords. *Spitting Image* provided viscera. Michael Palin provided a Biggles story similar to one in the *Bok*. Stephen Pile contributed some new *Heroic Failures*, while Adams, John Lloyd and Stephen Fry updated *The Meaning of Liff*. The Young Ones ruined the Nativity, Griff Rhys-Jones ruined an old joke, *Radio Active* got their facts wrong and spoof *Radio Times* listings appeared in cutout form.

This philanthropic collaboration was only tarnished by the Bishop of St Albans, who led assorted Christian pressure groups in protest against the 'blasphemous' content of the book, particularly the Young Ones' Nativity and Richard Curtis's Gospel According to a Sheep. Collins, publishers of the book who also happened to hold some particularly lucrative rights to the Bible, were cowed into cancelling a reprint, resulting in a large potential wodge of charity cash disappearing into the ether in the name of protecting the fragile sensibilities of a handful of people who were never likely to read the book anyway – a joke in poorer taste than anything in the book.

A new nest of ninnies

Glossy, all-colour comedy books may be perfect for programmes with armies of writers at their disposal, but the traditional stand-up comedian, who rose through the nation's chicken-in-a-basket circuit while the TV set were working their way through college, had fewer resources. The publishing equivalent of a mike stand and a glass of water was the bog standard comedy paper back, 4½ x 7 inches, Linotron printed in Aylesbury or Tiptree on fibrous off-white paper, illustrated by either Larry or Bill Tidy and yours for two quid all in.

Paradoxically, the comics who translated best to the silent format were ones of a musical bent. *Billy Connolly: the Authorized Version* (1976) was a collection of anecdotes from the fast-rising Big Yin collated by journalist Duncan Campbell, and graced with the hairy one's appearance on the cover in full leotard and banana boot regalia. As Connolly's fame spread worldwide, *Gullible's Travels* (1982) covered his global peregrinations from 'Doha to Bletchley, the surf of Sydney to Crawley Leisure Centre'.

Another comedian-singer who swapped guitar for typewriter was Jasper Carrott. The routines that helped him rise to national prominence from Midlands obscurity in the late 1970s, from the nutter on the bus to the indestructible mole were stuffed into *A Little Zit on the Side* (1979) in the same winningly rambling, digressive manner he employed on stage. By *Sweet and Sour Labrador* (1982) fame had opened up a jet-setting seam of new stories, including being mistaken for Trevor Brooking in Abu Dhabi, failing to buy a drink for Billy Connolly and the enduring Australian Durex/sticky tape confusion. Carrott also mused on the comedy world, prophesying Common Market regulation (the standard 'Englishman, Irishman, Scotsman' joke being recast with a Euroman, a Eurowoman and two Eurogays), predating the 1990s rash of 'politically correct joke books' by over a decade.

Labrador opens with the story of Jasper's repeated attempts to delay getting off his arse and writing the book, pestered by his publisher, Terence Blacker. 'I worked at Arrow Books as editorial director,' explains Blacker, 'and I helped put together a lot of these books. I don't think Arrow were necessarily very original, I just think we were quite good at it. The other thing about Arrow was there was no money, and these books were very cheap to put together.'

Taking the stand-up political manifesto a stage further was Mike Harding, the banjo-toting bard of Lower Crumpsall and Carrott's Arrow Books stable mate, with titles like *The Unluckiest Man in the World… and Similar Disasters* (1980) and *The 14½-Pound Budgie* (1981). In *The Armchair Anarchist's Almanac* (1981) he compiles a handy A-Z of weighty topics from sex to religion, written for those hungry for enlightenment, but 'impatient at having to plough through acres of highly stylised verbiage to get at whatever the getter-at's getting at'. If the result looks to the untrained eye like a compilation of facetious gags about British Rail gravy and the folk of Barrow-in-Furness, that's the untrained eye-owner's problem.

Third party manifestos

When the comedian retreats behind the curtain and pontificates in print through a fictional mouthpiece, the waters can get murky. Regardless of how many times Warren Mitchell appeared on chat shows relating the story of the skinhead who'd got *Till Death Us Do Part* all wrong, there was always the suspicion that the disclaimer attached to Alf Garnett to the effect that his views were not necessarily those of the management was printed too small for many to read. At least on screen the Bow bigot had a left-wing son-in-law to show him up, plus Mitchell's

own pantomime of vein-bursting mania undermining the
armchair authoritarian's authority. In print, Johnny Speight's
problematic creation sounds worryingly confident.

*The Thoughts of Chairman Alf: Alf Garnett's Little Blue Book, or
Where England Went Wrong – an Open Letter to the People of Britain*
(1973) assembles chunks of Garnett in full flight ('course, your
Welsh are your first original coons...', 'Not saying [Heath's]
Jewish. But he's not a proper Tory', 'I mean, your woman's brain
is hardly bigger than a coon's brain...') This is all introduced
with a big disclaimer comparing Speight to Jonathan Swift and
laying out the ground rules of the show once again, but the end
result seems more than ever like trying to satirise a brick wall out
of existence. Speight righteously denies Garnett the tiniest
amount of redeeming wit, with the awkward result that the
heated bigotry lies cold on the page once the initial 'he said
what?' shock has worn off. It's also, in this format, a long way
off being funny.

Closed minds are more likely to survive the printing press if
they're created with a little more affection, however ironic. *Dame
Edna's Coffee Table Book* (1976) is the gladioli fancier's self-
proclaimed 'guide to successful – and, above all, TASTEFUL –
living'. Opening with assorted commendations from the
glittering likes of Joan Bakewell, John Cleese and James Mason,
Edna Everage trots through her repertoire of tips on health,
beauty, catering and 'rude intimacy during marriage'. What's
really taking place on these luridly coloured pages is the
ransacking by puppet-master Barry Humphries of the staid,
conservative, inward-looking middle-class Melbourne childhood
he longed more than anything else to escape at the time, but can
now look back on with no small degree of wry nostalgia.

Nowhere is this more effective than a tabletop spread in
glutinous Technicolor of authentically stomach-churning
cuisine: beetroot and Vegemite sandwiches, curried rabbit in
grapefruit cases and Cambodian Camp Pie Surprise (luncheon
meat, tinned peaches and ketchup). The question of how much

is a grotesque exaggeration and how much grotesque reality is probably best left unanswered. After all this, a page of folk remedies featuring fresh urine ('that Cinderella of secretions') comes as blessed relief.

Further matriarchal advice on below-stairs business comes from *Entertaining at Home: 101 Party Hints from Britain's Most Popular Hostess* (1987), a guide to party-throwing from notorious luncheon voucher-taking tabloid favourite Cynthia Payne. In reality, most of the pen-work was done by Terence Blacker, who admits it was 'absolutely on the opportunistic and cynical side of non-books. She was in the news; it was decided to build a comedy book round her. The first problem we hit was that, beyond·the whole luncheon vouchers thing, there wasn't that much of a joke there. The other was that in order to get it into Smith's there could only be very marginal references to sex, which was really her only topic of conversation.' Broken-backed before the spines had even been bent, the resulting compromise failed to get booksellers' pulses racing.

Another one-track mind belonged to Nicholas Craig, the hyper-luvvy creation of Nigel Planer, occasional presenter of BBC TV acting masterclasses, immortalised in print with *I, an Actor* (1988). Craig's ego is so fragile it's touch and go whether he'll even make it past the foreword. ('No, it's no good. I can't possibly do this. Apart from anything else, I'm just absolutely completely bloody knackered.') Then there's an extraordinarily dull familial preamble (a favoured uncle 'worked for the Inland Revenue during the war and was a very keen blackberrier'), until the publishers tell him to get a move on. ('Well… into the bin it all goes and on I shall press. Satisfied, Lucinda?')

Once underway with the masterclass, Craig, that 'vagabond barometer of the human condition', accumulates actorly ticks at an alarming rate. There's the cloying namedropping. (Benny Kingsley, Nigey Havers, Whiffy Day Lewis.) The dewy-eyed memories of legendary productions of *School for Fops* and *The Dogs of T'blonsk*. A handy list of what first night prezzies to give.

('Michael Crawford: Nice bath smellies.') But most of all there's an endless stream of shrill pseudo-science about the job ('and it *is* a job, and a bloody hard one at that') of acting, filled with over-egged analogies and freshly minted terms such as 'perforgasm' and 'truthpumping'. It's all polished off with a comedy glossary. ('Sinden (n): Formally structured theatrical anecdote ending with the sentence, 'Amazingly, the audience were entirely unaware of anything amiss!')

'Let's Go!'

If there had to be a patron saint of toilet book authors, only one name would fit the bill. A well-bred intellectual who squandered his inheritance, failed spectacularly in the theatre and spent his autumn years as a crack-smoking ponce, William Donaldson was the toilet book's reputation of tarnished promise made flesh.

Wayward he may have been, but Donaldson's first major literary success was a piece of toilet textbook hackery – at least, on paper. (Or should that be off paper?) *The Henry Root Letters* (1980) was in Donaldson's own words 'a straight rip-off of a much funnier book', *The Lazlo Letters* (1977), an American bestseller in which comedian Don Novello, posing as unrepentant post-Watergate Nixonite and general ignoramus Lazlo Toth, sent deranged missives to everyone from Nixon to the CEO of the Mister Bubble bath foam company, and published them along with their painfully courteous responses.

Root had other antecedents. In 1948 Cambridge undergraduate Humphry Berkeley made postal mischief as H Rochester Sneath, eccentric headmaster of the fictional Selhurst public school, who sent missives by turns oleaginous and brusque to assorted figures in academe. Berkeley was eventually rumbled by the *News Review*, resulting in a two year suspension from college. He went on to become an MP for, by turns, the Conservative, Labour and SDP parties. He published the Sneath letters in 1974.

Donaldson was given the *Lazlo Letters* by his then wife and vaguely knew Berkeley ('the most unpleasant man I've ever met'), so Root was no original, but he was both delightfully timely and regrettably timeless. A brusque, over-proud bore who insults Esther Rantzen and regales Ted Dexter and Kenneth Kendall with the unsolicited, tedious minutiae of his life at 139 Elm Park Mansions, Park Walk, London SW10, Root's random missives (always superficially cheery, often signed off with a bouncy 'Let's go!' and accompanied by a pound note to grease the wheels of power) made for an amusing stocking filler, but aside from wasting the time of the Great and Good didn't, at face value, seem that subversive.

But Root was more than just a lairy saloon bar refugee, eternally bleating about his personal achievements, working himself up from living 'three-to-a-shirt and the outside bucket' via a string of wet fish shops. He was dangerous. Take his letter addressed, with typically unhinged applicability, to General Zia-ul-Haq, military dictator of Pakistan:

> Happily for us Margaret Thatcher – a strong man like yourself – has come to power. As she stomps the country, invoking the example of such great Englishmen from our island story as St Francis Drake and Sir Walter Pidgeon, the streets ring with the sound of do-gooders breaking wind and taking to the boats.

Donaldson wasn't the only person spotting signs of a shift in the country towards greed, xenophobia and witless parochial snobbery. But he gave it a voice that has proved indelible: clipped, clamorous, brimming with misapplied morsels of half-digested knowledge, angry and afraid in equal measure. The maniac contradictions in this tunnel vision comes out in his letter to Home Secretary Willie Whitelaw:

> I have two youngsters of my own, sir, and I can assure you that I would rather they exposed themselves to Mr

Enoch Powell than that they should be confronted in their local sweet shop by the naked bosoms of some so-called 'topless model'.

If there's a problem with the *Letters*, it's that the humour is sometimes too blunt – not through Donaldson overdoing it, but as part of the absurd nature of the beast. The thoughtless bigot with his array of obsessions arrayed like war medals is bound to dull over two volumes. By the end of *The Further Letters of Henry Root* (also 1980: the publishers didn't hang about when the balloon went up) the elements are familiar: the commendation of bigotry; the psychotic bonhomie; the ignorance of the victim's life, work, even name; the outrageous statement delivered in cheery 'hail-fellow-well-met' fashion.

But Donaldson's desire to milk the format shouldn't detract from its initial brilliance. While the working class bigotry of Alf Garnett failed to transfer to book form, Root's middle class equivalent is made for the job. Packaged and presented with deadpan aplomb, Root's letters take a scalpel to the rising tide of fog-brained Little Englandism and expose the screaming skull beneath the ruddy, well-fed flesh of the clubbable saloon bar droll.

'Delightful!'

As the *Letters* clung to the bestseller lists Donaldson mobilised his Chelsea crusader for what turned out to be his masterpiece. *Henry Root's World of Knowledge* (1982) was another 'straight rip-off', but this time of an altogether classier work. In the 1870s Gustave Flaubert amused himself by compiling a mock dictionary of the moronically sententious platitudes of the emergent Parisian bourgeoisie. This was eventually published as the *Dictionnaire des Idées Reçues* (1911). Flaubert, in deceptively guileless style, faithfully noted clichés on hot dinner party topics ('Stock Exchange: Barometer of public opinion.'); fashion tips

('Hats: complain of their shape.') and good honest idiocy ('Toad: Male of the frog. Its venom is very dangerous. Lives inside a stone.')

Donaldson had already updated Flaubert. Emma Jane Crampton, a nice, upper-middle-class prostitute based on a real call-girl of Donaldson's acquaintance, appeared in a book of fake letters predating Root. But *Letters to Emma Jane* (1977) was more playfully lascivious than Root would ever allow, and Donaldson was not above inventing lewd replies from celebrity targets, especially his eternal bete-noir Richard Ingrams. *Emma Jane's Reference Book* was a planned follow-up, a guide to life, love and the zeitgeist. Donaldson made great progress on it, but sales of *Letters to Emma Jane* were not enough for Eyre Methuen to commission it. But with the lucrative Root persona (and co-writer Anthony O'Hear) attached, the format was now revived.

World of Knowledge went even further than Root's *Letters* in encapsulating the reactionary doublethink of commonsense folksiness. Root was placed in the vanguard of Tory national reconstruction, along with a phalanx of generously quoted 'contributors' including James Anderton, Bill Grundy, John Motson and General Pinochet, ready to set down the tenets of the New British Order, in plain English prose a child of eight could understand.

Enemies were defined with reductive contempt. ('Democrats, The Social: Mention claret and canapés. Guaranteed to set the table on a roar.') Heroes were venerated. ('Ingrams, Richard (b. 1932): His prose is refreshingly unpretentious and puts into simple English the notions ordinary, ignorant people would express if only they could find the time.') Famous pundits crop up with alarming regularity to present their one solitary insight on various topics. Whatever the subject, we invariably find Michael Parkinson writes: 'That can't be bad!' (except when he writes: 'That can't be good!'); Christopher Booker 'was not deceived' and Arthur Marshall ('the merry Socrates of Myrtlebank') finds it all 'most agreeable'.

'Agreeable', that cosy Victorian word last seen propping up Hone's *Every-Day Book*, is a keyword for Donaldson and O'Hear. Along with other drowsy non-adjectives like 'tiresome', 'joyless' and 'estimable', they symbolised laziness of language as the chief symptom of complacency in thought. Try following the stylistic tips in *World of Knowledge* – always describing 'The Thin Blue Line' as 'stretched', academics as 'bearded' and Donald Duck as 'that estimable fowl' – and you too may find yourself in a snug bar musing: 'An old lag feels cheated if he doesn't do his porridge. We do him a favour by locking him up.' Or: 'Of course your proud black infinitely prefers to be lynched by a southern bigot than to be patronised by a self-appointed white liberal from New York. Two more gin and tonics over here, Winston. Chop chop!' Or even: 'What, I ask you, of the humble potato?' Luckily, should you find yourself doing any of this, you'll never be called upon to elaborate or justify it, as among this happy band there's always 'no need to explain why!'

World of Knowledge was the apotheosis of Root, and arguably of the toilet book itself. Sadly the book's rich, complex web of textures, conceits, running gags and varieties of antelope lacked the immediate hook of the *Letters* and failed to repeat their commercial success, and Donaldson left Root to fume and bellow in obscurity... for a few years, at least.

18

WHEN IS A BOOK NOT A BOOK

There are books, there are short books, and there are Very Short Books. The Very Short Book sneaks under the literary radar, masquerading as a 'greetings card plus', hopping into shoppers' baskets with an ease denied the 'proper' book. In the words of the Hallmark Corporation, crack American supplier of seasonal schmaltz worldwide, 'When a greeting card is too little and a dozen roses is too much, a Greetings Book is the perfect gift.'

At first they were hand-printed, virtuous affairs. *Happy Greetings 1926*, for instance, was a venerable pamphlet of Christian goodwill issued by the Lord's Day Observance Society, while Neville Hilditch's *A Christmas Greeting Book* (1933) and GV Butler's *An Eastertide Greeting Book* (1947) compiled spiritual nuggets in order to spread good cheer. Nanette Newman, of all people, kept up the trend for semi-devout sentimentality with the publication of *God Bless Love* (1972), a little square board book containing cute drawings and musings on peace, love and God harvested from primary school children, successful enough for its coffee-mad author to release a follow-up every other year until 1980's *The Facts of Love*.

Literature was chopped up for such delights as *Christmas Day at Kirkby Cottage – a Greetings Book* (1937), choice morsels of Trollope laid out in exquisite type inside a cannily designed illustrated jacket which doubled as an envelope in which to send it. In 1995 Penguin celebrated their 60th anniversary with 60 small-format condensed versions of their back catalogue classics, from Albert Camus to Spike Milligan, at 60p a throw. Plundering the past was a way of gift book life, with such whimsies as *Old Christmases* (1950), a cosy collection of Victorian yuletide ephemera, selling like hot chestnuts.

But the modern tiny book is primarily funny, and its British pioneer was Peter Wolfe. A heavyweight publisher of medical textbooks, Wolfe was nevertheless a man who liked to let his hair down, augmenting his worthy portfolio with tiny chunks of playful prose brought out on a whim. The most famous tale is of Wolfe's disgust at a waiter in an Italian restaurant who brought him soup with a thumb firmly planted in it. Wolfe angrily, but stiltedly, sent it back, and later regretted lacking sufficient Italian to fluently fume '*Togla il suo sudicio ditto dalla minestra!*' ('Get your dirty thumb out of the soup!') His publisher's brain kicking into gear, Wolfe conceived *The Insult Dictionary: How to Be Abusive in Five Languages* (1966), over 120 eloquently baroque insults in English, German, French, Italian and Spanish. It did rather well.

A notable Wolfe associate was Jonathan Routh, author of twelve board books in 1967, eight inches high, three across, with 32 pages of 'adult' content. There was *The Art of the Double Bed: For Sleeping Partners Only* and *A First Swear Book: A Beginner's Collection of Four Letter (and Other) Words Commonly in Use to Commemorate Moments of Joy, Botheration and Astonishment. Captain D'Arcy's Filthy Picture Book* assembled chaste Edwardian porn photos of voluptuous maidens in tiaras, high heels and little else, accompanied by the filthy thoughts and mucky fingerprints of the Captain, and rounded off with an advertisement for the Hounslow Knicker Works.

Wolfe's biggest hit was the bluffer's guide, a compact crib-sheet of impressive-sounding facts on various subjects, compiled by an expert in the field for the ignoramus to hold his own in polite conversation – an update of the 17th-century mis-cellanies. Between 1966 and 1974, Wolfe Publishing turned out guides on how to *Bluff Your Way in Literature, Finance, Music,*

Antiques, Teaching, Ballet, Accountancy and *PR* among many others. Wolfe eventually tired of his small book indulgence, but in the mid-1980s Ravette reignited the franchise, producing guides to *Golf, Philosophy, British Class, Hi-fi, Feminism, Publishing, Sex, Maths, Wine, Archaeology, Birdwatching, Espionage* (by one 'Phil Kimby'), *Weather Forecasting, The European Community,* and *The Quantum Universe.* In total, over sixty Wolfe/Ravette bluffer's guides have been produced to date, along with countless copycat works from other houses.

As with most 'adult' literature, the saucy small book is essentially juvenile. Hugh Silvey and Wally Jex were illustrators whose advertising portfolio included the KP Friars, the Homepride flour graders, the Country Life butter men and Access, your flexible friend. Pooling their resources and taking their brains off the hook, they came up with the heroically childish Bad Taste Books, beginning with *Bogies* (1980), which presented 28 snot-encrusted social situations for the delectation of overgrown schoolboys everywhere. Christmas, Flashers, Sport and Number Twos followed, as did the perennial theme of randy old toothless geezers lusting after pneumatic blondes, all 1980s humour staples.

The quintessential fad of 1981, the Rubik Cube, provided not only an ideal subject, but also the perfect format. Dozens of square paperbacks with complicated codes written by jumper-clad oddities on the art of twisting plastic lumps back to their pristine state in three seconds flat swamped the market. Before long, the backlash began. One WC Bindweed parodied the insanely complex jargon of corner flipping and face-alignment in *Not Another Cube Book!* (1981), while Miles O'Grady promised that *You Can Kick the Cube* (1982), and in a convoluted collision of fads, Jon Zales and John Stevens cooked up *101 Uses for a Dead Cube* (1981), taking its lead from Simon Bond's phenomenally successful *101 Uses for a Dead Cat* (1981), a ubiquitous collection of utilitarian ideas for the expired moggy in your life, with the emphasis on the versatile properties of the feline sphincter.

The standard shtick of the small book is cheery, cartoony, unassuming. One monolithic exception grew out of a writing holiday undertaken by *Hitch-Hiker's Guide to the Galaxy* author Douglas Adams and producer John Lloyd. Supposedly sequestered to the beach to write the second series of the science fiction radio comedy, they instead spent an inordinate amount of time getting drunk in wicker chairs. Adams recalled a school exercise from his youth,[16] in which British place names had to be redeployed as words with original definitions, and before long the two fell into long bouts of woozily coining new words such as: 'Shoeburyness (n.) The vague uncomfortable feeling you get when sitting on a seat which is still warm from somebody else's bottom'; 'Aberystwyth (n.) A nostalgic yearning which is in itself more pleasant than the thing being yearned for'; or indeed 'Matching Green (adj.) Any colour which Nigel Rees rejects as unsuitable for his trousers or jacket'.

Lloyd later published some definitions as The Oxtail English Dictionary, a feature in the *Not! 1982* calendar (1981), but the idea was transformed when Adams proposed *The Meaning of Liff* (1983). This was technically just another mock dictionary, but the presentation was something different. Using his clout as a bestselling novelist, Adams steered the book's design away from the brightly coloured standard template and towards an austere black book with sombre gold lettering, looking more like a religious text than a collection of gags. What Lloyd refers to as *Liff*'s 'Biblical smallness' was topped off with a large sticker proclaiming: 'This book will change your life'.[17] Adams's knack for mixing the provincially mundane with the absurdly cosmic had struck again, and the book became almost as big a cult as *Hitchhiker's*. '*Liff* has become a kind of bible for an enormous amount of people',' claims Lloyd, who tells of having meetings with people who 'pull out dog-eared editions of *Liff* and show me... they often haven't made a connection between the John Lloyd on the front of the book and the John Lloyd standing in front of them.'

In the 1990s a new frontline opened up in micropublishing. Never mind the shelves, that little flap of Formica in front of the tills was the ideal location for a miniature beachhead. Unexpectedly, the book that led the assault was neither filthy nor funny – at least, not intentionally. Paul Wilson's Little Book of Calm (1997), though of American origin, went through British shops like a dose of syrup of figs, and had the same effect on some of its more cynical readers. An unashamed self-help manual, each of its tiny pages contained a woolly relaxation tip of the 'visualise a calm blue ocean' variety. If this gave many punters an unsolicited reunion with the contents of their breakfast, still more lapped up its promise of stress-free nirvana. Copycat tomes on everything from excuses to farting deployed tillside, many sinking under the weight of mass indifference but a few hitting home. Inevitably, parodies abounded, the most acute being Craig Brown's Little Book of Chaos, which opens with a tip encapsulating the juvenile ethos of the Very Short Book: 'Regain the child within. Pull a colleague's hair, and when she yells "ARGH! HE HURT me!' remember to yell back, 'But she STARTED it!'"

Convenience tours

Everyone knows the old joke about the flushing lavatory being invented by Thomas Crapper. Except it isn't a joke – at least, Crapper was a very real, and respected, Victorian plumber. The confusion arises from the efforts of one Wallace Reyburn, who compiled a semi-satirical life of the great dunnyman. Flushed with Pride (1969), with its playful blend of fact and facetious fancy, muddied the waters (so to speak) to such an extent that received wisdom conspired to deny TC his place in engineering history for some time.[18]

Reyburn was neither the first nor the last to explore this taboo. War poet and friend of WH Auden John Pudney compiled The Smallest Room: a Discreet Survey Through the Ages

(1954), a frank and thorough history of That Place. In 1980 came *Are You Sitting Comfortably?*, a collection of defecatory epistles culled from Freud, Swift and the Ayatollah by hitherto patrician presenter of children's TV shindig *Magpie*, Susan Stranks, who claimed compiling the book had a life-changing effect – she learned to say 'shit' demurely.

In between the two, Jonathan Routh, whose grim countenance was familiar to fans of *Candid Camera*, took himself round the public conveniences of London (with Brigid Segrave investigating the ladies) for the eminently useful *Good Loo Guide: Where to Go in London* (1965). The result is a practical companion alerting the peripatetic penny-spender to 'where nature's call may be satisfied at the same time as your own spirit of adventure'. Each convenience is itemised (opening times, number of cubicles and stalls, 'choice of papers', 'fittings: Twyford's Adamant with automatic flusher', 'choice of four aftershave sprays in the gents' etc.) and awarded a star rating, or 'loo grade'. Routh notes which conveniences have jolly attendants, amusing graffiti and the presence of 'members of the tramping fraternity'.

He's on the side of the customer all the time, lamenting Westminster City Council's 'ridiculous charge of 6d to "use the mirror"', and not afraid to wax lyrical when the occasion suits. St Pancras gents 'resembles a vast ecclesiastical ballroom', while the Art Deco fittings at the Lyons Corner House on Tottenham Court Road are an 'absolutely ideal background for suddenly breaking into dance'. Buckingham Palace Road contains the most luxurious crapper, which costs half a crown to access and features a morning-coated attendant who 'will show you to the room you wish *and wait with you* while you transact your business'. For the most part, however, it's Soapamaster dispensers, Toilock paper holders and machines vending stomach powder.

In later years toilet connoisseurs looked more to the private, not to say the stately. Lucinda Lambton, architectural photographer and all-round eccentric truffler, provided the lavatory coffee table with its first glossy hardback in *Temples of Convenience* (1978), a National Trust brochure plus Bronco dispensers. In 1983 she moved into grand bathrooms with *Chambers of Delight*, pipping Frank Muir's *An Irreverent and Almost Complete Social History of the Bathroom* (1984) to the post.

Another widely disputed toilet fact is that the average person spends – wastes, even – 11 ½ minutes a day on the can. Bill Oddie to the rescue, joining forces with wife Laura Beaumont for *The Toilet Book, or 11 ½ Minutes a Day and How Not to Waste Them* (1984). Intended to be kept in the downstairs lav, it's a compendium of ludicrous 'activities' for the busy defecator, from keep-fit exercises, through ventriloquism (the loo brush makes a fine dummy), origami (plentiful supply of paper) and tap-dancing (tie toothpaste tubes to feet with dental floss). There's even a crisis guide to using unfamiliar loos, and page 97 is left blank 'for emergency use only'.

Bearded comedians seem drawn to the bog. *Kenny Everett's Ultimate Loo Book: an Astroloogical Guide* (1988) is a more straightforward day-by-day mixture of corny gags, humorous horoscopes and The Kenny Everett Guide to Survival in the Twentieth Century. ('Never insert a suppository with a fork.') Its greatest innovation is a loop of string threaded through the top left corner for hanging the book on a convenient nail.

19

LIFESTYLES OF THE RICH AND AIMLESS

The 1980s were nothing if not self-absorbed times. Sociology matured from being a much-mocked scourge of the universities and went legit. New social groups were being spotted, catalogued and analysed everywhere. Before long the toilet book joined the throng, wedding the arcane methods of the analyst to the anecdotal insights of the character writer. The first came from the unlikely house of society magazine *Harpers & Queen*, as Ann Barr and style editor Peter York presented *The Official Sloane Ranger Handbook: the First Guide to What Really Matters in Life* (1982).

> You round a corner, enter a room, pick up a telephone –
> and there are *that* voice, *those* mannerisms, *those* clothes,
> that *style*, THOSE PEOPLE. It all comes back. It never went
> away. It's all going on now, *still*.

So begins a journey into the world of England's well-bred urbanites, the men and women who operate in a tiny world centring on Kensington. The book's timing was masterful. Whereas for decades the upper classes would have been lucky to attract anything more substantial than general derision, suddenly the public couldn't get enough of well-bred gentlemen and ladies of leisure, and it was all thanks to the ascent of *that* woman.

Princess Di looms large over the book, as she did over TV, magazines, mugs and just about everything else at the time. But most of the book is wrapped up in propriety, tradition, and not a little arrested emotional development. Sloanes live in a bubble all of their own. 'You don't believe in The Future in the way other types do… The Good Stuff is here already and always has been. It *is* nice that now one can buy BMWs, powerboats and new garden machinery, and where would the City be without telex, but you certainly don't want to *live* in the Video Age.' Every tiny social detail matters, from drinking in the right pubs to playing the right party games. (Moriarty, for instance, which passed Francis Meynell by, involves lying on the floor and hitting each other with rolled-up copies of *Country Life*.)

If all this sounds familiar, the giveaway is there on page 71, where the Potterish word 'Sloanemanship' makes its appearance. Little magaziney box-outs deal with ideal Sloane dogs and how to paint your bicycle frame to look like bamboo. (One even advises on the ideal toilet books to furnish the smallest room: *Monty Python's Big Red Book* and *Not the Royal Wedding* figure highly, as of course does 'this book'.)

The tone is weirdly uneven: at first it mocks this strange breed, then it swings into 'so you want to be a Sloane' mode. Long lists of appropriate gents' outfitters, shops and prep schools run into multiple pages. The comedy book diehard scans these for concealed in-jokes and incongruities, but in vain – these are straight up itemries, designed to be useful. What started as a spoof becomes a genuine guide. The funniest things in the book are personal photographs of genuine Sloanes, contorting their mouths into cavernous braying voids.

The jet-lit boom

Barr and York's strange mongrel proved the Christmas hit of '82, precipitating a tidal wave of socially introspective comedy books, all chasing the zeitgeist at full pelt. Nicholas Monson and

Debra Scott's *The Nouveaux Pauvres: a Guide to Downward Nobility* (1984), picked over the same class, but added a touch of bathos in its interviews with various unfortunate nobs and nobesses caught in a cycle of – yes – 'one-downmanship', forced to close down huge drafty wings of their mansions, trade in the Bentley for a battered 2CV and, in the case of Old Harrovian Alistair Pirrie, swallow all pride and act as butler for the guitarist from Yes.

Most social groups were heading in the opposite direction. *Viviane Ventura's Guide to Social Climbing* (1983) is a decidedly rum case in point. As an actress, Ms Ventura was strictly Z-list. You may not remember her from such films as *Battle Beneath the Earth*, where she played a 'top expert on volcanic passages', mainly by standing about in a jumpsuit doing nothing, or *Carry On Jack*, in which she did nothing in Spanish. But as a member of the jet set and all-round toothily delightful piece of grade A arm candy, she was second to none, and here she doles out sage advice for Bianca Jagger wannabes from her Mallorcan retreat.

The trouble is, she's as accomplished a comic writer as she is an actress. A promising roll call of social climbing types – The Boring Rich, The Fun Rich, Showbusiness Royalty – is disappointingly fun-free. Where wit is attempted, it's via the all-purpose exclamation mark. ('Nowadays it's never a party without Julio Iglesias!') The book must have sounded like a scream when it was hatched with Roger Moore and Alana Stewart over après-ski cocktails on the bearskin rug in that Gstaad lodge, but on the page it resembles an in-joke which can't possibly have been that funny even at the time.

Social climbing grandmaster David Frost rattled through the same territory in *The Mid-Atlantic Companion* (1986), a glance at that age-old source of extremely limited humour, the cultural differences between Britain and America, this is possibly the most typically David Frost book of them all. It's designed to be read in those most Frost-y of environments, the departure lounges of Heathrow and JFK.

Frost's co-author is Michael Shea, the Queen's Press Secretary and not, perhaps, the first person most people would think of calling on for a bit of help with punching up their text. As a result, the book is a tissue of magpie borrowings. Here's George Mikes on the British penchant for queuing. Here's an extract from *1066 and All That*. A bit of rhyming slang appears, some familiar comical graffiti, a few heroic failures, even the infamous tea towel with a comically confusing precis of the rules of cricket on it. In a little over 150 pages, there are well over 200 attributed quotes. Nothing wrong with this, but it all adds up to a strange sort of non-book, written by people busy doing other things to be read by people busy doing other things. Still, it's a healthier way to pass flight-delayed time than loitering in World of Whiskies.

Mobile clones

With this sort of book, timing is everything. Too late, and you miss the boat. Too early, on the other hand, and you get nothing but odd looks. This was the fate of *The Official British Yuppie Handbook* (1984), a transatlantic migration of an American dissection of all things upwardly mobile. Landed with the task of Anglicising the text was Russell Ash, who soon discovered how thankless it was. This wasn't just a case of inserting references to Battersea Power Station and Jeffrey Archer. No one in the UK at the time actually knew what a Yuppie was. Ash bolted on a bet-hedging explanatory introduction, but to no avail. Nobody wanted to read about a social phenomenon that hadn't happened yet, and the humble little paperback tanked, but Ash received some consolation years later by appearing in the OED as the first known British printed source of the word.

Further down the sophistication ladder, and staying there, is the coarse social type first isolated by Theophrastus, the unapologetically prattish lummox with the furry dice and the mighty consumption of Black Label, whose Bible is Paul

Manning's *How to be a Wally* (1983). It's uncertain when and where the appellation 'Wally' arose, but by the early 1980s it was everywhere: in Jasper Carrott routines, the *Wogan* show, an ad campaign for Midland car dealer Swithland Motors starring Samantha Fox, and a ZX Spectrum computer game to name a few. It meant loutishness, crassness, gaucheness, and a general lack of taste. A badge of honour it was not.

Manning, a junior publishing editor, was something of a company bard, famed for penning raucous mock epic poems for staff weddings. Finally he sat down to write a book proper, and *How to Spot a Wally* was the result. Colleague Mark Lucas loved the sample pages, but disliked the tone. 'I decided it lacked affection. The point, I felt, should have been that we're all Wallys if we're honest, but there's no point being just a bit of a Wally, and you might as well go the whole hog… and here's how to do it. So it became about the thrill of recognition rather than idea of watching these strange characters from the other side of the road.' Manning agreed to re-draft, and it paid off – Lucas took the handful of sample pages to Tim Healy-Hutchinson at New Futura, who bought them for a then-whopping ten thousand pounds. Get in!

Within the finished book (and its sequel, 1984's *Superwally*) can be found the great clichés of the age. Names on car windscreens. 'I'm with stupid' T-shirts. Fake plastic tits. The great smell of Brut. The Ford Cortina with the go-faster stripe. 'Over the moon!' 'Sick as a parrot!' 'A'wight, John?' It's hard to imagine the 1980s British comic landscape without the Wally. The Wally lifestyle offered endless potential for amusingly naff cultural references. Manning's Wally knows the plot of *Smokey and the Bandit*, the words to every Cinzano ad and Barbara Windsor's bust measurement by heart. His favourite book is *101 Uses for a Dead Cat*. Favourite band: The Barron Knights. Favourite bit of DIY: adding Wild West saloon doors to the lounge. Favourite pastime: standing outside DER showrooms in the rain watching *Game for a Laugh*.

The nation's Wallys couldn't resist such a tempting concoction, and it shot to the top of the *Sunday Times* bestseller list. Sales topped 750,000, pretty much on word of mouth alone, though Manning and Lucas cooked up some low-rent publicity. 'The whole campaign cost something like five hundred pounds in total,' claims Lucas. 'There was the distinctive "moon and parrot" logo which caught people's eye and a DIY Wally Pack, including a beer mat printed with instructions for flipping it into your pint in the Wally manner. We made up a few dozen and sent them out to radio DJs, who opened them live on air, which was great publicity. But mostly the book sold itself.' Vindication for an idea that had originally been rejected by several publishers on the grounds it 'couldn't possibly work north of Watford'.

An oven glove shaped like a crocodile's head

Out on the fringes of sanity, *Max Headroom's Guide to Life* (1985) was the literary wing of commercial designers Rocky Morton and Annabel Jankel's ubiquitous multimedia zeitgeist-worrying creation. Headroom was conceived as a vehicle to link music videos in a Channel Four version of MTV – a pineapple-headed, stuttering transatlantic showbiz show-off created entirely by computer (though in reality played by a latex-scalped Matt Frewer). To accompany the programmes, a dystopian sci-fi film explained the character's origins and bolstered the element of media satire. A novelty hit single became part of the package too. Before that, the obligatory comedy book reared its head, allowing the smarmily superior *ubermensch* to berate us Ordinary People for failing to live up to his glamorous golfing lifestyle. But take away the supercilious, exclamation mark-festooned style of the programme, and the book pans out into a series of social observation lists suspended midway between the *Yuppie Handbook* and *How to be a Wally*, with its litany of white Speedo swimming trunks, dry roasted peanuts and glass tubes of coloured sand from Alum Bay, Isle of Wight.

Taking itemised humour to the limit, *The Complete Naff Guide* (1983), written by the formidable-sounding trio of Dr Kit Bryson, Selina Fitzherbert and Jean-Luc Legris, is nothing but a series of lists of what to avoid doing, buying, saying or being if you wanted to make it in 'Mrs Thatcher's Britain, with mean-minded egalitarians in retreat and the stage-army of compassion lobbyists routed'. If the reactionary tone of that sentence sounds vaguely familiar, it's because this was yet another Willie Donaldson enterprise, teaming up with Simon Carr for a wild and offensive round of common sense-bashing, obscure in-jokes and dangerous pursuit of personal vendettas (the publishers had to settle out of court over one libellous statement which naturally involved Richard Ingrams.)

The Naff Guide rambles all over the place. Some of the lists border on the Wallyish. ('Naff expressions: A bit on the side, this is it, I'm a tit-man myself.') Others delineate the foibles of the age. ('Naff household objects: Wall heaters, coal tidies, crouching Atlas holding TV on back, black bath with gold taps, notice board for silly messages from woman of house to herself, Christmas books, esp. by Frank Muir.') Most of it is apropos of nothing. ('Naff things to teach your parrot to say: Fuck the Pope. Naff things to do with parts of the body: Comb hair in public, adjust lie of penis through trouser pocket, clench and unclench buttock muscles when standing at bar in tightish trousers.') Naff Guide saw Donaldson simultaneously leaping on a literary bandwagon, lampooning its lazier, snobbier aspects, and doing it better than anyone else.

Entertainers entertain

The cookery book – straightforward, practical, slightly prim – had rattled along just fine for centuries, until the frill of celebrity arrived to muss up its well-ordered cupboards and sling far too many glace cherries on top. Take *How to Be a Good Hostess* (1950) – a wipe-kleen guide to party throwing in the pre-Suez suburban manner, introduced by Anna Neagle, the actress who single-handedly secured victory in Europe, in a charming foreword ('How lovely to see you!'). Here the boil-washed formality of old mixes uneasily with the first knockings of the Technicolor free living to come. It's a world where a 'teenage get-together' may be 'a shirts and slacks evening,' but a fork lunch is still 'an occasion for friendly rivalry in smart hats! The hostess will not wear a hat if the lunch takes place in her own home: but if it is given in a private room at an hotel, at a club or in committee rooms, she will.'

When the non-cooking famous enter the fray, dull utilitarianism goes out of the window. Multimedia current affairs behemoth *Nationwide* spawned a fair few cookery books in its time, but the best of the bunch was a dollop of pure amateurism. *Cooking with Nationwide* (1974) is a treasure house of celeb-grub riches, wherein the entire *Nationwide* family spill the kidney beans. The hungry current affairs groupie can swoon over Frank Bough's Gougère with Chicken Livers, or Bob Wellings's Fish Pie Penelopé. These are the *'Wide'*'s sophisticates. (The blurb reveals, 'Bob Wellings and Gregory Peck have more in common than height, dark good looks and a kind of gentle firmness.') Valerie Singleton goes for elegant Sautéed Kidneys with Soured Cream, while Sue Lawley offers a homely 'Uncheesey Cheesecake'. But it's studio führer Michael Barratt, looking incredibly uncomfortable peeling an onion on the cover, who takes the teacake plugging his vegetable broth.

Unlike most of my colleagues I can't stomach fancy foods – foreign foods especially. Wild horses wouldn't drag me into a Chinese or Indian restaurant. Well, my wife does sometimes, but even she can't twist my arm to taste their sweet and sour pork, their bamboo shoots and other abominations. The furthest I'll go is to toy with their tomato soup (preferably out of a British tin) and a chicken omelette, with chips of course. Bob Wellings is ashamed of me. Each day in the *Nationwide* canteen he reddens with embarrassment as I queue patiently for fish fingers or sausage and mash in preference to palate-rotting mixtures like moussaka. (I've an idea that's Greek.)

Some celebrity cook books have no editorial content whatsoever but still manage to be bonkers. Random collections of favourite dishes of the great and good like the showroom-sponsored *Cook With the Stars (and North Thames Gas)* (1968) give readers the opportunity to sample Eric and Ernie's Fruit Chiffon Pie at their leisure. For *Alton Douglas's Celebrity Recipes* (1984), the 'former quizmaster of top-rated BBC TV series Know Your Place' sent out a form request for a favourite recipe to every celebrity in the world, if the selection of those who replied is anything to go by. Bob Hope's Lemon Pie precedes Geoffrey Howe's Avocado Mousse. Liberace's Grand Marnier Soufflé jostles with Little and Large's Tea-Time Special. Brian Cant's Chicken Tamara nuzzles up to Ronald Reagan's Macaroni Cheese. Neil Kinnock's Rogan Josh vies for supremacy with Enoch Powell's Crème Brulée. You want world cuisine? Chew on this.

'It's a recipe for lots of fun!'

Kenny Everett's *Cook Book* (1976) epitomises the traditional division of labour between practical and frivolous. Ev's wife Lee cracks the eggs while Ev himself cracks wise. Humble fare is on the menu – Everyday Tripe and Onions, Meat and Tater Pie, Kippers Plain – with Ken popping out from behind the Moulinex with zany comments betimes. 'Dear Bisto, my wife uses your stuff, so how about a TV commercial? Tessa Blackburn's gravy looks like the Mersey compared with ours!' More sedate culinary DJ-ing comes courtesy of the *Jimmy Young Cook Book* (1968-72), a regular round up of the man's famed radio recipe feature that was inexplicably introduced by high-pitched cod-Italian Raymondo, who sadly fails to transfer into print.

More ambitiously, *Dick Emery's Cookbook* (1979) tries its arm at heavy concept cookery. Each of Emery's TV characters present straight recipes in their own inimitable fashion. Lampwick does Roast Beef wif' Yorkshire Puddin' ('while chattin' up your butcher, get 'im to take out the backbone'), Ton-Up Boy offers 'Erbed Buns ('these are easy to 'andle with one 'and when doin' the ton up the 'ighways'), Mandy attempts Lobster Paella à la Michael ('I wonder who Michael is? I bet he's awful. But I know I'd like him!') and Clarence, perhaps predictably, plumps for Spotted Dick ('you don't see these too often these days, more's the pity!')

Who better to coach the reluctant bachelor into culinary maturity than Richard O'Sullivan, on-screen proprietor of the *Robin's Nest* bistro and off-screen bloke-friendly actor *sans pareil*? *Man About the Kitchen: a Book for People Who Can't Cook – Much* (1980) takes the culinary dunce through a series of simple recipes, accompanied by O'Sullivan (clad in regulation 'lady in underwear' apron) who lards the book with anecdotes about Liz Taylor swearing her head off on the set of *Cleopatra* and the legendarily hot chili con carne served up by Mrs Dennis Waterman. O'Sullivan's not above the odd Delia-ish sleight of hand – there's not a kitchen slip-up that can't be cured by adding a dash of instant mashed potato.

Len Deighton's Action Cook Book (1965) is a more flattering bachelor's crib sheet. The foil-embossed thriller writer, gazing cheekily from the cover as he strains his pasta in front of the ladies, compiles his stylish, self-drawn 'cookstrips' from the *Observer*, leading the novice from chopping an onion to concocting Cervelle de Veau au Buerre Noir for an alluring Soviet lady double agent. Recipe titles like The Profiterole Motive and Tripe and Onions: a Stirring Tale allow the kitchenette klutz to fondly imagine himself as a Bond-esque man of the world in training. Harry Palmer had a Deighton cookstrip on his kitchen wall in the film of Deighton's *The Ipcress File*. The book ends, as every good MI5 meal should, with cheese, coffee and fine cigars. Follow-ups included the Frenchified *Ou Est Le Garlic?* (1965).

On the sauce

'Ever since I was fifteen, and persuaded to neck with a boy who gave me a frozen Milky Way, I have been aware of the seductive powers of food.' Mimi Sheraton's 1963 opus *The Seducer's Cookbook: Helpful And Hilarious Hints For 20 Situations Into Which Men May Lure Women, And Vice Versa* folds the age-old mixture of food and sex into a smoothly cheeky sauce. Lionel H Braun increased the temperature with *Fanny Hill's Cook Book* (1971), seventy recipes adorned with *fin-de-siecle* nudes and sporting sportive titles like Nutcracker Sweet and Cock in Hand.

Venturing into coffee-table territory, David Thorpe's *Rude Food* (1978) is a collection of photographic gags, which combine the solemn elan of the perfume advert with the coy impropriety of the seaside postcard. Photographed in the sumptuous style of *Vogue* cover shoots, various 'saucy' visual puns are created with the help of complaint models, some artfully reflective glass surfaces and a gallon of Hollandaise sauce. A model in black lipstick holds a spear of asparagus licentiously between her teeth. Sole Colbert, a suggestive assembly of sole fillets and prawns is inspected by a wandering finger. ('The trick is to arrange everything so that the soft white fillets curve gently round the creamy sauce rather like two long lips.') Deft hands pour oil and balsamic vinegar onto a reclining female model's groin-mounted curly endive salad. A banana does pretty much what you'd expect. In the stifling world of up-market 'erotica', *Rude Food*'s burst of playful silliness is immensely refreshing.

Sequels had to happen. The *Rude Food 1985 Erotic Calendar* (1984) introduced a spaghetti-based bondage element to the slickly obscene proceedings. *Rude Health* (1981) went to the gym and 'accidentally' forgot its PE kit. *Vin Rude: An Alcoholic Alphabet, Photographed at Room Temperature* (1980), with its fluted glasses of red deftly obscuring the downstairs details, brings on a whole new sub-genre – the booze book. There's a default setting for the wry alcoholic writer: upmarket, convivial and on the verge of falling into the cups. Kingsley Amis was ideally suited, writing his own *How's Your Glass? A Quizzical Look at Drinks and Drinking* (1985) and being one of the contributors, along with George Melly, for *Drinks-Man-Ship: Town's Album of Fine Wines and High Spirits* (1964), a debonair anthology of half-cut prose commissioned by Michael Heseltine's suave *Town* magazine and marshaled by the ubiquitous Len Deighton, leering woozily from the cover behind a bare-backed model in true Dean Martin style.

More akin to Jerry Lewis, Willie Rushton sought to take wine from the clutches of the sophisticated and out to the Whitbread-bibbing masses with *The Naughty French Wine Book* (1980), a comic tour of France's wine-producing regions with a continentally saucy front cover. This alcoholic evangelism wasn't entirely altruistic. The intro fesses up to no small degree of patronage from G & J Greenall Ltd, the distillers behind Vladivar vodka and a three-litre bumper box of *vin de table* called – yes – Naughty French Wine, which featured Rushton on the box in comedy Frenchman garb, complete with Gallic 'friend' Vicki Michelle. 'About time I had a top-up!'

What of drinking holes? *The Doncella Book of Pubmanship* (1972) is a weird little book sponsored by the eponymous John Player & Sons cigar brand. Your guide to the ins and outs of communal drinking is Ronnie Corbett, attempting to do for pubs what Stephen Potter did for everything else. There's a handy pub score chart. ('Plastic pineapples containing ice: 10 points. Out-of-date calendar retained only for nude on it: 5 points.') There are dodgy methods of conning free drinks on the house. Corbett namechecks endless bar products in the brazen hope of being sent a free case. Women, once again, don't get a look-in unless they're pulling the pints.

Finally come the inevitable *Hangovers* (1981), which the gregarious Clement Freud guides us through with a bracing dose of lachrymose wisdom. After a ramble through historical cures (including the old favourite of burnt frog's liver) and a few drunken anecdotes concerning National Servicemen and Gilbert Harding (though not together) Freud apologetically admits to not having a better solution than 'drink some water'. There is, however, a nifty three-day 'bender planner' wall chart which plots inebriation against next-morning roughness, allowing one to time that pre-dinner comeback highball to perfection.

20

'LET'S DANCE AROUND THE BREAKFAST TABLE, UNCLE CORNFLAKES!'

Pop has inspired a host of toilet books, but rock 'n' roll's fanatical solemnity excludes the stars themselves from paperback wackiness. Fortunately, radio provides the remedy. Who embodies the gaucheness of British pop music better than the DJ? And, unlike the inscrutable musicians, they're only too keen to get it all down on paper. Tony Blackburn appended his name and grin to the *Pop Special* (1970-3) series, in direct competition with a swarm of fellow jocks, among them the happy author of *Stewpot's Book of Pop* (1973), which, it's fair to say, is typical of the genre. (That the genre consists of nothing but typical examples saves a lot of bother.) Stewpot is your intrepid investigator out to grill the popperati and answer the questions that matter, even if the answers give rise to yet more questions. ('Ed Stewart got the nickname "Stewpot" from his otherwise unusable talent of rolling his stomach muscles to resemble a cooking utensil.')

Stomach rippling fearlessly, our intrepid reporter exclusively reveals that Slade's Noddy Holder likes pizza, the colour black and Susannah York, 'and he's got a pet tarantula called Sooty!' Jim Lea, by contrast, prefers Brigitte Bardot and eating egg and chips. Lynsey De Paul got her big break while designing Pipkins album covers. Gilbert O'Sullivan's name is actually a clever joke. With his audience's jaws smacking onto the floor like a dozen rounds of buttered toast, Ed turns the conversation round to the chaps who really matter, his fellow jocks. 'That looney-humorist Noel Edmonds... is busier than ever now, having opened two branches of The Noel Edmonds Record Shop, one in Chelsea and one in Orpington, Kent. A busy and successful man-about-records.' All very impressive, but a bit cliquey, is it not? How does one join this record-spinning elite?

Glad you asked, man. A one-stop shop for the would-be disc jock, *Emperor Rosko's DJ Book* (1976) promises to be the definitive guide for the nation's countless aspiring DLTs. Unfortunately for them, but fortunately for the rest of us, the book is put together in a strange variant of the Emperor's breathless transatlantic patter, 'translated into English and written down by Johnny Beerling'. From a sensational opening ('To a Neanderthal man the idea of switching on a small black box in the corner of his cave to produce music would have seemed like one heap good trick!') Rosko whizzes us through a potted history of his unique career.

> My mother was a Hollywood lady... compulsory military service... one day I came across a quite "blue" LP... taking care of Chuck Berry... there was plenty of French crumpet about of course... soon set off for Lowestoft... one of the largest mobile discotheques in existence... incorporated three lovely sensuous sexy galloping Go-Go girls... I said to them, "Listen, Rosko is Rosko"... just heavy bass and good vibes.

For Rosko, image is everything. 'Is your destiny to be a "smokin' jokin' disco duke" or a "super sophisticat" of major airwave communication?' His destiny decided, the reader is permitted access to the divine secrets of the Radio 1 inner sanctum, such as the arcane practice of stealing another station's exclusive (er, tape it off the radio and fade out the bit where Simon Bates starts talking). There's also a little look and learn as Rosko crafts an ILR commercial for shampoo. ('Lemon Up and make peace with grease. Yeah!') Job done, the Emperor rides off into the sunset, his parting words slowly fading on an evening wave of cross-Channel static. 'All enquiries for disco bookings for me, Emperor Rosko, should be made to Bunny Lewis at 108 Frobisher House…'

'My idol at thirteen was Emperor Rosko. I used to copy him all the time. He was the original rapper.' So says the voice of Radio 1's next generation, painstakingly profiled as he goes about his daily duties in *What a Week! With Bruno Brookes* (1988). At the height of his pomp, the Compact Disc Jockey is trailed for seven chaotic days, fuelled by a potent cocktail of Royal Jelly and ham sandwiches. ('He's not terribly fit.')

It's a hectic week. Bruno comperes the international ladies' hockey final in a Poco Loco sweatshirt. ('Translation: "A Little Mad!" Does he realise what it says?') Bruno cocks up the scoring on *Beat the Teacher*. Bruno gets an answer phone message from the singer off Johnny Hates Jazz. Bruno is disappointed by the original Batmobile. Bruno poses for a photographer in 'thoughtful' manner, and loses all feeling in his legs. Bruno broadcasts live from the Ideal Home Exhibition. Bruno broadcasts live from an elephant's head. Bruno plays Michael Jackson to Mike Read's Tina Turner for Comic Relief. Bruno is given a fly fishing magazine by Steve Wright. Bruno is presented to Fatima Whitbread. Bruno gets coffee all down him on the 3.15 to Carlisle. Bruno has calmed down a lot 'since Anthea sorted him out'.

Most DJs wisely confined their printed efforts to fluff like *The Tony Blackburn Sensational Joke Book* (1984). Jimmy Savile took up the pen for a collection of cartoons in *Savile's Selection* (1976), while a shutter-happy BBC breakfast mainstay coaxed the likes of Joanna Lumley, Kim Wilde and Faith Brown into posing for the Kodak-sponsored *A Bit of a Star: Media Women, Their Fine-Points and Phobias as Photographed by Dave Lee Travis* (1986).

Boys to entertain you

No self-respecting band would dream of producing a funny book, so the running has to be made by the parodists – see *Private Eye* collection *Private Pop Eye: the Life and Times of Spiggy Topes, or Not; with an Introduction by Hans Killer* (1969) – and that maligned institution, the comedy group. *The Instant Sunshine Book: with Hints for Struggling Supergroups* (1980) is a case in point. A supper club quartet comprising three showbiz doctors and one showbiz Miles Kington, the 'Sunshine's whimsical songs were all over British TV and radio throughout the 1970s and beyond, notably on Stephen Potter adaptation *One-Upmanship* (1974-8). Clad in cheery yellow, this 'how to' guide for putative bands is by turns over-specific ('If you lean a double bass up anywhere, it will sooner or later fall over'), didactic ('Poor reviews in the *Leeds Advertiser* are unlikely to haunt what remains of your professional career as you will never play Leeds again. *Supergroups never play Leeds again.*') and reliably mundane, with constant overtures to the VATman and the mantra: 'Do remember that the recording industry is in a particularly bad way at the moment.'

One of the oddest pieces of printed rock merchandise is *The Book Of Bilk: 41 Characters In Search Of An Acker* (1961). It's masterminded by Peter Leslie, the Svengali who took 'Mr Acker Bilk' to the top by dressing his trad jazz in trad rags and plugging it with Edwardian heartiness. Before Acker's career peaked with Stranger on the Shore, his publicity reached a summit of absurdity with this book, purporting to trace the remarkable Mr B's ancestors, 'from Ackermemnon to Ackawatha, from King Ackered the Unsteady to John Osbilk, the Ackery Young Man'. Despite Leslie's toiling prose, and the accompanying photos Mr Bilk himself in historical garb, what may have sounded funny down the Two I's coffee bar assumes the dour relentlessness of an especially sodden Aldermaston march. Ban the pun!

In the 1990s a few representatives of the more conceptual side of rock 'n' roll saw fit to get out the jumbo jotters. KLF kingpin Bill Drummond, holed up in Aylesbury Public Library, compiled *45* (2000) a journal-cum-mental-shopping-list of his 45th year. It's packed with art projects that redefine 'esoteric' (including 'a private joke that's so private I don't even get it myself'), some reminiscences of his little million quid burning spree, and hymns to council houses and the down escalators in Friars' Square shopping centre. Former peacock of electronica turned conceptual studio guru Brian Eno collated the same mix of weighty and feather-light in *A Year with Swollen Appendices* (1996). The main headlines here are 'generative music', producing U2 and curating endless exhibitions, but there's enough time out to muse on oyster sauce, women's arses and being so transfixed by an edition of BBC2 comedy *The Saturday Night Armistice* he's forced to wee into a wine bottle, then inquisitively sips the result. Such is the life of the pop intellectual.

'I'd like to stroke Debbie Harry's bum.'

Over on the coke-dusted coffee table, *Rock Dreams* (1973) flops languidly. This collection of candy-coloured pop star portraits from the airbrush of Belgian comics artist Guy Peellaert has become notorious in rock circles, and receives regular reprints to this day, despite being as '1973' as 1973 got.

The most famous picture is a mock-up Sinatra news story; the headline 'Frankie Goes Hollywood' paraphrased a decade later by some leather-happy scousers. Elsewhere, literalism rules. The Drifters are pictured... under a boardwalk! The Chairmen of the Board... well, have a guess. Semi-surreal juxtapositions abound. The Beatles take tea with the Queen, Cilla knits on the doorstep as Brian Epstein's Roller bundles down the street, and the Stones get kitted out in bondage drag and Nazi storm trooper outfits while some underage naked girls learn the piano. A polite cough just won't cover it.

The same applies to Paula Yates's *Rock Stars in Their Underpants* (1980), the definitive coffee table/toilet crossover. Inspired by a pair of Bob Geldof's clag-stiffened crackers hanging off the end of the bed, La Yates takes a Polaroid camera round the haunts of music's elite to snap them *sans culottes* for a dirty giggle. The results, grainy and amateurish (Yates admits her 'models' had to help her load the camera) are more telling than a thousand airbrushed 'fan-tasies'. Some stars wisely go for the comedy route (Jools Holland in bow tie, Macca in frilly knicks over trousers and comedy beard). Many genuinely fancy themselves (Richard Jobson, Phil Lynott, David Lee Roth). If nothing else, it's a valuable record of a time when male underwear design remained an unsolved engineering problem, as one glimpse of the translucent lycra straining to envelop Rod Stewart's battered saveloy startlingly demonstrates. Andy Warhol, predictably enough, dubbed the book 'the greatest work of art in the last decade'. Peter Cook, on the other hand, wrote: 'At a time when two million people are out of work it is sickening that this woman should get rich with this hastily assembled bunch of snaps.' An interesting way to round off the book's foreword.

But what about the fans? They're surely the randiest of all. Media-savvy academics Fred and Judy Vermorel ransacked reams of fan correspondence and placed small ads in the music press collecting frenzied confessionals for the definitive compendium of mid-1980s pop fandom, *Starlust: the Secret Fantasies of Fans* (1985). The results are verbally all over the shop, but they all point to the same truth – the real driving force of rock 'n' roll is not musical progression or even corporate expansion but, well, provincial teenage masturbation.

The pop scene's a mixed bag at this point. Duran Duran may be on the rise, but Bowie still adorns many a wall, and reminiscences of the front rows of his concerts descending into mass tug-offs loom scarily large. Barry Manilow commands an international community of hormonal fundamentalists who sign off their delirious inter-fan correspondence with 'Lots and lots of Barryhugs, Manilove, and as always Manilust.' In amongst the tweeness tragedy does arise, usually involving female fans. Groupies get their dreams fulfilled only to have them trashed in a mire of backstage sweat and disdain. One girl's perpetually unanswered daily letters to Nick Heyward tip from obsession into madness and, we're told, end in a suicide attempt.

Boys, their emotional illiteracy granting them immunity from most worst-case scenarios, tend to avoid the soulful anguish and get straight down to business… or not as the case may be. One young lad is so shy he keeps making excuses to leave his own Sheena Easton fantasy. ('Sheena said: "Come back to my hotel room." I told her I had to be back. Then she touched my hand and said: "It's all right, I'm not that much of a Modern Girl."') Another finds the perfect fantasy partner in the pink negligee-clad form of Bucks Fizz's Cheryl Baker.

> I bite her ears and that makes her laugh even more. She's
> a torment and a tease. She just laughs all the way
> through. She doesn't encourage you but she doesn't
> exactly put you off. She lets you get on with it. She
> doesn't put up any resistance at all.
> She smells good – she smells of Cheryl.

Apart from the occasional pretentious tool ('I WORSHIP CELESTIAL LIGHTSHIPS'), it's all so sweetly gauche. Awed teenagers from the sticks drop the Vermorels a line in the businesslike tones of a job application. ('My secret sexual fantasy is with Bruce Foxton of The Jam and it is as follows.') Letters to Nick Heyward pepper their authors' humdrum domestic routine with star-spangled pop lust. ('Your sperm would last me through breakfast, lunch, dinner, tea and supper!') Anyone seriously worried about rock's evil influence on our pop kids would find more to dispute their thesis than back it up here. It's a testament to the harmlessly life-affirming, if often slightly messy, powers of music. 'At the moment I am masturbating and I've just come. Bye!'

21

GOING OUTSIDE

Tour guides, being sober and useful books, have no place in this survey. The celebrity tour guide, a chummy attempt to leaven the dry litany of place names with the personable reminiscences of a local famous face – that's a different matter. Often the celebrity's just a bit of garnish. Landscape photographer Derry Brabbs paired off with well-known writers in such books as *James Herriot's Yorkshire*. Respectable enough coffee-table fare, but the joins in the cut-'n'-shut format begin to show by the time we reach *Angela Rippon's West Country* (1982).

It's no fault of Rippon's. She keeps her side of the bargain with the good taste you'd expect from the veteran journalist, evoking her middle-class Plymouth childhood vividly. Trouble is, it's not terribly exciting stuff, despite the occasional reckless interlude of 'hanging upside down on the ornamental railings', and it's hard to keep coming up with new visual metaphors for the endless procession of cliffs and tors delicately snapped by Brabbs. Still, nobody bought *The Country Diary of an Edwardian Lady* for the diary bit, and Angela seems content to let her name and riding britches do the talking.

Fred Trueman's Yorkshire (1984), by contrast, is a text intended to merit serious consideration, as indicated by the jacket photo of a remote and rugged dale gazed upon by Fred's remote and rugged features, and the imposing, no-nonsense foreword by the Earl of Scarborough. ('I commend this book.') Don Mosey is on call to provide the basic quilt of Tourist Office information onto which Fred, fading in and out of proceedings like Mithering Hour on Radio Luxembourg, applies his common sense. Fred rounds off a passage on Dick Whittington prototype William Craven with a brusque: 'Not bad for a lad from Appletreewick!' and insists *Ilkla Moor Baht 'at* 'is, in all truth, a long and rather boring song and not a particularly good advertisement for those moorland breezes.'

Trueman the cricketer is keen on employing stats to give his regional musings the weight of authority. ('In Harry Ramsden's chandeliered dining room, decorated in cream, orange and brown, 31,000 bottles of sauce are emptied onto the plates of fish and chips, and the sideplates of bread and butter take up 39,400 loaves a year…') He crowns champions of every activity from fast bowling to tea drinking. ('The greatest pot-of-tea man I've ever known was my good friend Brian Close.') Elsewhere, there are pages to be filled. A casual mention that Fred enjoys 'nothing better than breakfasting outside and watching the finches frolic on the bird table' allows a list of garden birds spotted in Yorkshire to pad out a good four pages. Even Harold Wilson is roped in for some Huddersfield Town reminiscences. ('I used to go every Saturday morning… it was a penny each way on the tram… I usually had a pie.')

Capital offence

After the career blow dealt by an ill advised chat with the Sex Pistols, bluff ITV kingpin Bill Grundy led the hapless reader of *Grundy's London* (1979) a merry dance through the capital and, inevitably, his own obsessions. He's a matey if slightly gruff guide, wringing droll copy from historical quirks, lovable landlords and the haunted toilet roll holder of St Paul's cathedral. It's liberally seasoned with Grundy's own musings, which can seem rather odd. Historical intrigue in the house of Mayfair landowner Sir Thomas Grosvenor prompts Grundy to aver: 'some people have all the luck. If I had married a girl of twelve, they would have put me in prison.'

Elsewhere the bitter voice of experience warns the unwary tourist away from the more nefarious areas of Soho. ('Do not be drawn by the provocative pictures outside the clubs. They bear no relation to the contents and could probably be comfortably "done" under the Trades Description Act.') And the youth are forever mocking him with their unapologetic presence, giving him palpitations of rage on 'the dreaded Carnaby Street… reminds me of nothing so much as one of the outer circles of Hell.' The King's Road fares little better. 'The young people who frequent it do not seem much troubled by the need to earn a living.'

Recourse is to be had in the city's pubs. Despite such modern curses as 'juke boxes, pin tables and electronic tennis', Grundy upholds the boozer in all its forms. Ye Olde Cheshire Cheese gets an unsurprising rave review ('the size of the portions is apt to be a trifle overwhelming to all but hearty trenchermen.') Another pub is so small 'entering it is like putting on a comfortable pair of old slippers'. Handy boozing tips abound. Many London pubs can become crowded, 'so arrange to arrive there as they open, which is 11.30 AM on weekdays.' A trip round Portobello Road market can be easily livened up. 'There's nothing to stop you taking your own [booze] if you feel you'll be needing a drop before the law allows the pubs to open.' And inevitably, nothing tugs his heartstrings more than the closing of a decent old hostelry. 'We have lost a piece of England.'

'Come with me if you will…'

The deliberately amusing guide is harder to pull off, but *Les Dawson's Lancashire* (1983) leads the field. Taking his home county's superlative status for granted, Dawson's verbose 'Ramble in Arcadia' is an unofficial by-product of an edition of the BBC's well-loved *Comic Roots* series of reminiscences by strolling comedians revisiting their old haunts. *Roy Hudd's Croydon* and *Paul Shane's Rotherham* may have made fine telly, but only Dawson's trek to meet the lip-reading factory girls of Collyhurst had a book in it.

No genuine guidebook could hope to be a tenth as roundly written. 'The air is so bracing as it buffets your cheeks, and cajoles out a reddish hue, you will soon feel like a coy maiden hurrying to a tryst.' On New Brighton: 'the drink flowed like a faulty sluice and the girls left morality behind.' And Southport: 'I have seen little children walk out to find the sea, usually with a packed lunch under one arm, and they have returned fully matured and ready for the knackers.' Where Angela Rippon struggled for metaphors, Les has difficulty passing a paragraph without dropping one off. 'I was a cub reporter with a small newspaper, the circulation of which was smaller than the network of veins in a prawn's leg.'

Tour guides can arise from the unlikeliest alliances. By his own admission, Chelsea-born Old Salopian Willie Rushton was surprised when he was approached by the distillers of 100 Pipers ('the de-luxe Scotch whisky') to write a guide to Scotland. *Sassenach's Scotland* (1975) is an odd little book that begins, as required by law, with a mock conversation with the publishers, in which Rushton envisions a leisurely jaunt down celeb guidebook easy street. 'Ah well, I thought. I shall relive some old memories. Thumb through Dr Johnson's Highland Jaunts or whatever, cull some deathless prose from the Scottish Tourist Board's offerings, interlace it all with many a dash of Rushtonian smut, and be back here on Thursday.' What actually takes place is a series of bemusing Highland adventures for Rushton and his five-year-old son Toby, involving tall tales and a lot of whisky. It's lightweight fun above and beyond the call of the average booze promotion, festooned with the man's own sketches of affably bearded boiling lunacy.

Language lab

After the comedy tour guide comes the comedy phrasebook.

Dialectical humour can be ready-made, as anyone compiling a stocking-sized primer in Cockney rhyming slang will attest. Jack Jones' *Rhyming Cockney Slang* (1971) remains ubiquitous in its London bus cover, having seen off short-lived pretenders like Ronnie Barker's *Porridge* cash-in *Fletcher's Book of Rhyming Slang* (1979). Bob Aylwin's *A Load of Cockney Cobblers* (1973), a slightly more scholarly tome, grew out of an especially swinging Press Club lunch (as all great literary endeavours should) and combined a smattering of linguistic history with a comprehensive list of rhymes for swearwords (from 'Hampton Wick' to 'Sharp and Blunt') and a foreword by Leslie Crowther.

Stanley Baxter was the first to cast a thick regional accent as a foreign language in its own right with *Parliamo Glasgow*, BBC radio language course *Parliamo Italiano* relocated to the Gorbals, in the early '50s. Television and print followed in the early '80s, the last allowing close textural appreciation of Glaswegian compound words such as JIWANNABELTOANRAMOOTH? and JEEZYURSTOCIOUS! The idea was applied widely outside Glasgow, as nearby as Dundee and as far afield as Australia, where Alastair Murdoch's *Let's Talk Strine* (1965, 'compiled by Afferbeck Lauder') achieved international notoriety.

Similarly, the BBC's *Look North* news magazine was peppered in the late '60s by wry items on the Geordie tongue, presented by Mike Neville. These were the work of Tyneside humorist Scott Dobson, who corralled Mike and pals into a spin-off spoof language record and phrasebook *Larn Yersel' Geordie* (1969). The book's publisher Frank Graham hooked up two years later with Yorkshire Television's regional round-up *Calendar*, which ran a feature entitled *Yorksher Speyks*. Producer Sid Waddell and presenter Austin Mitchell guided viewers round the rockier points of God's Own Dialect, explaining such choice phrases as 'If ee fell oft Co-op eed fall int Divi Ole' ('He is a remarkably fortunate person.') An LP and booklet, *Teach Thissen Tyke* (1971) followed, adding a lot of slightly forced punny humour about 'Tykonian Man'. ('He arrived in the first (Pre

Bird's Eye) Ice Age'.)

The book remained a source of pride for Mitchell long after he left television behind for the House of Commons. He updated it to 'celebrate' the marriage of Sarah Ferguson to the Duke of York, and was still plugging it on Tuesday 20 March 2007. During the Commons debate on the proposed Draft Corporation Tax (Taxation of Films) (Transitional Provisions) Regulations bill, he mused: 'I am delighted, my Right Hon. Friend will be pleased to hear, that up to four points may be awarded, depending on "the percentage of the original dialogue that is recorded in the English language or in a recognised regional or minority language". As the author of *Teach Thissen Tyke*, which is the people's guide to Yorkshire grammar and language – to speaking Yorkshire – I expect that my sales will be enormously increased by that concession to regional language, so I welcome it.' Mitchell, Austin: see also 'Brassneck'.

Gentlemen with odd-shaped balls

As Vivian Stanshall nearly sang, it's an odd boy who writes about sport. How can you do justice to purely physical feats with a few motionless words on the page? Then there are the lengthy publishing lead times that keep *Guinness Book of Records* editors awake at night – a week is a long time in sport, never mind the best part of a year. So what's left for the sporting author? You can mock with affection, as when Geoffrey Atkinson ghosted *How to be Really Interesting by Steve Davis* (1988), but that was showbiz, not recreation. Something more is needed.

Sports writers can go the serious, statistical route; or take a baroque ramble through the highways and byways of the game, with plenty of hearty Victorian clubroom bonding. Willie Rushton, unsurprisingly, was the master of the latter. *Pigsticking, a Joy for Life: a Gentleman's Guide to Sporting Pastimes* (1977) is his avuncular illustrated catalogue of sporting life from hunting to hang-gliding. It's intended as a useful book. Rushton gives copious practical details for each pastime, including costs (it's £1,000-£1,500 p.a. to run a show-jumping horse, and 55p to get started at marbles).

The trademark Rushton bufferish ebullience abounds. He takes in elephant racing, real tennis, octopush and of course pigsticking, a vicious-looking colonial pursuit of wild boar with spear on horseback, discovered in an ancient book by Sir Robert Baden-Powell. Facts are generously garnished with digressive detours into the Elgin marbles, the *Gidget* films and the Japanese women's volleyball team. It's not all post-prandial frivolity – he's genuinely passionate about rampant Formula One sponsorship, the rotten state of British athletics, and... well, the Japanese women's volleyball team.

One of Rushton's keenest comments concerns golf. 'One favourable aspect of the game is that it transfers well to print... On the other hand, it has the largest fund of awful jokes, many oddly starring God or his eldest.' Sure enough, each Christmas brings a new wave of nineteenth hole ephemera, varying wildly in quality. Golf is as much an amateur pastime as a professional sport, and it's this, along with the eternal showbiz connection, that's to blame. *How to Become a Scratch Golfer* (1963) is a fine early example, with Patrick Campbell donning his usual 'baffled stumblebum' mantle for a flat-footed faltering tour of the amateur game. But it's a long way down the ladder of wit, via Tim Brooke-Taylor's *Golf Bag* (1989), Ronnie Corbett's *Armchair Golf* (1986), Cliff Michelmore's *Businessman's Book of Golf* (1981) and the inevitable *Tarbuck on Golf* (1984), to *The Good Golf Guide to Scotland* (1985), a meeting of minds between Sean Connery and 'Diddy' David Hamilton.

All very cosy and Pringle-clad,so it's no surprise to see the word 'bedside' surface here. *The Golfer's Bedside Book* (1971) is an anthology of amusing golfiana with golf course architect Donald Steel as club secretary. Unsurprisingly, velvet-lined wordsmith Peter Alliss takes centre stage. Half the time, he's not even talking about golf: 'I get as much pleasure out of looking at the *Radio Times* as Dean Martin must get when reaching for his first martini of the day... stocked up with plenty of cold meat and coleslaw... I put my feet up on my favourite television pouffe, and settle back.' It's all charming as hell, and thunderously irrelevant.

Bedside Bedser

Cricket's another sport of gift book note. Like golf, it's conducted at a pace leisurely enough to allow funny things to happen. The word 'anthology' follows the word 'cricketing' as naturally as the word 'whites' or the word 'disaster'. Any fan looking to kit out his smallest room as a miniature Long Room can pluck out weighty cornucopia like Gerald Brodribb's *All Round the Wicket: a Miscellany of Facts and Fancies of First-Class Cricket* (1951) and Leslie Frewin's *The Boundary Book: A Lord's Taverners' Miscellany Of Cricket* (1962), while those with a taste for sporting whimsy might take a chance with *LBW: Laughter Before Wicket!* (1990) or *Nicely Nurdled, Sir!* (1986). If an MCC tie could talk, you fear, it would sound like this.

The first thing to ask about *The Thoughts of Trueman Now: Every Cricket Maniac's Anthology* (1978) is what the hell they were playing at with that title. Was there a cultural revolution about to emanate from the boardroom of the Yorkshire CCC? Things make a little more sense when the book's cast are announced on the inner flap. There's 'a bloody fast bowler' – Trueman of course. He's aided by 'a wise supporter', ie Eric Morecambe (geddit?), 'a celebrity square-leg' Willie Rushton (geddit redux) and 'a rightish left-arm mediator', that is to say editor Fred Rumsey (Derbyshire & England).

This over-manning is a cunning attempt to get over the main problem with humorous sporting anthologies. Nearly all sportsmen's humour is of one variety (just as, to be fair, nearly all comedians' cricket is of one variety). It's the amusing on-pitch story, told in hearty after dinner style, full of forthright 'or so I thought's, 'unbeknownst to them's and the odd 'to this day I'll never know how…' Fine for public engagements, but on the page all that best bib and tucker loses its congenial character. You can say this shit, Geoffrey, but you can't type it.

Thoughts solves the problem by having Morecambe 'interrupt' Fred's flow of rugged wisdom with little jokey boxouts. ('Fred holds records – one was by Des O'Connor, which I broke!') Willie weaves his cartoons around the two in best *Pigsticking* style and Fred R, presumably, held the jumpers and tried to keep score. Trueman's musings on the technical side of the game are livened up by the odd Morecambe quip, and later on, when talk turns to broader issues and Fred's expertise runs out, the gags are stepped up to fill the void. On streakers, Fred blames 'the permissive society we have found ourselves living in.' Eric, meanwhile, recalls, 'as she ran away from the police she looked like Kojak with a deep frown.' But Morecambe avoids penning a whimsical coda to Fred's reminiscences of cricket masseur Bright Heyhurst. 'A nice little man who liked to smoke his pipe, he was definitely a character. Mind you, he would only rub the players he liked!' There's no answer to that.

Bobby Hope is better than Eusebio

The beautiful game has produced more literature than any sport, but light-hearted romps are thin on the ground. *Shack's Guide to Soccer* (1956) by Len Shackleton followed hard on the heels of his autobiography *The Clown Prince of Soccer* which, in the PR vernacular of that vintage, 'rocked the game to its foundations with its frankness'. A wry aside in a chapter called The Average Director's Knowledge of Football (consisting of – yes – a blank page) convinced someone a full-on Shack gigglefest was a good idea, but with free rein to clown, Shack over-eggs the pudding. We get gags, all right. Too many bloody gags.

Shackleton had a good comic ear and could certainly write, but the jokiness rapidly wears thin. He tries to do a

Beachcomber with whole chapters of whimsical predictions of the state of soccer ten years hence featuring whimsical names like Sir Odd Lee-Enough. There's even a touch of surrealism in footnotes like: 'If you have read up to this point you should ask yourself this question: "Have I read up to this point?" If the answer is "No", what reason did you have for asking that question?' He's on surer ground looking at aspects of the game that are silly to begin with, like the obsessive nature of pools panelists.

But Len could be forgiven for trying too hard, judging by the dourness of his contemporaries. Most football books are deadly serious, but that doesn't mean you can't still have fun. In *Striking for Soccer* (1961) Jimmy Hill gives us an earnest appraisal of the modern game in all its red-shinned glory. We begin with a potted biography of the man himself. 'I was so keen on football that I would play for my school team in the morning, go home covered in mud, have lunch, and then go to play for the Boys' Brigade team in the afternoon. All of this only needed one bath, but what a bath it was!' Sadly he fails to specify which items of clothing were used to mark the goals.

Once past that, things start to get interesting. Chapter Eight, 'Kissing and Cuddling', gives the Hill verdict on the eponymous modern form of on-pitch gratification – he's 'not against the occasional "cuddle", which can be manly,' but kissing is best left to 'our Continental and Latin friends'. Best of all, however, is Chapter Six, 'Beard Versus Chin', chronicling his rise to national eminence after donning the hitherto un-soccer-like facial hair (which, excitingly, came about when he decided not to bother with shaving in order to free up precious morning time that could be better spent watching his goldfish).

> Advertisers became interested in me. The beard photographed well on television. People wanted to listen to what I had to say... Previously I had just been the long-chinned, rangy, lanky, long-striding Jimmy Hill; now they

could embellish their reports with such phrases as 'the bold buccaneer', 'the plundering pirate', 'Mephistopheles running wild', 'the beatnik with the ball', etc.

Michael Parkinson cast a shadow of dour pride over both cricket and football in fairly straight anthologies, but with *The A-Z of Soccer* (1970) his lachrymose parochialism was ameliorated by the sprightly humour of playwright Willis Hall. For good measure, Bob Monkhouse added nifty cartoons. Overcome with pre-match anticipation, the jacket blurb overplays its hand. 'All three make a living out of being funny.' This is either being weirdly generous, or snidely caustic, about the lad from Barnsley.

It's tempting to try and spot the division of labour. Closet Wingers, a paean to the peripheral footballer's traditional training regime of booting a ball against a row of outside khazis, has to be the work of Parky, while Hall is most likely the one pouring elegant scorn on the 'sniggering songs of rugby oafs', and praising the unbawdy purity of soccer chants in which 'the true intent of foul language is that of honest insult and pure abuse.' This book is a lot bawdier than previous football anthologies. Firey Fred's permissive society has let broad humour invade the after-dinner pitch. There's also an early sighting of the perennial complaint of the game's inept colonisation by the middle class intelligentsia.

Professional humourists snuck onto the football pitch, but the surface cut up pretty rough. Eric Morecambe tried to repeat his Freddie-boosted success with *Over the Moon... Sick as a Parrot* (1982), but got an early bath instead. The book comes to you live from a Bilbao hotel room during the Spanish World Cup, allegedly, but turns out to consist of photos of the great man in a series of wacky spectacles-akimbo poses. Also letting the pictures take the strain was Willie Rushton, but *How to Play Football* (1968) is at least smile-inducing, being as it is a paper-thin excuse for Rushton, Richard Ingrams and special guest Roy Hudd to pranny about in baggy Edwardian football shorts, caps and comedy moustaches. Surely Ingrams in shorts is worth 12/6 of anyone's money?

It's up to the dark horse of the tournament, Willie Donaldson, to provide a suitably strange coda. *The Meaning of Cantona: Meditations on Life, Art and Perfectly Weighted Balls* (1997) is a mock philosophical tract written with Terence Blacker under Donaldson's perennial alias of Dr Kit Bryson, purporting to dissect the towering psyche of that most gnomic of international footballers. It's full of nicely judged aphorisms ('When the fox plays badminton with the goose, the shuttlecock is the loser') but the real coup is the book's discovery of an earlier French counterpart, *Que Signifie Gazza? Les Pensees d'un Idiot Savant* (1990). This, of course, never existed, but according to Donaldson (salt at the ready, chaps) many readers who didn't quite 'get' the book assumed it did, and 'one of WH Smith's thin, ambitious women (formerly of paper-clips)' even phoned the alleged publishers to try and obtain English translation rights. As the book itself says, 'Do you see? Well, you're mistaken. Never read another football book again.'

'They're putting the fun back into sport!'

The more frivolous the sport, the more serious the books. David Vine's celebration of the first four years of television's all-comers celebrity decathlon *The Superstars* (1977) is a case in point, breathlessly belting through the programme's milestone events as if we're witnessing the acme of sporting endeavour. With intensely furrowed brow, Dave brings us the skinny on the Joe Bugner-Jackie Stewart feud! David Hemery's obsessive personal best chart making! Malcolm Macdonald's canoe capsizing! Jonah Barrington lobbing his Adidas bag at the wall in protest at disallowed squat thrusts!

Vine uses every weapon in his commentator's armoury to make the reader feel he's actually there at Rotterdam's Ahoy Stadium counting JPR Williams's pull-ups. He phoneticises foreign accents for amusing local colour. ('Zat ees anudder event we will 'ave to forget eef we want to stop 'im winnin' again next year!') And of course the defining moment of the series, Kevin Keegan's vest-shredding cycle crash at Bracknell, is brought to life in classically taut Vinian prose. ('There's a lump of skin missing from his elbow about the size of a small beer mat.') It all ends with a puff for the Palitoy *Superstars* board game.

Wearing its prose at an altogether jauntier angle is *To Horse! To Horse!* (1982), a spin-off from Terry Wogan's Radio Two racing feature *Wogan's Winner*, a notoriously slipshod betting roundup denounced by Wogan himself as a perpetual failure. Aiding the betting on the wireless was Tony Fairbairn, who provides the informative meat of the book to accompany Tel's crinkle-cut chippy asides. ('Shout it from your crenellated castle ramparts! Royal Ascot! Morning suits and toppers! Good old Moss Bros! Smoked salmon and champoo! Roly-polys as far as the eye can see!') Wogan's in his element here, if not his cups. Anecdotes include the day Sarah Kennedy was obliged to read out the carefully worded racing tip: 'Mai Pussy, triumphant at Doncaster earlier this week, is looking for further success this afternoon.' Fiery Fred would not be amused.

22

LOOSE WOMEN

After being refused entry to the 1960s countercultural party, feminism finally got a foot inside the door come the turn of the decade. Revolutionary manifestoes leapt from university humanities labs to op-ed pages and panel discussion programmes. Wild-haired liberationist sisters clashed with tweedy establishment bastions whose condescending tones gave an air of unimpressed amusement only slightly betrayed by their rigidly clamped-together knees. But feminist literature really troubled the tills when Shirley Conran, women's editor of the *Observer* and high profile equal opportunities campaigner, published *Superwoman* (1975). This wasn't a socio-political call to arms. It was about washing up.

Conran spent 18 months distilling twenty years of domestic know-how via 500,000 words of notes into 200 pages, plus endpapers emblazoned with imperial-to-metric hat size conversion tables. (Although some pages are left blank, for the reader's own additions: *'please deface this book.'*) Add in some reminiscences from veteran parlour maids, and you've got something that wouldn't look out of place on an 18th-century gentlewoman's scullery shelf. This didn't look like empowerment, at least as the feminist intellectuals had described it, but that's exactly what it claimed to be.

The tips can seem daunting, especially when delivered in Conran's patrician, clipped sentences. ('Don't put away jars or tins with drips on them. Clean floor and shelves with warm, damp spongecloth. Fold packet tops over *before* putting away and regularly wipe out bread, cake and biscuit tins.') Lesser mortals baulked at what looked like a pinafore-clad version of National Service, but Conran was only being practical. ('Let's face it *someone's* got to do the dirty work and anyone who thinks they're going to chuck a dirty bra at a man and tell him to sew on a hook and eye is an idealist, or daft.') As the book's motto famously said, life's too short to stuff a mushroom.

These misgivings had little effect on the book's tremendous success. *The Times* called it 'the most practical *aide memoire* to feminism on the market'. An excitable Tina Brown described Conran as 'a revved-up Mrs Beeton… who, even in an apron, exudes nervy sexuality.' *Superwoman* became the number one gift for newlywed women that Christmas. Follow-ups proliferated. The shocking pink *Superwoman Yearbook* (1976) contained twelve months of weekly recipes, gardening hints and middle class gags ('New Beaujolais arrives this month; throw away Old Beaujolais.') *Superwoman 2* (1977), *Futurewoman: How to Survive Life After Thirty* (1979) and *Superwoman in Action* (1979) followed in a flurry of authorial activity that, though intense, never stopped Conran having a good go at the taps with liquid Gumption.

Not everyone was impressed. *The Times* Diary cynically described her as 'a woman who writes a book of household hints and, by thinking up a catchy title… manages to promote it as some kind of breakthrough'. The *Guardian's* Suzanne Lowry predicted that the book signalled 'a PS: a last crow, or perhaps cheep, of the dizzy hen journalism launched so brilliantly when she taught us to own up to being sluts, to giggle and brow-mop, and somehow, gosh, to cope'. (She couldn't have been more wrong.) Polly Toynbee laid into the mad frenzy of activity described in the book ('I wash my light bulbs, every one, every week, because you say that you can lose 25 per cent of your light with a grimy bulb, and I soak my acrylic lampshades in the bath') and wondered why the index omitted an entry for 'divorce'. Conran herself married and divorced three times, most famously in 1963 from philandering Habitat major-domo Terence Conran. She later conceded that

Superwoman's domestic maelstrom might have been a tad unrealistic, and published the downwardly revised *Down with Superwoman* in 1990.

On November 3, 1975, *Superwoman* received one of the oddest publicity puffs ever devised. Publishers Secker and Warberg invited the world's press to an exhibition of three 'superkitchens', designed around the bespoke whims of three celebrities: Conran, who was celebrating sales of 50,000; Michael Crawford, and Jilly Cooper. Cooper, who'd spent the first half of the decade carving a deep niche in the dead centre of Lowry's hated 'dizzy hen' school of journalism, was no stranger to the 'super' epithet herself, combining it in various ways with her second favourite word, 'jolly', for a series of paperback collections from *Jolly Super!* (1971) to *Superjilly* (1977).

In contrast to her often bloated romantic novels, Cooper's twin books on the battle of the sexes, *Men and Super Men* (1972) and *Women and Super Women* (1974), crack along like extended columns, a light-hearted shopping list of half-sentences laying down the lore on gender stereotypes old and new ('men in television brush their hair forwards'), peppered with symptoms of compulsive punning disorder (housework is 'the tortures of Sissy-fuss'). Despite the Christmas cracker feel, Cooper wrings a cheery corrective to the 'joyless outpourings' of women's lib lit, 'the biggest bore of the century, only rivalled by the Common Market,' with breezy upper-crust confidence, epitomised by her claim that the manuscript for Women… was dashed off longhand in the pages of a blank publisher's dummy of Winston Churchill's *The Gathering Storm*.

'God bless Shirley Cooklin!'

Predictably, parodies of *Superwoman* were not far behind. But in this case, the parodies had the grace to be useful in their own right. *Superpig* (1976) was a 'what about the fellers?' answer from Willie Rushton. All very well the single working mum grabbing the domestic goddess cake and stuffing it into her mouth on the way to one of her three full-time jobs, mused the dapper humorist, but what about the other side of the equation? Where there's an estranged wife, there's an estranged husband. Finding himself in that position, Rushton makes his own guide as sincere as Conran's, and a lot more amusing to boot. ('Men, simply look upon this as your life support system. I have before me as I write a picture of Shirley Conran, rather as Monty used to keep Rommel tacked to the wall of his caravan.')

Rather than leer bitterly ('There's no vinism, like chauvinism, like no vinism I know…') Rushton decides the best revenge is living well, and guides his sock-sniffing bachelor charges through a theoretical 'worst 24 hours a lone man could possibly enjoy… it's the Book of Job for non-starters in the race of life.' He's got the initiative of Conran too, catching wasps with a Hoover, ironing frozen bread and knocking up Nepalese scrambled eggs for one. He even branches out into party-throwing, parenting and, indeed, pulling, arguing that a Superpig is surely irresistible to women: 'Gracious lady, viewing him across a room, breathes huskily "Now there is a man, he knits, he sews, he cooks Crepes Suzettes, he changes nappies, he gives excellent suck, he knows his Hoover, he shaves his legs, there is a man".'

It might be advisable to start mending your slovenly ways before the big split. Who better to advise on the finer points of manly responsibility than Gyles Brandreth, in *The Complete Husband* (1978)? Dedicated to his wife Michèle Brown, whom he wooed over a Chinese meal (set menu 4/6d), Brandreth's book is a painstakingly researched compendium of domestic budgeting, DIY, cooking ('no slicing butter out of the packet!') and cleaning (a bottle of Handy Andy to the fore). Further chapters deal with fitness and sex ('with age the quality (if not the quantity) definitely improves'). Towards the end of the book the subjects get unnervingly personal. Sexually transmitted diseases and mental illness (slovenly housekeeping, apparently, is an early warning sign of the latter) are a long way from the TV-am comfort zone. But the desire to help is genuine, even if, as Brandreth himself admits, he'd 'do it differently nowadays'.

Pottering in the other direction, women's refuge charity founder Erin Pizzey parried the Conranisation of domesticity with *The Slut's Cook Book* (1981), an unashamedly easygoing guide to early '80s NW1 social life. ('If you find that you have accidentally invited a sociologist, you may as well let him deliver a lecture and get down to drinking straight out of the bottle.') Dismantling militaristic housekeeping maxims one by one ('the old method of putting the lettuce into a tea-towel and swinging it round one's head must have given British women peculiarly lopsided breasts'), Pizzey puts the case for knocking the fearful pursuit of domestic perfection on the head and just enjoying yourself. 'Sluts of the world unite! You have nothing to lose except your Valium.'

They're out to get us, chaps!

The typical humour book had a typical hero – the suburban, middle-aged, married everyman. All aspects of life weighed heavily on his mind, but none more so than marriage. The stereotypical nagging wife is older than history, and her restless tongue has been a feature of toilet book comedy from the *Hundred Merry Tales* onward. *Punch* founder Douglas Jerrold set the modern incarnation of the matrimonial harpy rolling with *Mrs Caudle's Curtain Lectures* (1846), the collected memoirs of Job Caudle, a hapless toy seller nagged to sleep every evening by his wife Margaret on 'the joys, griefs, duties and vicissitudes comprised within that seemingly small circle – the wedding ring'. Whatever Job has got up to that day – losing a shirt button, lending an umbrella, coming home slightly late – he puts up with a lengthy bedtime lecture from the missus, starting out with steamrolling rhetoric, but gradually becoming more sympathetic, even tragic in her last lecture, delivered in the throes of a fatal cold brought on by 'getting wet in thin shoes'.

By the 1970s, the phrase 'Women's Lib' introduced a good ten percent of all British stand-up comedy routines. *The Cosmo*

Smallpiece Guide to Male Liberation (1979) is subtitled 'a fantasy by
Les Dawson', which is either a tacit distancing of the great
comedian from his slimiest creation – a walking bollock in bottle
top glasses whose surname speaks volumes – or a way for the dour
old gagsmith to have his cake and eat it. The arguments for and
against the mother-in-law gag as natural product of working class
existence are as old as the back-to-backs from which they sprang,
but it's clear Dawson's fear and distrust of women only comes
about as a subset of his fear and distrust of everything. Besides,
no genuine misogynist, fortunately, is ever this quotable. On
marriage: 'I've been married nearly twenty years and you know
something? It only seems like yesterday. If it was tomorrow I'd
cancel the bloody thing.' On sex: 'A woman, when hubby finally
gets her on the boil, prefers to make love in the dark, so that as the
poor old coot pants like a station horse on the vinegar stroke, she
can bury her indifference by pretending she's being raped by Burt
Lancaster.' It all ends up in a nightmare year 2000 where men are
kept in concentration camps by Prime Minister Angela Rippon.

Speaking of small pieces, the premise of cartoonist Gray
Jolliffe's *Wicked Willie: Man's Best Friend* (1984) was simple.
Bumbling, bald, big-nosed man attempts to cop off with
simpering, blonde, big-nosed woman, only to have his sarky, big-
nosed penis make lewd interjections and generally louse things up.
Once the concept of a book featuring several dozen wobbly
cartoons of an erect penis had somehow got past the moral
guardians at WH Smith's, the stage was set for several consecutive
Christmases of bestselling glans-related merchandise. Providing
the linking text in these endeavours was Peter Mayle, a former
writer of sex education manuals who would hit more respectable
paydirt a few years later with pastoral Middle England romp *A
Year in Provence*, and presumably had a lot of explaining to do to his
new fanbase. (He was once reprimanded: 'Your dreadful little
books are in every lavatory in Wiltshire!') In 1988, the inevitable
distaff version was floated onto the seasonal humour table. *Pussy
Pie Hits Town*, however, despite passing the textual baton from

Mayle to Laurie Graham, was a bit of a non-starter, not helped by the inelegant solution to the visual problem of representing the organ in question without being blackballed by Smith's. The resulting sort of pink furry cat thing with high heels and tits wasn't, let's say, quite so iconic.

Naughty pictures of a more decorous kind were the hobby of Ronnie Barker, who brought out half a dozen books for the boudoir coffee table over ten years, showing off his collection of coy pre-war erotica, from *Ronnie Barker's Bathing Beauties* (1974) to *Ooh La-La! The Ladies of Paris* (1983). Barker took his cue from Victorian erotica like publisher R March's *A Jolly Book for Jolly Folks: All About Girls and Their Doings* (1880), which boasted plates of 'big girls at school, big girls at home, girls who are fast, girls who are wicked, sensible girls, silly girls, dirty girls' in glorious colour. A serious collector, Barker toned down the jokes and let the pictures do the talking. (...*Paris* claimed 'you can read this book in an hour. But you can look at it for the rest of your life'.) Another girlie coffee table affair was more verbose. Paula Yates, high on Warholian approbation for her Polaroid pop-grot investigation *Rock Stars in Their Underpants*, took her next coffee table commission a bit more seriously.

For *Blondes: a History from their Earliest Roots* (1983), Yates, in a self-styled impression of AJP Taylor, puts in the legwork researching her subject. Copious photographs and paintings are surrounded by reams of unstoppably chatty text. We romp through Helen of Troy, Boadicea ('the Janet Street Porter of the Northern Tribes'), the legend of Lady Godiva ('which appears to have been written by typesetters on a day off from the *Guardian*') and Madame de Pompadour ('bore a distressing resemblance to Dame Flora Robson had Dame Flora ever run in the Grand National'). The jokes are all this good. She's on firmer ground with film stars (Marilyn Monroe's chronic wind and toothbrush-and-toilet pubic bleaching method) royals ('If only Koo Stark were blonde I could type for as long as Norman Mailer') and advertising ('What does happen after a Badedas bath?') It's forgettable fluff, and naturally critics queued up to patronise its author on release. 'Well tried!' She was never going to win this one.

Man-size issues

Anna Ford, journalist, newsreader and all-round getter-up of chauvinist broadcasting backs, also attempted a sociological survey, though this was a tad more serious. *Men: a Documentary* (1985) collated three years' research of 120 male subjects from all walks of life. 'Of those approached only four declined to see me: Denis Thatcher, the Archbishop of Canterbury, Sir Freddie Laker and Oliver Reed.' If this whets the appetite for some kind of celebrity confessional, tough luck: all names have been diligently altered. So it's 'Chris, bank clerk', 'George, CID officer', and 'Fred, dustman' to you, Mr Prurient.

This gives rise to a tempting round of 'guess the grandee' among the more high-profile subjects. Who, for instance, is 'Philip', a fifty-year-old tycoon who muses 'Women like you to give it to them hard and regular'? Or 'Phil', a pop singer aged 20, confessing to having 'always worried about my penis just not satisfying her. I know all the magazines say that when they're erect there's not much difference, but I don't think that's true'? Or 'Paul', the forty-year-old actor with the secret toupee? Or the seventysomething Lord who used homosexuality to get off games at school? ('I wasn't a real homosexual, it was just convenient.') Only Ford knows for sure, and she's not telling.

All titillation ruled out, Ford, a social anthropology graduate from Manchester University, lays on the academic rigour. No stone is left unturned. Unfortunately no stone is left unedited either, and the endless transcribed confessions soon become tedious. Sometimes a revealing phrase stands out. ('I really have no criticism of women as a race and of course they are a different race. But I dislike some of the species. For example, small, fluttery, "poor little me" women I can do without.') Mostly though, it's an unremarkable litany of clichés and prejudices. Ford earnestly ponders the eternal question of what men really *are*. On this evidence, a bunch of boring bastards might be one conclusion.

The press trashed the book. ('Godforsaken' – *The Times*.) It was seen as unprofessional, lazy and dull. Some of these claims held weight, but there was also an element of chauvinism at work. Not just between male and female journalists, but between pressmen and a 'celebrity' television (and therefore not really legit) journo. The *Times* Diary contented itself with trying to identify the sissy cabinet minister who cries at the national anthem. (For the record, it was probably Geoffrey Howe.)

Ford's much-trumpeted work had a parodic answer in the works before it was even published. Again, this was no ordinary parody. The premise of *Henry Root's A-Z of Women: 'The Definitive Guide'* (1985) was simple: Root has been commissioned by 'Lord Weidenfeld of Nicholson' to write a 'rival' book to Ford's *Men*. The stage is seemingly set for a gender-based *World of Knowledge*, but the book in question never gets written. Instead, we're treated to the diaries of Root's young collaborator Kim Kindersley, a foppish, proto-metrosexual Old Etonian with a penchant for high-top boots and *Cosmo* stress guides, who accompanies Root on a series of lewd adventures at a sex shop, a massage parlour and finally an attempt to entrap two *Daily Mirror* journalists in a CCTV-equipped bondage dungeon at Elm Park Mansions. Aside from a few dictated letters for old times' sake, this 'A-Z' turns out to be a moderately funny bedroom farce in the Tom Sharpe mould, albeit the only sex farce in publishing history to come with a fully annotated index ('Ford, Anna: on men, vi; ejaculated, 2; says 'masturbate' in the early afternoon, 2; head-first down backstairs, 3; back end of a panto horse, 4; asks impertinent questions, 88; and bondage, 214').

23

FALL AND RISE

From its mid-1980s peak, the only way for the toilet book was down the pan. Various factors conspired to dent the market. The collapse of the Net Book Agreement, and the subsequent rise of the mega-chains, shook the industry in general. But for the humour market, the biggest impact was due to the rise of the video. The 1990s saw the sell-through VHS market take off, with novelty titles such as car accident compilation *Police Stop!* (1994) and footballing pratfall miscellany *Danny Baker's Own Goals and Gaffes* (1992) stealing the humour book's thunder by appearing on crowd-drawing in-store monitors on a constant loop. The static antics of Larry were no competition: the 1990s novelty gift of choice was all singing, all dancing, and all falling over.

As VHS gave way to DVD, the impact on comedy TV tie-in books was felt too. Increasingly, fans of comedy programmes could own the original broadcasts, rather than a paper translation. Why expend acres of new material and design expense on a book, when you can call the stars into a screening room for an afternoon's commentary recording, stick a 'making of' featurette on the end and charge fifteen quid for it? But comedy traditions have always died hard, and the craft of the comedy book weathered the commercial onslaught.

Original formats helped some tie-ins stand out. The show itself may have given rise to the overused aphorism that comedy was the new rock-'n'-roll, but *The Mary Whitehouse Experience*

Encyclopaedia (1991) took the form of a studious, *Guinness Book*-style children's fact file. The book was, however, marred by rock-style ego battles – various members of the fragmenting four-strong team chose to distance themselves from the others' content by labelling, without a shred of irony, their own favourite contributions with their initials.

Less prone to vanity were the stand-up duo Stewart Lee and Richard Herring, who made literary capital of their cult BBC2 series *Lee and Herring's Fist of Fun* (1995), which took the form of another hoary old children's format, the 'why not try…?' activity book. Here, however, the enthusiasm was genuine, as Herring explains. 'As teenage comedy fans, we spotted which comedy books were ripping us off and which were done with love. I really liked the *Monty Python* books. Stew really liked the *Goodies* books. These were the benchmarks we were aiming at.'

Amateurish in the best sense, the duo pitched into their task with great energy. 'We were very hands-on with everything,' recalls Herring. 'It came together pretty quickly, partly because we had lots of resources to draw on. Some of it was stuff we had done as students – the page of doctored Panini football stickers was something Stew had done at University.' They weren't entirely free from BBC Books's censure, though: 'We wanted to do a couple of pages parodying the books by John McCarthy and Brian Keenan, which our editor didn't like at all. She was working on a book with John McCarthy and showed it to him, and he read it down the phone to Brian Keenan, who was offended. (It was a routine about different attitudes to imprisonment, rather than any kind of attack on them.) We had to cut it.'

The golden rule remained: because of the amount of work involved, if the comedians' hearts weren't in the project, the wheels came off. 'It is an awful lot of work writing a book,' admits Herring. 'You need a lot of material. Unless you just fill it with scripts and photos of you in funny hats.' The DIY aesthetic that characterised much of 1990s British comedy helped in this respect. *Vic Reeves' Big Night In* (1991) was

festooned with the same surreal, childlike scrawls as Reeves and
Bob Mortimer's groundbreaking TV series. Following in Lee
and Herring's footsteps, no-budget bedroom comedians Adam
Buxton and Joe Cornish put *The Adam and Joe Book* (1999)
together with lashings of childlike thrift. Sadly, sales were so disappointing that the pair resorted to the self-flagellating gesture
of cutting up and frying remaindered copies on air. (Perhaps
unsurprisingly, copies that escaped the frying pan now go for
tidy sums on eBay.) Equally high on low-rent charm was *Buygones*
(1988), a spin-off from Victor Lewis Smith and Paul Sparkes's
ramshackle nostalgic segment on unlamented Channel Four arts
magazine *Club X*, which almost single-handedly bent the trend
for media nostalgia away from the misty-eyed armchair reminis-
cence to the acidly cynical deconstruction of such long-gone
ephemera as I-Spy books, Wonderloaf and the mysteriously dis-
continued Ayds slimming biscuit.

The odd sitcom could still be bent into book shape, as
Graham Linehan and Arthur Mathews demonstrated with *Father
Ted: the Craggy Island Parish Magazines* (1998), which focussed on
the ecumenical comedy's lead character's slowly evolving
attempts to edit the threadbare 'Our Parish' newsletter, high-
lighting Ted's combination of naïve enthusiasm and tetchy
egotism over the show's other, broader characters (with the odd
appearance from Mrs Doyle, advising on the best way to 'clean
shite out of the carpet'). But what would perhaps have the most
interesting 1990s comedy tie-in book never happened at all.
After the landslide critical success of BBC2's pixel-perfect
rolling current affairs spoof *The Day Today*, plans were advanced
for a paper companion, but due to that old saw of 'artistic
differences' within the programme's already fragmenting
creative team, what could well have been the most original and
mind-boggling screen-to-print comedy transfer since *Monty
Python's Big Red Book* came to nothing.

The Further Adventures of Henry Root

Willie Donaldson remained busy, both as Root and a variety of other characters. *Bitov's Britain* (1985) was a collaboration with Anthony O'Hear and Terence Blacker, who recalls it as 'probably the most unsuccessful toilet book ever written. It was based on the idea that Oleg Bitov, a KGB spy, had defected to England. He was writing a book about Britain and was so demoralised by what he found he got the first plane back to the USSR. It was basically a dictionary of everything that annoyed us about modern life. It was really a rather good idea. Auberon Waugh liked it, and I think somebody else liked it, but no one else seemed to. It was the first and last book I've known where the publisher asked to revert rights back to the authors within six months of publication. They just couldn't wash their hands of the thing quickly enough.'

This state of affairs was far from unusual for a Donaldson enterprise. Blacker continues: 'The thing about Willie – which I found very laudable but made him very difficult to publish – was that he wanted his non-books to take people in. He didn't like the idea of announcing them as jokes. And when people were taken in, that was far better than people saying "Oh, what a marvellous joke that was". The problem was that, quite often, if people didn't get the fact that it was a joke they didn't buy the book. So it wasn't a very commercial position to take.'

Things got less commercial still with *The Soap Letters* (1988). Ostensibly a return to Henry's correspondence roots, it begins in familiar style with Root writing to the chairman of Twyford's Toilets re: sponsoring a Booker-style prize for toilet books, but veers off on a tangent when Root receives a letter from an 81-year-old spinster wanting his opinion on a script she's written. Spying a moneymaking chance, Root re-titles the play *Crack-Up*, claims the tale of privilege, corruption and crack abuse as his own, and gets embroiled with a shady bunch of American TV producers, who pester the likes of Jeffrey Archer, Mary

Whitehouse and Cecil Parkinson over putative roles in the production.

A few replies come back, some twigging the ruse and some not, and a small amount of controversy is generated in the *Today* newspaper, but the main interest here is the warping of the *Letters* concept into a strange sort of narrative, with fictional characters corresponding with, threatening and even killing other fictional characters, all told via the medium of photocopied letters, until the whole queer business ends with journalist Geoffrey Wheatcroft launching hundreds of turkeys out of a light aircraft onto Trafalgar Square. There's plenty to enjoy here, especially in the hilariously on-the-nose dialogue of the enclosed *Crack-Up* scripts, but unlike *World of Knowledge* or even the original *Letters*, there's little in the way of broad appeal, just a virtuoso display of prose tomfoolery – a *Tales from Topographic Oceans* of toilet lit.

The Root franchise came to a halt with lacklustre TV spin-offs *Root Into Europe* (1992) and *Root Around Britain: Henry Root's Guide to Englishness* (1994), marking the final literary resting place of the prophet of Park Walk. But Donaldson continued to pester the unwary. Andy and Fergie cash-in *101 Things You Didn't Know About the Royal Lovebirds* (1986) bewildered an unsuspecting public with mad tales of Prince Andrew levitating over a gas ring, written under the *nom de plume* of Talbot Church. 'It's my favourite of the non-books I've been involved with,' says Blacker. 'It was such fun to do, and Talbot Church was a good character: that sleazy sort of "royal expert" who's always talking about Prince Charles as if he knows what he's thinking.' Naturally such spot-on parody of oleaginous society namedroppers went right under the meagre bullshit detectors of many newspapers, and parts of the book were paraded as hard fact by some of the more gullible journalists.

The Heart Felt Letters!: A Tragedy Aired Is a Tragedy Shared (1998) was a collection of hysterical missives from gushingly tasteless TV producer 'Liz Reed' to the country's TV stations and production houses. *I'm Leaving You, Simon – You Disgust Me: The Dictionary of Received Ideas* (2003) re-worked and recycled *World of Knowledge*, updating the milieu from a suburban saloon bar to an Islington tapas bar, and working one last conceptual trick: though taking the usual A-Z format, the book, if read through from start to finish, reveals a slowly developing narrative between the assorted undesirable diners at the restaurant, who eventually either cop off with each other in the toilets or leave home in dejection and despair.

The most successful of Donaldson's non-Root books was one of his last, the dementedly comprehensive *Brewer's Rogues, Villains and Eccentrics* (2002), a doorstep gazetteer of ne'er-do-wells from ancient and recent history. In a perfect match of subject and author, Donaldson catalogues criminals, misers, mad MPs, courtesans, drug dealers and cricketers of note, in perfectly deadpan tones and with almost complete disregard for factual reliability. It's all cross-referenced with the sort of dummy entries guaranteed to stop the most jaded Waterstone's browser in his tracks:

> Buggery, self-improvement through mystic. *See* CROWLEY, ALEISTER.
> Codpiece, using a tortoise as a. *See* MOON, KEITH.
> Magnetic, believing oneself to be. *See* EDINBURGH, PRINCE PHILIP, DUKE OF.
> Penis in the heavens, assertion that the God of the Old Testament was a mighty. *See* ALLEGRO JOHN.
> Two pounds of Wall's pork sausages and a week in Bournemouth. *See* BELCHER HARRY.

The net book agreement

Another perceived threat to the publishing industry during the 1990s was the rise of the Internet. As with predictions of the 'paperless office', which had been heralded as imminent since at least 1981, doom-laden voices in the book trade pointed at the rapid advance of the web as the final nail in the coffin of the printed word. Certainly the public's ease of access to, and corresponding appetite for, silly bits of ephemeral humour and cosmically pointless in-jokes went through the roof with the advent of the viral email.

Before long, the new medium attracted more disciplined and distinctive humour merchants, who would take things in the opposite direction. In the USA, *The Onion* began life at the University of Wisconsin-Madison as an on-campus newsletter spoofing the style and ludicrous content of American newspapers. An Internet presence in 1996 brought its distinctive parodic voice to international attention, and in 2000 it made the journey back into print, via the softcover compendium *The Onion's Finest News Reporting Vol. 1*. For all the talk of the internet's liberation of intellectual property from the shackles of commercial reproduction, the old-fashioned desire for a tangible product, not to mention a tangible profit, died hard indeed.

The following year, the first authored British web-to-print comedy book appeared, taking a very familiar guise. In 1999 Charlie Brooker, journalist, cartoonist and all-round TV obsessive, initiated *TV Go Home*, a weekly JPEG purporting to be a scan of a *Radio Times* schedule which featured such unlikely programmes as *Daily Mail Island, Get Hen!, Mick Hucknall's Pink Pancakes* and the adventures of London media hotshot Nathan Barley, succinctly titled *Cunt*. Word of mouth spread the site's popularity with alarming speed, and in 2001 Brooker found himself editing both a book of the site's highlights and a TV series bringing some of the programme ideas to fitful life.

Brooker's mixture of foul-mouthed misanthropy and meticulous attention to detail (he spent ages getting the fake *Radio Times* fonts just so) set the tone for subsequent internet-based comedy books. Brooker followed *TVGH* with *Unnovations* (2002), a warped parody of the ubiquitous *Innovations* Christmas catalogues full of tawdry 'gift ideas', including an ingenious kit to help you 'convince miniature whores your face is a shop'. In the same year, a collective of comedy writers transferred *The Framley Examiner*, their very British take on *The Onion* in the form of a stultifyingly parochial local newspaper, into print.

All toilet book traditions must turn in on themselves before long, and the Internet book trade was no exception. By 2005 David McCandless, journalist for techno Bible *Wired* magazine, had amassed a number of pastiches of popular websites, mainly for his own amusement. Then he had the idea of turning them into a book. 'I punted it excitedly to a senior editor friend of mine,' he remembers. 'He said, "nice idea, but what's the concept linking it all?" At the time, I had pitched it as "The Internet Is Shit", which neither he nor his sales team warmed to. Then I came up with "The Internet Annual", in honour of those Christmas kids' books. He didn't buy that either. I couldn't come up with another concept so I thought, "Oh, that's that then" and shelved it. A few years later, I came across the proposal during a big purge of my possessions and ideas. A friend asked me what it was all about. I said, "Oh, it's the internet in a book".'

The Internet: Now in Handy Book Form! (2007) was born, a full-colour *Dunciad* of web idiocy, front pages of dubious websites like search engine Bahoogle and one-stop shop Amasszone.com were convincing frameworks for a plethora of net-picking gags. The design was key, and after getting through a few professional graphics people, McCandless took on the job himself. 'It was quite a job,' he admits. 'In the end, I sort of hacked it, really. I found a way of exporting web pages as hi-res PDF files. Then I'd import them into Photoshop and trace them to get the layout bang on. Then I'd wipe the text and pictures and insert my own. It worked out really well in the end, because I was still writing the gags as I was designing, and a lot of good stuff was written "on the page".'

But for all the technological innovation, McCandless agrees

that the print tradition still holds sway, at least for another generation or two. 'Print is still more "real". People are still impressed if you say you've got a book out. Say you've done a website and they barely blink. In fact, they usually walk away, I've found.'

Filth Renaissance

By the end of the 20th century, the plucky British toilet book was down, but not out. As ever, a resurgence in its fortunes depended as much on successful marketing as original ideas, and this was what the entire book trade received in the closing years of the millennium from the unlikely area of children's literature. Bloomsbury's runaway success with *Harry Potter and the Philosopher's Stone* (1997) and its sequels did more than revitalise the children's book market. Suddenly books were back in the news. The media turned on to the idea of big new literary releases in fiction and non-fiction alike, especially around Christmas. The 'must have' book was back on the shelves, and gift book authors scrambled to write the next stocking filler.

The breakthrough was made by Bloomsbury once again, who published *Schott's Original Miscellany* (2002). With its smart dust jacket, antique typesetting and tidy red ribbon bookmark, it moved the gift book's physical appearance decisively away from the garish paperback hangover of the 1980s. For the first time in a generation, here was a toilet book that looked as at home on the study's mahogany bookshelves as it did propped up against the Harpic. In an aspirational marketplace, the non-book was no longer non-U. To put it in terms of other media, it was a perceptual shift from Saturday night ITV to Sunday night BBC2, Radio 1 to Radio 4.

The next novelty bestseller came straight from the bosom of that very genteel BBC station. *Cutting a Dash* was a modest series of fifteen-minute programmes broadcast on Radio 4 in 2002, in which journalist Lynne Truss fulminated over the country's declining grasp on the nuances of punctuation, from the gross misuse of the apostrophe to the death of the semi-colon. Neatly transferred into an elegant Schott-style hardback, *Eats, Shoots & Leaves: The Zero-Tolerance Approach to Punctuation* (2003) looked set for modest but respectable five-figure sales. Instead, a combination of Home Counties word-of-mouth and the newly book-aware media circus took it right to the top of that year's bestseller list. From then on, every Christmas played host to at least one slice of well-mannered non-fiction wryness, from Simon Barnes's amateur twitching paean *How to Be a Bad Birdwatcher* (2004) to Gavin Pretor-Hinney's madly esoteric *Cloudspotter's Guide* (2006).

The emphasis was now firmly on esoteric knowledge, amusingly conveyed. Heavyweight scientific journal *New Scientist* weighed in with *Does Anything Eat Wasps? And 101 Other Questions* (2005), a compilation of its question-and-answer column, which did for publishing what Magnus Pyke's 1970s ITV programme *Don't Ask Me!* did for television – gave a scientifically challenged public the chance to have those many childlike questions about the natural world answered for them in an accessible, interesting and, importantly, non-condescending way. (*New Scientist* had previous form in this field: David EH Jones's *The Inventions of Daedalus: a Compendium of Plausible Schemes* (1982) was another compilation of columns, this time detailing a series of wild, yet scientifically plausible, imaginary inventions, from a chamber filled with inert gasses dense enough to allow humans to 'swim' in a breathable atmosphere, to a bus with a steering wheel in front of every seat, which turned in the direction of the passengers' majority will.)

Another magazine spin-off was less genteel. *The Idler Book of Crap Towns: the 50 Worst Places to Live in the UK* (2005) was a tiny-format collection of regional fear and loathing compiled by Sam Jordison and Dan Kiernan via the readership of the titular periodical aimed at the intelligent loafer (with a nod to Dr Johnson's original). A combination of those two great British traits, miserablism and parochialism, ensured the authors barely needed to get off their arses to publicise the book: an army of outraged councillors from the towns near the top of the chart did the dirty work for them. The only kink in the pipeline came when the owner of a mobile phone number which appeared in the book as part of a piece of graffiti in an Ipswich underpass, suggesting homoerotic delights for those who called it, leading to a hefty payout for the aggrieved victim.

Crap Towns jockeyed for position that Christmas with another barrage of foul-mouthed *weltschmerz*, *Is It Just Me or is Everything Shit?*, Steve Lowe and Alan McArthur's A-Z of petty irritations from 'Adult editions of children's books' (step forward, H Potter) to 'Z-list celebrities as fuckwit pundits' (step forward, everyone with a ghost-written autobiography out that Christmas). The language may have been a bit coarser, but the principle was exactly the same as that of the Reverend James Beresford's *Miseries of Human Life* some 200 years earlier. The book even inspired a couple of optimistic 'answer' books in the following years, such as the mysterious Steve Stack's *It Is Just You, Everything's Not Shit* (2007), just as Beresford's original had done. In fact, after that brief breath of Radio 4-friendly fresh air, the seasonal humour table was once again drowning in shit – non-book specialist Michael O'Mara in particular dragging the more respectable non-books back down into the sewer with parodies like *Shite's Unoriginal Miscellany* (2003) and *Eats, Shites & Leaves* (2004), the first one selling almost as many copies as its target. You can take the book out of the toilet, but you can't take the toilet out of the book.

Any Questions?

Toilet book history repeats itself with almost clockwork regularity. Three hundred years after John Dunton went mad with his various publications dedicated to Athenianism, the endless thirst for arcane knowledge, another insanely ambitious franchise-cum-philosophy would bring an educational mission to the world of publishing. This time, fortunately, the research was rather better quality.

On one level, *Quite Interesting*, or *QI*, is an amiable BBC2 panel game in which Stephen Fry challenges assorted wits on their knowledge of out-of-the-way subjects. But the programme is just the tip of a vast iceberg of projects envisioned by its creator, John Lloyd. In fact, books came first. 'We spent six years thinking of how to make a book from *QI*, before there was even a series,' he recalls. 'The original idea was to do an Encyclopaedia of Everything, but all of it interesting – the world's first non-dull reference book. It soon became obvious that would take 25 years to write.' Something simpler was in order.

'Often a good title can do the work for you. *The Book of General Ignorance* is a good title, and that's where we started.' The book, a distillation of the show's hunger for obscure information and intelligent entertainment, was the publishing hit of 2006. A sequel beckoned. 'The obvious thing would have been *General Ignorance 2*, says Lloyd. '"Screw the public, we'll just give them another one." And if we'd done that, the second book would have been half as thick and half as good. We'd used four or five years' worth of material in the first one and only had a couple of years to spare. So that was rejected. Then the plan was to apply the "Ignorance" brand to everything – animal ignorance, botanical ignorance, international ignorance, biographical ignorance and so on, building up a kind of *Reader's Digest* library of broad single subjects.' So *The Book of Animal Ignorance* was planned for autumn 2007 but, it was felt, something more was needed.

'Steven Page, who runs Faber, is a very bright guy. Most publishers would leap at the idea, because you can run that series forever. Steven said, "It's not very original though. *QI* is surprising, so it should be a surprising second book." And it was one of those things where everyone's been in a meeting for hours, and it's a bit of a struggle – "Well, we've sort of come to a decision, let's do that then" – and then as everyone's getting up to get their coats, Steven said, "What about an annual?" And everyone said, "Ah! Of course!" I think there should be a word in *The Meaning of Liff* for that – a remark someone makes at the end of the meeting that means you have to start all over again.'

The first *QI Annual* (2007) – half *Look and Learn*, half *Beano* in style – harked back to Lloyd's love of the 'treasure trove' childhood sensation on opening a fact and fancy-filled book on Christmas morning. That sensation proved as strong for the present young generation as it ever was, and a new demographic was added to *QI*'s scope. 'The things you get really excited about are thirteen-year-old boys who literally know *General Ignorance* off by heart,' Lloyd enthuses. 'What *QI* is about is education. We think everybody should have as interesting a life as we do. There's a lot to know.'

2008 saw two QI books launched: the 2008 annual, and *The Book of Advanced Banter*, a collection of memorable quotes that grew out of a far more ambitious project. 'We were supposed to do a book called *The Book of the Dead*, a book of biographies,' says Lloyd. 'Again, we liked the title. But that's a really difficult book to write, because you've got 90 billion people to choose from. The problem was one of research: if you're researching a mandrill or a hedgehog, there's not that much to say about them. But if you want to research, say, Newton, there are about fifty books written about him, two of them huge and all of them very interesting.

'It became clear in March that we weren't going to make the deadline, so we took the file of quotations which we use on the show – Stephen closes the show with them – and suggested that. They were rather disappointed. They said, "Well, it's just a book of quotations, they won't sell," which they don't generally. One of the reasons they don't is they're usually not very good. But we had this fabulous file of stuff where the problem was choosing what not to put in. When they saw the final collection they were really excited about it.'

Ambitions for the brand don't stop there. 'There are hundreds of pages of *QI* theory, which far outrun what we've managed to achieve. There are all sorts of ideas we haven't had the chance, time or money to do. In the long term that encyclopaedia remains an objective. It would be a big fat book – say, 1600 pages. The trouble is, when you've been doing *QI* for ten years, a 1600-page encyclopaedia's simply not good enough. You want something that's ten times that size. Then it gets interesting. But again, that means it's years away. Then there's *The Book of the Dead*, *The QI Atlas*, and ambitious plans to completely rewrite the National Curriculum, getting all the Stage 3, Stage 2 books, in all subjects, and doing a companion volume to each of them.'

Despite such grand schemes, Lloyd is well aware that, to most people, *QI* will remain a comedy panel game and a series of toilet books. 'As long as they're done well and they give people pleasure, I don't mind if people keep them in their loo,' he accepts. 'I keep some of my favourite books in the loo. (Even though there's something slightly grubby about thumbing through a book that's been thumbed through by a lot of other people who haven't washed their hands yet.)'

In fact, Lloyd argues, in many cases a book's tour of duty bogside is not an embarrassed attempt to hide it away, but a perverse form of proud display. After all, what room are most guests guaranteed to visit? 'It's slightly vain. If you put books on the loo you're saying to your friends, "This is the kind of person I am." It's self-advertisement.' And as long as people feel the need to show off their taste, intelligence, quirkiness or sense of humour, however questionable, to others, the future of the market for books to fill the little porcelain shelf seems assured.

POSTSCRIPT

Shoppers, gird your loins. Stoke your wallets. Brush up your four-yards-an-hour crowd shuffle. Today is no ordinary day in British retail. This is Shop West End VIP Day (sponsored by Visa), an annual transformation of London's Oxford and Regent Streets into a committee-designed orgy of festive fun and frolic aimed at getting the hapless shopper to part with their hard-earned lucre in a bilious mixture of theme park traditional and tin foil contemporary. Pipe organs, roast chestnuts, Sally Army bands, break-dancing Santas and 'the world's best musical Christmas nun' mingle with giant Simpsons characters urging sceptical teens to pop into Zavvi, and the metallic mauve Mariah Carey Beauty Truck. The ideal setting, then, in which to assess the state of the toilet book art.

12:05. Oxford Street. Ruddy-faced gents in stovepipe hats and buggergrip sidewhiskers rattle along on penny-farthing mountain bikes to the seasonal strains of the Kaiser Chiefs. This is what it's all about.

Pop into Waterstones, and a host of familiar names greet the eye. Books from *Private Eye* and *QI* hold steady at the front. Russell Ash's *Potty, Fartwell and Knob* catalogues people with unfortunate names. Leigh and Lepine offer *Pets with Tourettes*, a tiny collection of pictures of hamsters shouting 'bollocks!' *Schott's Almanac* is here, as is *The Meaning of Liff*, biblically small as ever. Alan Coren's posthumous *69 for 1* looks sideways from the other side. Wogan's got yet another one out. The humour table groans under the weight of post-Lynne Truss language trifles: *My Grammar and I (or Should that be 'Me'?): Old-School Ways to Sharpen Your English, Pop Goes the Weasel: the Secret Meanings of Nursery Rhymes, Damp Squid: the English Language Laid Bare, My Gonads Roar* (anagrams*)*, and *A Steroid Hit the Earth* (misprints and howlers). Julian Henby's *Dear Celebrity* is the latest entry in the 250-year-old parade of spoof letter collections. There's even a coffee table collection of vintage *Punch* cartoons. *Plus ça change*, indeed.

13:15. A punk Scotsman up a stepladder outside Foot Locker inflates a rubber glove pulled over his head to tumultuous applause.

One reasonably new trend is the nostalgic reprint. Hardback collections of *Look-In, Jackie, The Broons* and Ladybird books litter the shelves. Doorstop collections of war stories from *Commando* comic pile up everywhere. Fandom has always provided a niche for this sort of thing, but these collections are mainstream, placed front and centre in plain view, where once they were hidden in a corner like a teenager's porn stash. Post-Potter, the childish things we once put away are now turfed out of the attic at a frantic pace. Nowadays you're never to old for an annual, as evinced by *The Big Book of Top Gear*, an unashamedly childish compendium of illustrated whimsy from the stable of the once solidly middle-aged motoring programme. Act your age, not your engine capacity, lads.

14:02. Oxford Circus. A flying squad of boobish, eager-to-please performing arts students offer 'free hugs' at top volume, and garner from passing shoppers the sourest looks since the Nuremberg trials.

Amongst all the till-friendly trend following, there's one unlikely revival worth a small cheer. Against all the odds, the TV comedy tie-in book is back in town. It started last year with *The Pub Landlord's Book of British Common Sense*, a gallimaufry of admissible bigotry from Al Murray's hugely popular bullet-headed lager tout, assembled in the lavish, detail-packed style of the great comedy books of the 1970s and 1980s (Murray himself namechecked the *Python* books and *The Rutland Dirty Weekend Book* in dewy-eyed terms when plugging his tome). This year he's joined by efforts from *The Mighty Boosh* and *Gavin and Stacey*. Whatever you might think of the content, it would be a hard heart indeed that didn't warm to the resurgence of this labour-intensive format in an entertainment landscape otherwise increasingly set on the path of least resistance.

15:35. At the bottom of Regent Street, a crowd has gathered. Geriatric barbershop choirs, cod-Edwardian unicyclists and a dancing panda have been comprehensively outclassed by James Bond's original Aston Martin DB7 (or something a bit like it) doing nothing but sitting in the middle of the road being famous, while all around, struggling acrobats knock themselves out. Perhaps there's a lesson here.

Sure enough, the bookshop bestseller charts point to a waning of the toilet book's 21st-century dominance. Aside from the expected *Guinness Book* in residence at number one, the top ten is dominated by the celebrity autobiography. Nothing new about that genre, but we're in the middle of a particularly virulent strain here. Stars younger than a first edition copy of *The Moon's a Balloon*, some with careers shorter than the year, bring out life stories they happily admit to not having read, let alone written. The parade of grinning faces and chins cheekily balanced on wrists covers the bookshop wall like an unusually benevolent county jail 'wanted' display: From Parky's *My Story* to Julie Walters's *That's Another Story*, Barack Obama's *Dreams from My Father* to *Just Biggins*. Only in this case, the suspects themselves are the ones collecting the bounty. Industry scorn has, consequently, been diverted away from the toilet book. Cynical pundits maintain most of these books never even get as far as the smallest room, being given as mere tokens of recognition ('Here you are, you like him, don't you?') with barely a word of the content skimmed by either giver or receiver. With unrecoupable six-figure advances being doled out to all and sundry, this wasteful charade can't go on much longer, but while it does, the humble paperback of bitty whimsy suddenly finds itself in the unfamiliar position of being only the *second* most despised genre in publishing. That can't be bad.

16.58. An oddly emaciated and rather unconfident Father Christmas who's been making a poor fist of enticing shoppers into Boots all afternoon ('Er, hello. Merry Christmas, obviously...') finally switches off his under-beard microphone and collapses, exhausted, under a welter of consumer indifference. Same time next year?

SELECT BIBLIOGRAPHY
(REAL BOOKS)

Allen, Robert J: *The Clubs of Augustan London* (Harvard University Press, 1933)

Blacker, Terence: *You Cannot Live as I Have Lived and Not End Up Like This: the Thoroughly Disgraceful Life and Times of Willie Donaldson* (Random House, 2007)

Carpenter, Humphrey: *That Was Satire That Was* (Gollancz, 2000)

Hewison, Robert: *Monty Python: the Case Against* (Methuen, 1981)

Hunt, Cecil: *Ink in My Veins* (Robert Hale, 1948)

Jenkins, Alan: *Stephen Potter: Inventor of Gamesmanship* (Weidenfeld & Nicholson, 1980)

Law, Roger: *Still Spitting at Sixty* (Harpercollins, 2005)

Marnham, Patrick: *The Private Eye Story* (Andre Deutsch, 1982)

Marr, George S: *The Periodical Essayists of the Eighteenth Century* (James Clarke, 1923)

Meynell, Francis: *My Lives* (Bodley Head, 1971)

Palin, Michael: *Diaries 1969-1979* (Weidenfeld & Nicholson, 2006)

Price, RGG: *A History of Punch* (Collins, 1957)

Raven, James: *The Business of Books* (Yale University Press, 2007)

Sherbo, Arthur: *Christopher Smart: Scholar of the University* (Michigan State University Press, 1967)

Smyth, Adam: *Profit and Delight: Printed Miscellanies in England, 1640-1682* (Wayne State University Press, 2004)

Southworth, John: *Fools and Jesters at the English Court* (Sutton, 1998)

Spufford, Margaret: *Small Books and Pleasant Histories* (Cambridge University Press, 1981)

Thompson, Roger: *Unfit for Modest Ears* (Macmillan, 1979)

Troyer, Howard William: *Ned Ward of Grub Street* (Frank Cass, 1946)

Wilmut, Roger: *From Fringe to Flying Circus* (Eyre Methuen, 1980)

Wilson, Ben: *The Laughter of Triumph: William Hone and the Fight for the Free Press* (Faber, 2005)

NOTES
(ESSENTIAL)

1 'Gotham' was a notional county town whose inhabitants were traditionally a few councillors short of a parish. Their probable origin in a 13th century poem called *Descriptus Norfolciensum* suggests that, as so often, the good folk of East Anglia were the ones being ribbed.

2 Though this in turn brought counter-insurgency with such books as Ned Ward's *Female Policy Detected. Or, The Arts of a Designing Woman Laid Open.* (1695), a 'pocket piece' for young men to keep ready armed against female low cunning.

3 That title continues, with mounting gruesomeness: ... *Or, the Fundament-all Cause of the Distempers Incident to the Fair-sex, Enquired into. Proving à Posteriori Most of the Dis-ordures In-tail'd Upon Them, are Owning to Flatulencies not Seasonably Vented. Written in Spanish by Don Fart-in-Hando Puff-indorst, Professor of Bombast in the University of Crackow. And Translated into English at the Request, and for the Use, of the Lady Damp-fart of Her-fart-shire. By Obadiah Fizzle, Groom of the Stool to the Princess of Arsimini in Sardinia. Long-Fart: (Longford in Ireland), Printed by Simon Bumbubbard, at the sign of the Wind-Mill Opposite Twattling-Street, 1722.* More scatological Swiftian punnery of dubious attribution was to be had in *The Wonderful Wonder of Wonders, Being an Accurate Description Of the Birth, Education, Manner of Living, Religion, Politicks, Learning, &c. Of Mine Arse* (1720) and *A Curious Dissertation on Pissing; Written by Piss-A-Bed Scat-Her-Water, Countess of Piss-in-Ford, and Lady of the Manor of Piss-Pot-Hall* (1726). Small wonder Swift huffed with dismissive annoyance whenever these were brought up in his presence.

4 Mrs Midnight's scholarship was later quoted in *The New Boghouse Miscellany* (1761), a further collection of dirty poetry that had no input from Mad Sam Johnson, but was 'printed on an excellent soft Paper; and absolutely necessary for all those, who read with a View to Convience, as well as Delight.'

5 She even spawned several bandwagon-hopping publications not linked with Smart. *Mother Midnight's Comical Pocket-Book* (1763) was 'Carefully Cook'd-Up by Mother Midnight's Merry Grandson, Humphrey Humdrum, Esq'. *Mother Midnight's Miscellany* (1751) claimed, in its full, 194-word title, to contain 'more than all the Wit, and all the Humour, and all the Learning, and all the Judgement, that has ever been, or ever will be', including 'the marriage ceremony of a Flying Man to a Flying Woman' and was dedicated to 'the King of the Fidlers, and to his Queen... and to Bajazet the Famous Race-Horse'. It makes a cameo appearance in Sir Walter Scott's swashbuckling *Redgauntlet* (1824), when the pious Alan Fairford happens across a copy, and flings it in disgust into the Solway Firth.

6 As in 'denizen of the Greek island of Lesbos', clearly.

7 I.e., he ran a pub in between sonnets.

8 'Shrdlu' was a word often seen in old newspapers, being the second line of keys on the old 'hot metal' Linotype typesetting machines, the first being 'Etaoin', as 'Qwerty' is on a typewriter. (In Lintoype the keys are arranged according to their frequency of use in English.) The appearance of one or more shrdlus in a newspaper meant something had gone wrong with the type, and the typesetter was 'striking out' the error by running his finger along the keys, as a signal for the line not to be used in the paper, which of course was often ignored.

9 One of the most resilient of humour formats, this canon of classroom errors ('History is not what you thought. *It is what you can remember*. All other history defeats iself.') has been 'updated' several times by such lavatorial greats as Craig Brown (*1966 and All That* (2005) – the last third of the 20th century), Paul Manning (*1984 and All That* (1984) – extending the original from the Great War to the End of History), Willie Donaldson (*1992 and All That* (1992) – a topical spoof on EU paranoia) and *All the World's a Globe: the National Theatre of Brent's Concise History of the Human Race from Lemur to Cosmonaut* (1987), the print incarnation of Patrick Barlow's pretentious yet touchingly naïve multimedia historian manqué Desmond Olivier Dingle.

10 Fry also takes the self-flagellating foreword to new heights of apologetic abasement, profusely begging forgiveness for his 'publishing atrocity' and recommending its immediate installment in the smallest room, musing 'it may be that each article of the book should have been flagged with a number or symbol indicating the length of time the article would take to read, that number or symbol corresponding with the health of the reader's bowel'.

11 This expense was parodied in the script book of Python film *The Life of Brian* (1979). A TV-shaped hole proving prohibitive, a cut-out dotted line was printed instead with the instruction: 'We wanted to cut this space out for you but unfortunately the publisher said this would cost an extra 11 pence per copy… In order to increase the value of your copy all you have to do is cut along the dotted lines where indicated.'

12 Lloyd picks as his exception to the script book rule *The Diaries of a Cabinet Minister* (1981-3), Jonathan Lynn and Anthony Jay's adaptation of *Yes, Minister*, which recast the series' episodes as chapters in Jim Hacker's diary, republished in 2019AD with countless footnotes and inter-jections from the programme's other characters.

13 Lloyd didn't exactly make matters easier by adding, in *Not! 1982*, two extra days to March and the government-initiated productivity-boosting month of Thatch, while *Not! 1983* came with three spare February 29ths.

14 The product of reclusive painter Kit Williams, *Masquerade* was 1979's Christmas publishing phenomenon. In the book, fifteen of Williams's dense, surreal canvases revealed, via an elaborate secret code, the whereabouts in the UK of a jewel-encrusted hare, which had been buried accordingly. 'Thoughtful' children and their grumpy, spade-wielding fathers the nation over went briefly insane.

15 Thus bringing the puzzle to a slightly more satisfactory end than *Masquerade*, whose eventual winner was later shown to have cheated, quizzing an ex-girlfriend of Williams as to the hare's likely whereabouts.

16 The teacher who set the exercise may have been reading Paul Jennings, whose 1950s essay Ware, Wye and Watford laid out the signpost method of etymology in more delicately wry terms.

17 'Liff (n.) A book, the contents of which are totally belied by its cover. For instance, any book the dust jacket of which bears the words, "This book will change your life".'

18 Ironically, Reyburn's next book along similar lines, *Bust-Up* (1971), which did the same thing for the invention of the bra, was taken at face value, with the result that early editions of Trivial Pursuit confidently stated that the first such garment was created by one Otto Titzling.

INDEX